MW00622652

Blessings!
Emilia (Emily)
Zecchino

only in
America

By

Emilia Zecchino

Llumina
Press

Family photos courtesy of the Zecchino family.

Not to be reproduced or excerpted without permission of the author
This work is a memoir. It is the author's recollection of her experiences over many years. At times, certain names and identifying characteristics have been changed.

© 2011 Emilia Zecchino

All rights reserved. No part of this publication may be reproduced or transmitted in any form or by any means electronic or mechanical, including photocopy, recording, or any information storage and retrieval system, without permission in writing from both the copyright owner and the publisher.

Requests for permission to make copies of any part of this work should be mailed to Permissions Department, Llumina Press, 7101 W. Commercial BLVD., Ste 4E Tamarac, FL 33319

ISBN: 978-1-60594-658-0

Printed in the United States of America by Llumina Press

Library of Congress Control Number: 2010917493

DEDICATION

"Give me your tired, your poor, your huddled masses yearning to breathe free, the wretched refuse of your teeming shore. I lift my lamp beside the "Golden Door."
I dedicate this book to you, America. You opened that "Golden Door" to me when I arrived alone, tired and poor, a WWII war bride sixty-three years ago. Today I am living that much sought after "American dream."
To you, beautiful Italy, for giving me roots and a passion for music, arts, cooking, food, faith in God, love of family, and hard work. There will always be a large part of you deep in my heart!
To all of you that endure life's struggles, have courage and pray. I hope my story will encourage you to listen to that little voice inside of you, to never give up, and I hope that it demonstrates that ordinary people can do extraordinary things. Earnest prayers are always answered!

ACKNOWLEDGEMENTS

With my deepest gratitude, I thank you, Lord Jesus and you my gentle dove, the Holy Spirit, for letting me be in your presence and for the inspiration you lavished on my thoughts and words as I wrote this book. It is only through your intersession that I was able to open my heart and mind to put on paper the ups and downs, the defeats and victories, the failures and successes, and the tragedies and accomplishments that follow me to this day. May this story bring all glory to my Father in Heaven.

My deepest thanks to you, Riccie, my husband and companion for the twenty five years of love and devotion to our family, giving us all your best in spite of your limited physical abilities and for the valuable business skills you imparted me while working together.

My deepest thanks to you, my beloved mom and dad, for giving me life, for all the sacrifices made to keep me safe, and for nourishing my soul with all the fervor you could master. Your strength and love has been the pattern I have tried to emulate. Thanks to you, Andrea and Pierino, my deceased brothers, for all the happy moments we shared growing up during time, both good and bad. And to you, Antonietta, my dearest sister, for sharing my pains and joys, and for all the comfort you have given me through the years. God bless you in all your efforts.

A special thanks to Carolyn Goss, my dear friend and editor. For two years, you had the patience to wait for my pages to be ready for your corrections. You always know how to make words sound better in a sentence.

Many thanks to all of you—relatives living near me and those far away, but still very close to my heart. Many thanks to all the friends who have encouraged and supported me in this endeavor. Deep thanks to you, deceased friends and relatives. You have been such a part of my life, and without your help, my dear Ruth and Sam, I could not enjoy my retirement now.

Finally, I owe gratitude and appreciation to my sons Ricky and Vinnie and to my beautiful daughter Linda, for giving me the pleasure and joy of motherhood. I believe the greatest moment in a woman's life is when she holds her newborn babies in her arms. You guys gave me such immense joy when you were born and I held you in my arms for the first time. Miraculously, I became your mother. Thank you! Thank you! And thank you, God for this privilege. I give you, my children, this book as a legacy of my past and your ancestors' past. I pray you will read between the lines and understand the meaning of my actions and the reasons I became the person that I am. As I look back on the journey, all along God has been the potter; I have been the clay in His hands.

TABLE OF CONTENTS

Introduction

"Only in America"—do these three words sound like a cliché to you?

One morning, I started to write the introduction to my memoir. I had decided to call it *Only in America*. That evening, the TV was on in my family room, and I caught a new show hosted by former Arkansas governor, Mike Huckabee. He played electric guitar in a band he had formed with some of the camera people and other TV crew. They sang the Brooks & Dunn song "Only in America." What a wonderful coincidence, I thought! That song captures the hope that still endures in this country, where a child with no pedigree can become president.

"Only in America"—that phrase resonates in my life. Having lived on three continents and endured for five years the perils of World War II, in Ethiopia first and then in Italy before coming to America, I believe it reflects the accomplishments I was able to achieve because I seized the opportunities available *only here in America.*

Many of my friends have encouraged me to share my uncommon life with others who have the audacity to believe that if we pause to consider the possibilities available in America, we can dream the impossible dream and reap the benefits.

The purpose of this book is to share with you the ups and the downs, the victories and the defeats, the downfalls and near failures, and finally the success that made me stronger and yet more humble. In the inevitable unfolding of our lives, we face hardships of all varieties, and I have had tons to face ever since I was a little girl. Looking back, I believe every episode of my life molded my character and brought new visions that enabled me to face challenges and choose a better path. I know I am the happiest when I accomplish the best with what I have. I have learned to focus on the solutions instead of wasting time on the problems and to take responsibility for my choices.

So it is with deep gratitude that I thank God for bringing me to America, and although the "Italy" in me will always have a very special place in my heart, I am blessed to have jumped into that proverbial melting pot and come out *an American.* To those born here, who have never experienced life in another country, I say, "How fortunate you are! Your land has been exceedingly blessed." Countless success stories make up the fabric of this country, but to appreciate their value, you have to travel the world and try to make a living somewhere else. How different it is here! No wonder everyone wants to come and live in America.

When I first arrived from Italy as a war bride in September 1947 to live with a wonderful Italian family in Flushing, New York, I was amazed at the abundance of food on the dinner table. I was shocked to see how much leftover food was dumped in the garbage. I would look at the food and cry because I knew that many miles away in Italy, my mother, father, two brothers, and little sister were going to bed hungry. I wished I could send them those leftovers. Tears running down my cheeks, I swore I would do anything to bring them to America. By the grace of God, I did.

Only in America could I have found the opportunities I have had. Those opportunities are still abundant.

In these pages, you will walk with me as I do my best to convey the meaning of *Only in America* and try to inspire you to feel some of the same wonder, hope, and thankfulness that I have felt since I arrived on this soil.

Emilia "Emily" Zecchino

CHAPTER 1
RAGS TO RICHES

January 20, 2006—a beautiful morning, as most January mornings are in South Florida. A balmy 55 degrees just before dawn. Waking from a deep sleep, I glanced at the glowing numbers on the clock on my bedside table. 4:45 A.M.!

I jumped out of bed as expectation gripped my mind. Today—yes, today—something extraordinary was going to change my life. I had prayed for months and envisioned the change with expectant glee. Did I say "glee"? Yes, I did. Glee and exuberant joy. Suddenly, there they were—three little words bouncing against the walls of my mind: *Only in America!*

Awestruck, I heard them over and over. *Only in America.* Why did those words resonate so much with me, a seventy-eight-year-old woman?

I grabbed a robe and went into the kitchen. The pot of coffee was ready to be plugged in, and in a few minutes, the strong, enticing aroma filled the kitchen. I went to the window. A myriad of stars were happily blinking in the black sky above, and it seemed that the whole world was still asleep. I sipped a cup and thought, soon the sun would make its appearance as it always does , and the silence of the night would give way to the sounds of the day, as they always do. But today, there would be one awesome difference. In a few hours, by the grace of God, I would be signing a contract to transfer ownership of my small company to a multi-billion dollar company! Holiday Foods, my specialty frozen food company, would be acquired by the Schwan Food Company—at a price that would instantly make me a millionaire!

Such things happen many times in America, you say, but in my case, there is a difference. I am a little seventy-eight-year-old lady who still works a full schedule. You might say that is not so spectacular. So do many other old ladies. But some things make my story different from other successful business people. In November 1982, Holiday Foods was a small catering company began with an investment of just *one thousand dollars*. (I kept the cancelled check as a memory of that day.) It occupied 2,500 square feet of warehouse space and gradually evolved into a USDA-inspected frozen food manufacturing company. Over the years, the plant grew to cover 46,000 square feet of warehouse space, and the payroll grew from a handful of people to about 150 employees.

At the time of Holiday Foods' inception, I was fifty-five years old, a time when many of my friends and acquaintances were retiring. I had no formal training in the culinary arts, no chef's degree, and no gold medals to adorn my chef's uniform, only a great flair for entertaining and a great passion for cooking.

My amazement at the success of my company was unending. Small catering jobs became large affairs. After our conversion to food manufacturing, Holiday Foods began serving some of the most prestigious hotels and country clubs in the country. My products, through distributors, found their way to Air Force One, and Disney World became one of my best customers.

How did it happen? It certainly was not luck! Hard work and sacrifice? Yes, plenty of both. But it happened mainly because here in America, opportunity exists for anyone with a vision to start small and make it big. Only in America—if you can dream it and work hard for it, you can make it happen!

Another very important element played a big role in my success: I kept God involved in every decision. Every morning at 4:30, I grounded myself in the Bible for an hour and, like King Solomon centuries ago, I prayed for His presence and wisdom.

"God, thank you for what you have done with my life," I prayed as I dressed, and as I prepared for this most special occasion, my thoughts suddenly flashed back. The years rolled backwards at great speed as I tried to make some sense and find some logic for the present moment. Could this really be happening to me?

I saw myself on the deck of the *S.S. Saturnia* as it made its unforgettable entrance into the grand port of New York City. That day was September 6, 1947, and I was a very frightened, bewildered, and yet excited nineteen-year-old entering America as a war bride under the War Bride Act of 1945.

I remember hugging the rail on an upper deck, resolved to take in as much of the panorama as possible. The breeze felt cool as it kissed my cheeks and ruffled my hair, and a haze hung heavy over the impressive skyline of the city. Skyscrapers that I remembered from scenes in movies suddenly appeared in all their solemn grandeur.

I remember when the Statue of Liberty came into view, how the crowd around me, broke into shouts of joy, and I cried, yes, cried in gratitude, as fantasy became reality. I had seen pictures of this fabulous lady many times, and I knew well her history, but to actually see her so close, looking at me with her stretched arm holding the torch, so majestic and tall? It seemed impossible that this was happening, and yet a dream was about to come true at that moment.

I ran down the stairs that led to the cabin I shared with two other Italian ladies and grabbed the one suitcase that contained everything I owned in the world. I clutched a bag that held the impossibly large sum of $50 as I made my way towards the immigration office on board. I had my passport properly stamped and I raced down the gangway, thinking that finally I could hope for a free, peaceful, and maybe prosperous future. But who could have guessed that $50 would someday grow into millions?

"Are you ready yet?" Linda's voice from down the hall suddenly brought me back to the present. And today, as on that day long ago, another dream was coming true. I wanted someone to pinch me. The thought that my life was to take such a drastic change again gave me pangs of nervous excitement.

"I'm almost ready!" I replied.

"Well, let's get going!" My daughter, part owner of the company, wanted to waste no time. After all, this was a special day for her, too. I heard the tapping of her heels on the tile floor and she soon appeared, all dressed up and ready to leave, sporting a big smile of satisfaction.

"Well, we made it, Mom! Can you believe it? In a few hours, our lives will be changed. Come on, let's hurry!" She sounded excited and anxious. I grabbed my handbag, and we walked through the front door. I locked it and started towards the front steps. Linda grabbed my arm and helped me climb into the SUV parked in the driveway. I don't think either of us thought that what was happening was real.

Linda's hands firmly clutched the steering wheel as she backed out of the driveway and headed toward the exit of our complex and on to the main highway. We were both silent, concentrating on the direction and movements of the cars around us. Once on the ramp to Highway 595 we joined the already heavy traffic heading east. I glanced at the clock under the panel board and sighed a wisper of relief. 6:55 A.M. Good.! I thought. We will have plenty of time to stop at the plant and make sure everything is running smoothly.

It was almost 7:30 when we pulled into the parking lot of Holiday Foods' 46,000-square-foot complex. Linda parked the SUV in her designated spot and helped me out. The front parking lot was almost full; the early shift employees had been there since seven A.M. getting the plant ready to open for the day's food production. The rest of the employees were trickling in, getting to their assigned locations.

The front building of Holiday Foods had four production rooms, four packing rooms, three full commercial kitchens, and one sample room. In the shape of an inverted L, the second building hugged the side of the first. It housed our many freezers, supply storage, and lunchrooms. As I walked towards the front door of the offices, I noticed the USDA inspector's car in its assigned spot, so I knew she was making the rounds in the plant. A prayer quickly formed in my head: "Lord, please, please, let everything go smooth this morning! You know how pressed for time I am. Let everything be in your control and bless every hand that is working under this roof."

I feared that if someone made a mistake or forgot to clean any surface of the processing equipment, the inspector would hold up the opening until all surfaces were cleaned and sanitized. This seldom happened thanks to the efficiency of the employees, but occasionally, it did. The inspectors were meticulous in carrying out their tasks, and sometimes production was held up for an hour or two.

"Do you think our employees suspect what is about to happen?" Linda's voice brought me back to reality.

"They must know that something is going on," I replied. "Especially when they saw all those people from Schwan come in and spend all their time in the accounting department with Don Franza." I hesitated a moment. "I am sure when they know we are selling the company, they will have mixed feelings, just as we have."

I left it at that. In my heart, I knew an era was ending and a new beginning was approaching with all its wonders. Part of me was exuberant as I contemplated my future. Finally, this big mountain would be lifted from my shoulders, and at the age of seventy-eight, I was extremely encouraged. Getting up at 4:30 every morning and working until six or seven in the evening six days a week had become a burden, even though I had a lot of help. Holiday Foods had 145 employees on its payroll. Many of them had been with the company as long as fifteen years. Finally, I saw myself relaxing for days and days at a time on the slopes of the picturesque Amalfi coast, on the beaches of Capri, Venice, or in Bari, my native city. Free at last, free from the responsibility of leading a demanding enterprise.

On the other hand, here it was, Holiday Foods, this special company, *my baby,* which I had birthed twenty-four years ago, this company that had given me the greatest of pleasures and the greatest of worries, this company that had become such an integral part of me—it was going to take wings and fly into the sunset.

Was this possible? I felt something painful nibbling at my heart, and I wanted to cry. Am I going to miss this? What about all these people with whom I had had such a warm association for so many years?

I felt like a mother hen attending her brood. I was going to miss my association with Holiday Foods. However, as I stepped out of the car and began to walk toward my office, my feeble knees and aching feet told me softly, "Emily, it's time to quit." Arthritis pains were increasing with a vengeance, and my body was beginning to slow down. "Yes, Emily, it is time to go." I heard my bones express their grim agreement.

And then a thought reassured me: Holiday Foods would soon be part of the Schwan Food Company, a multi-billion-dollar enterprise, and my people, my very dear employees, would be well taken care of. I felt some of the guilt melt away. After all, I was getting too old to carry on, and Linda, after several years of intense work, was in need of a change.

I walked into the lobby of our office compound and greeted the staff with my usual "Hello, everybody." Then I opened the door to my office, and Linda made her way into hers.

I wanted to feel and act as normal as I could, but my mind was scurrying in many directions and my heart was pounding inside my chest. I finally bridled my wandering thoughts, and walking around the desk, slumped into the swivel chair. I picked up the phone, cleared my throat, pressed the intercom button, and called Fausto Mello, my supervisor.

"Fausto, I need you in my office."

I think my voice carried a hint of weakness in its tone. There were papers everywhere on my desk, wire baskets full of catalogs, and notes lined up in order of the importance of their content. Impaled on spikes were my most special notes with dates and itineraries scribbled in haste. One thing was missing on my desk—that marvelous, extraordinary machine called "the computer." To my shame, I had never learned to use one. I was always too busy with everything else.

Waiting for Fausto to make his way from the plant, I stepped out of my office and into the cluster of offices that made up the brain of Holiday Foods. It was here that business was conducted with great care and precision. It was in this place that orders for our products were received and scrupulously filled. On this floor, four girls were assigned to customer service, and Danny Kucera, our executive chef, had a desk in the far corner on the right side of the room. On my left, just past the door connecting to the vestibule, was Linda, our receptionist, who also took customer service calls. Further down was Francine, and just behind her, Mary had her own section dedicated to the development of product and nutrition labels. On the other side of the room, Chef Danny, already at his desk, was busy collecting from his computer the recipes needed for the day's production while Ronda and Liz, stationed between partitions next to him, were busy answering the phones and entering orders in the computers. Orders were also coming through the fax machine. January was the top of the season, and we expected to be busy. Orders poured in from local distributors as well as from out of state, so the clicks of keyboards and the rings of the phones were music to my ears. The second floor above the office housed the accounting department, overseen by Don Franza, our C.F.O., assisted by Nikki on accounts receivable and payable.

As I made my habitual survey of the operations, I peeked over Linda's shoulder and followed on her computer the order coming through from our distributor in Texas. Good! I thought. That is a large one. Business is booming. From another desk, Ronda's voice reached my ear as she reassured the person on the other end that his three hundred cases had been shipped and would be in his warehouse in Pennsylvania the following day. On the other side of Ronda, I saw Liz and listened as she had an anxious discussion with the person on the other end.

"Yes, chef," she said reassuringly. "I have everything down. Your order of 1200 canapés will be delivered to you, as you have requested, at four P.M. tomorrow." I heard her go over the selection to be sure she had made no mistakes. She then called for Lisa Ming our garde-manger chef in charge of the cold canapé production. In a few minutes, Lisa walked into the office and Liz handed her a copy of the order. Lisa glanced at it, and in her unmistakable and enthusiastic Chinese accent, she assured me she had no problem filling it.

God bless Lisa, I said to myself. What a wonderful, remarkable, and talented person she turned out to be. Her alabaster cheeks, almond shaped eyes, and sweet smile reminded me of a delicate China doll on display in shops that sell items made in Asia. Lisa, as we had found out after we hired her, had a marvelous soprano voice, and before coming to America, had appeared in many operas on the Beijing stage. What made her even more special was her ability to use her porcelain hands to create the most exquisite garnishes for all types of canapés.

As Lisa turned towards the back rooms, Fausto was on his way in. "Good morning, Emily!" Fausto's arms warmly embraced me as a big smile formed on his face. He informed me that he was satisfied that everything was under his control.

"Of course, Fausto! You're the best of the best! I can always depend on you." Fausto was my very special and precious employee. A special bond held us together very much as one between mother and son. It seemed we were made to work at the same place and same time.

From the moment Fausto was hired several years before, he had shown a loyalty and integrity far beyond the capacity expected from a good employee. Wearing as many hats at a time as necessary, Fausto has been always there, giving his all for the benefit of everyone in the company. He worked very hard with his hands and brain, but above all, he worked with his heart. When he first arrived from New York City, where he had worked as a cab driver for five years, he applied for a driver's position. Not needing a driver, I offered him a position in the receiving department, which he immediately accepted. In no time at all, he had learned all the names of our products and organized the receiving refrigerators and freezers. When his job was done, he drifted around the processing rooms, looking for things to do and learn.

Before long, I realized he would be more valuable controlling the flow of production than in the receiving department. With great precision, Fausto learned to do just that and became very efficient at supervising the 150 workers in the processing plant. He was able to follow the orders to be filled from the moment we received them. He learned each step of the process: first the recipes were produced in the kitchens in large batches, then placed in refrigeration units for cooling down, and then taken out again onto working tables, where dozens of nimble hands rolled, folded, dipped, and brushed the thousands of mini Wellingtons, spanakopitas, crab rangoons, brie with raspberry puffs, lobster turnovers, and scallops wrapped in bacon, just to name a few. Next, these mouth-watering little bites were put in order on sanitized plastic trays, then transferred from the trays to metal racks, and then wheeled into blast freezers, where temperatures reached as low as twenty degrees below zero. It took not quite an hour for the hors d'oeuvres to freeze solid. Next, the racks were then wheeled into the packing rooms. There, expert hands packed them, sealed them, labeled the boxes, and put them back in nearby holding freezers, where they remained until other personnel picked them up and transferred them into enormous storage freezers at the far corner of the building. Fausto diligently followed the orders as they were processed—from the beginning until they were ready to be shipped. He always gave extreme care to any special order. What a worker!

"Did everything go well with the inspection?" I asked Fausto.

"Yes, Emily. Everything went well!" Fausto was quick to reassure me.

7

Holiday Foods is a USDA-inspected plant. To clarify what that label means, by law, every plant manufacturing meat products has to be inspected daily by the United States Department of Agriculture. We had to follow a strict set of rules. We had to provide the inspectors with an office, complete with desk, file cabinets, and telephone. There was no set time for their arrival, and when they showed up, they put on their white helmets and white smocks, and with a flashlight in one hand and a pen and pegboard clipped with all kinds of forms in the other hand, they entered the plant and looked *everywhere*—behind every cabinet, every piece of equipment, under every table, inside every refrigerator and freezer, in dark corners and behind stoves, ovens, and deep fryers. They used the flashlight to search for any crumb left behind by the cleaners. I am telling you they were strict with a capital S. If they found a trace of dirt on any surface, we had to close the processing room, scrub it down, and sanitize it before the inspectors would allow us to reopen it for production again, and that could not occur before another meticulous inspection. This morning, thank God, everything went smoothly!

"Thanks, Fausto, for taking care of everything. I will be leaving soon with Linda, and we'll be back in a few hours. If you need to reach me, call me on my cell or Linda's, but before leaving, we want to join you guys for prayer".."

I had instituted that ritual years ago. We all assembled for prayer in the large processing room, Room #3, before the start of the workday.

Fausto nodded as the bell signaling the start of production blasted behind the office door. At the sound of this bell, employees assigned to production made their way into the processing rooms. The women wore clean white smocks, aprons, bouffant white nets on their heads, and white latex gloves that they changed several times during the day. Most wore white sneakers with rubber soles to prevent slipping on the bare cement floors. USDA regulations had the processing rooms hold temperatures not higher than 55 degrees at all times, so the women wore heavy sweaters and long warm pants under their smocks. For the men, the same rules applied. Though the kitchens feeding the processing rooms were a little bit warmer, strict clothing rules applied there, too.

This morning's routine was no different from many others. I reached for my own smock and hair net and then took off my earrings, watch, rings, and bracelets, as the USDA rules specified. Followed by Linda and Fausto, I made my way into Production Room #3, the largest of the plant's processing rooms, for prayers as usual.

CHAPTER 2

MY ITALIAN ROOTS

As we prayed together, sadness gripped my heart. This was the last day these people would have me as their boss, and I knew they would be both saddened and apprehensive for their future. I wished it did not have to be this way, but I had no other choice. None of them yet, not even Fausto, had a clue that soon Holiday Foods would be part of a huge *multi billion-dollar* company.

Prayers ended, and I walked back to my office hiding my tears. I could not help wondering how a little old lady born in Italy seventy-eight years before could have come this far. My life, with all its pains and tragedies, its dangers and crises, had several turns that still mystify me. It is here that I feel free to open my album of memories and tell you how it all began.

I was born on March 5, 1928, in Bari, Italy. To be exact, I was born, on the second floor of an ancient, and quite massive building that over-looks Piazza Mercantile, one of the principal entrances to the famous Bari Vecchia.

Bari is the second largest city in Southern Italy and a leading com-mercial port on the heel of Italy's "boot." Bari is unique because the city is actually two distinct cities, the old one called "Bari Vecchia" (Old Bari) and the new and very modern Bari. Together they open their arms, join hands, and for several miles gently hug the coastline as they reach out to kiss the Adriatic Sea and put on display their very ancient history.

Piazza Mercantile, where Mom and Dad ("Mamma" and "Babbo") resided at the time of my birth, is one of the many *piazzas* (public squares) that one will encounter in the maze of narrow streets, twisted alleys, and numerous Romanesque churches that make up the very ancient Bari Vec-chia. At my entrance into the world, Mamma and Babbo were temporar-ily sharing living quarters with Nonna Antonia, my grandmother on my mother's side. Nonna owned a four-room, second-story apartment in a building attached to many other buildings of varied styles and heights that surrounded the famous piazza. Nonna had owned the apartment for many years, and she lived there with her youngest son, Zio (Uncle) Nino. Her husband, Nonno Andrea Capozzi, had died suddenly of a heart attack a few years back when Nino, my mother's only brother, was barely fifteen years old. My mother's older sisters, Zia (Aunt) Giuditta, Zia Elisa, and Zia Serafina, were already married and had gone to live in other parts of the city. My mother, Carmelina, was the last to get married.

You could blame the rise of the fascist regime that was rapidly changing the fabric of the Italian lifestyle, or you could blame the depression that was raising its ugly head all over Europe and America. You could blame the world war that ended in 1918, leaving much destruction and a worldwide depression. Whatever the reason, my father could not find a job. He could not support his family, and they had to live somewhere, so they moved in with Nonna Antonia and Zio Nino.

My father, Vittorio Lorusso, was the youngest in a family of four sons and one daughter. His father, Pietro Lorusso, was president of the court of appeals when he died in 1923 in Trani, a nearby town. His mother, Emilia Vavalle, was a member of a prominent and wealthy family from Conversano, another town of Bari province.

Little I know of my paternal grandparents' lives, for Babbo seldom spoke about them and his years growing up in Conversano. I know very little of my father's oldest brother Peppino, a lawyer who lived in Fiume, or of his other brother Carlo, also a lawyer, who lived in Trieste. Both those cities are in Northern Italy, and both are a long train journey from Bari. I heard Babbo mention more often his brother Amedeo, with whom he kept in contact by mail. Amedeo lived in Rome, which is about twenty miles from the coast of the Tyrrenian Sea on the western side of Italy. He also corresponded with his sister Anna, who lived in Naples, about 120 miles south of Rome on the Tyrrenian coast.

Once in a great while, he told us a little about his boyhood. His family had lived very comfortably, enjoying a spacious home on the outskirts of town. It was surrounded by manicured lawns and colorful flowerbeds. He told us he enjoyed picking ripe red tomatoes, green zucchini, long, plump eggplants, fragrant basil, and sage cultivated in their vegetable gardens and attended by several farm hands (*contadini*). He also alluded to the maids who had attended the children's needs and the lavish vacations the family enjoyed every summer. With a twinkle in his eyes, he recounted some of the mischievous adventures he perpetrated with the help of his brothers. He didn't talk of those days often, though. In retrospect, I think Babbo deliberately avoided dwelling in the past and made every effort to forget it. Remembering all he had lost would have been too painful.

Wars, like wild fires, have a way of destroying everything in their path—a terrible reality my father would experience and I would learn a few years later. The great times ended for Babbo when, in 1917, at the tender age of eighteen, he was called to serve in the Italian army and go to war. Since 1914, World War I had been raging in Europe and the Balkans, and in April 1915, Italy entered the hostilities. Soon, the Italian army was mobilized to defend Northern Italy. The war was brutal and fierce. Italy sustained many defeats and casualties. By 1917, men as young as eighteen years old were being drafted into the army. They later became known as "Ragazzi del '99" (Boys of '99—1899, the year they had been born). In this group, my dad was mobilized and sent to the front lines.

Vividly, he described those dangerous days and nights in the trenches. He and the men in his platoon rode horseback as part of the mounted artillery and had to maneuver heavy pieces of equipment with wide barreled cannons into strategic positions to hit designated targets. There were times, he told us, that he thought he was going to heaven at best, or losing some limbs at worst. Thank God, neither happened.

The war ended in 1918. All over Europe, drastic changes were occurring. Babbo's world was changed forever. His family had sustained enormous material and financial losses. Gone were the fields they once owned. Gone was their big home with its luscious gardens, and gone were all the hired hands.

Babbo was faced with serious choices. Was he going to apply to the university in Bari and pursue a degree in law as his father and brothers had done? Would he stay in the army and make a career of it? He was not and never would be a bookworm.

It didn't take long for him to make up his mind and choose the army. He had acquired a fondness for the beautiful stallions that were part of his outfit, and he had no problem tending the stables. After his decision to stay in the army, my father was transferred to the Corpo di Armata in Bari, a large army base on the Corso Vittorio Emmanuele in the center of the city, and assigned to training new recruits in the skill of horseback riding.

The stage was set, and soon the curtains of a dramatic romance would rise in Bari. Mamma and Babbo's romantic story began in the summer of 1924. My father was about twenty-five years old, tall, slender, and of very light complexion, with light brown, almost reddish hair.

He was so darn good looking that when he attended gatherings, all the girls scrambled for his attention. My mother was about twenty years old, a slim and attractive brunette with a very sexy figure and a warm smile. One day, while watering the plants on the balcony in Piazza Mercantile, a "miracle" happened, as she frequently called it later.

On that day, the man who would become her husband, dressed in his uniform, and riding his majestic stallion, led a platoon of mounted soldiers from the training camp through the piazza. He happened to look up, and their eyes met! It was love at first sight. Mamma used to tell me that the first glance of Babbo seated on a gorgeous brown horse with a white streak running down the middle of its head made her feel like the heroine in the pages of the fairy tales where "Prince Charming" appears and sweeps the beautiful young girl away.

Carmelina and Vittorio communicated with each other for a few months, but they kept very secret the way they met. We were never told how they managed to sneak out and see each other for ten or fifteen minutes at a time, and they never mentioned whether their meetings were during the day or the night. One thing they knew—they were in love and wanted to get married.

That goal seemed simple and obtainable—to everyone else, perhaps. Not to Nonna Antonia, though. Nonna, although very petite, was a determined woman. In her fifties, my grandmother appeared much older and seemed to be always in mourning. She always dressed in black, long pleated skirts that reached the floor and black tunics buttoned high on her neck. In public, she always wore a soft black scarf that framed her much wrinkled face and covered her salt and pepper hair.

Her hair was very long, almost down to her waist. With fast movements of her fingers, she would twist her hair into a braid and wrap it into a bun at the back of her head, and then she would secure it with long pins and wide combs. She wore black socks and flat, high-laced black shoes. Yet she was very light in her stride, and she had a silent, fast way of moving around.

When her husband Andrea died of a sudden heart attack, Nonna Antonia took over their business constructing handmade belts for bulging hernias. She had worked with him as a ladies' corsetiere, and she kept the business they had built together operating. There was a good market for the belts, because farmers from neighboring towns toiled hard with their hands and lifted heavy bundles, which often caused them to develop enlarged hernias. Nonno Andrea had become locally famous for his skill in making the belts, and he was much sought after by farmers all around the countryside. He was probably one of the few in the city with this unique occupation.

He was also a kind man. Many times, when a farmer could not afford to pay, Nonno would not charge him for the belt. This kindness was largely compensated during the celebration of the Christmas holidays, when the farmers showered him with the best of their produce. In their apartment, Nonno had separated off a small bedroom that he kept under lock and key, which no one was allowed to enter, not even Nonna. A few weeks before Christmas, Nonno would take everything out of that room, even the bed, and store it in every available space in the other rooms, so that he could fill the empty room with gifts from the contadini.

They gave him vats of refined olive oil, terra cotta vessels filled with all kinds of olives cured in special brines, and even small barrels of the most exquisite fine and rare wines kept aging for many years. There were also jars filled with marmalades, *confetture* (jams), and smooth fruit jellies. On special shelves, he stored baskets of dry figs layered with chocolate. When it came to baked goods, every town boasted its own specialty, and the farmers brought in boxes and boxes of sweet delights—sweet breads, biscotti, cookies of every flavor and texture, fruit cakes, and specialty candies.

After he died, Nonna managed to keep her husband's business going with the assistance of her youngest son, Nino. Though only fifteen, he had been in the habit of helping his father after school and was already familiar with the sewing machines used in their tiny factory behind the retail store they rented on Via Argiro. Zio Nino had to quit school to help Nonna, but when Nonna later passed away, he operated the business very profitably for many years.

My widowed grandmother, by then a businesswoman and entrepreneur, had become the undisputed authority in a household comprised of Nonna, Zio Nino, and my mother. When Nonna learned of her daughter's affair with Vittorio, she opposed it and fought desperately to keep them apart.

She tried arguing. "He will make a very bad husband. He is much too good-looking. Many women will go after him and try to steal him from you. Don't you see the signs? He seems to enjoy the adulation he is getting now. What will he do when you are home raising the kids?"

Nonna's motives were good. She wanted to spare her daughter the pain of having to deal with infidelity. Carmelina would not listen, though, and she begged for her blessing. Nonna would not budge.

Losing all hope for a future with her handsome soldier, my mother decided there was no sense in living without the man she loved. She saw only one way out: to take her own life. She almost succeeded. One day, she found a bottle of iodine in one of the kitchen cabinets and swallowed almost all of its contents.

What saved her from sure death was the quick intervention of Zio Nino, who happened to walk into the kitchen just as she slumped to the floor. Mother was still clutching the bottle of iodine in her hands and Zio Nino realized what had happened. He picked her up off the floor and ran down the stairs and out on the sidewalk.

A horse and buggy was approaching from down the street and Zio Nino commandeered the driver to rush them to the nearby hospital. Seeing the emergency, the driver took off. At the hospital, after feverish attempts, the doctors brought her back to life. The event shook Nonna so much that she finally gave in and consented to their marriage.

On October 16, 1926, Vittorio and Carmelina were married, and after a brief honeymoon, they moved into a very small apartment on the outskirts of Bari. Mamma, like most other married women of her community, did not work outside the home. Her time was spent cleaning house, shopping for food, and cooking. There were no refrigerators in those days, so every morning she made the rounds from the open vegetable market, to the fish market, on to the butcher, and finally to the *fornaio* (the baker), where she bought fresh bread just out of the shop's wood-burning ovens. (To this day, if you walk the streets of Bari, you can smell the pleasant fragrance emanating from those storefronts from several blocks away.)

Babbo's day was a little more complicated. He was up by 6 A.M. He washed and donned his uniform and then caught an early bus to take him to his office at the Corpo di Armata, where his day started punctually at 7:30. He had a special office where he gathered his assigned men, a dozen at a time, and after completing his paperwork, took them to the stables, where they had to groom the horses. Then they had to go down to the training field, where they learned horseback riding.

My mother and father were very happy and loved each other deeply. Life was good. Then suddenly Babbo came home from work one evening with some bitter news. His job was being eliminated!

My mother never forgot the pain and anguish of that moment. Could it be possible? How could it happen just as they were expecting their first baby? In Italy, as in most of Europe in 1927, unemployment was rampant and jobs were nowhere to be found, unless you joined the Fascist Party. My father wanted no part of it.

The totalitarian state that Mussolini imposed on the Italian people gave my father no hope for a secure future. He did not agree with the repressive measures being introduced by il Duce. He had already witnessed the end of the free press, the banning of political parties, the replacement of elected local officials with those appointed by the central government, the banning of trade unions, and the creation of a secret police force, just to name a few. He could not adhere to such extreme views.

My mother agreed with him, and when my father could not pay the rent and they were faced with eviction, Mamma had no choice but to turn to her mother for help. "Could we please move in with you?" Mamma pleaded, swallowing her pride.

Nonna had no choice but to say yes. After all, she loved her daughter very much, and there was a baby coming. Mamma and Babbo moved in with Nonna, and Babbo kept hunting for jobs. In his desperate search he could only find temporary or part-time employment, which gave him and his family very little to live on. But anything was better than nothing.

The year 1927 passed, and on March 5, 1928, I made my entrance into the world. I had a humble and disadvantaged beginning, but I had something that has always been of higher value, though. What was not lacking in my family was love.

Months rolled by, and mother gave birth to my brother Pierino on January 21, 1930. My father was still shifting from job to job, when, in the early part of 1932, a letter arrived from Zio Amedeo in Rome that brought a spark of joy and hope for our future.

Zio Amedeo had secured for my father a very good paying job in one of the offices of a reputable enterprise in Rome. Babbo had to leave immediately. Mamma was left behind, waiting for Babbo to get settled and to find an apartment big enough for the family.

The notice arrived a few months later, and Mamma lost no time in packing our clothes in a pair of suitcases. We boarded the train for Rome. Babbo was waiting at the station for us, unaware of a surprise that my mother was bringing.

Yes! She was pregnant again! And when was the baby due? Very soon.

CHAPTER 3

SNAPSHOTS OF ROME FROM MY ALBUM OF MEMORIES

I was about four years old when we moved to Rome. I remember little of the few years we spent there. Like beams of sunlight breaking through the clouds, certain memories flicker here and there. Those snapshots are buried in the past, , and they curiously resurface from time to time, bringing me back to a time and place that, without my knowledge, shaped my personality.

One of the earliest snapshots in this phantom album of my memories is an image of the dirigible Hindenburg flying over Rome. I was attending kindergarten then and had many friends. Babbo had to work that day, but Mamma, pregnant for the third time, but still curious about important events, took my brother Pierino and me to the nearby park, where most of our neighbors were assembling to see the famous blimp.

The Hindenburg was scheduled to pass over the city around two P.M. When we got there, the park was already full of people scanning the blue sky above with anticipation. Mamma held Pierino's hand and I skipped behind her, searching the crowd in the hope of encountering some of my little friends from school as we walked the twisted pathways hemmed in by lush green hills.

The park was like an oasis in a desert, located in the center of a bustling part of the beautiful city of Rome. For whatever reason, its completion was still months or years away, and big boulders were scattered here and there from previous excavations. On one side of the park, a steep cliff was still open. It was dangerous for passersby to walk beside it, especially because about twenty feet down were boulders of many sizes piled up on each other.

After a short wait in our place among the crowd, we heard a rumble as the dirigible appeared in all its majesty, an enormous long, gray balloon, slowly cruising above our heads and below the puffy white clouds

17

that dotted the brilliant blue sky. The people cheered and waved at the historic event taking place before our very eyes. Suddenly from the direction of the cliff, just a short distance from where we were standing, a scream pierced the air. I ran with other people towards the cliff, not minding my Mamma's supplications to wait. Although I was almost trampled by the crowd, I managed to reach the edge of the cliff, and in horror, I recognized my dear friend Marina sprawled on top of a huge boulder at the bottom, her face covered with blood.

She lay motionless. There was a deep gash in her forehead, and her mouth was wide open and toothless, her clothing blood-spattered. She'd hit the boulder first with her face and then rolled over another one, knocking all her front teeth out. She was a mess and certainly not something small children like me should have witnessed. We returned home, and for many nights, nightmares woke me in a sweat and my loud screams brought Mamma or Babbo charging to my side to quench and calm my fears. Marina's fall and the sighting of the Hindenburg occupied the neighborhood conversations for many months. The sight of my friend's bleeding face occasionally still makes its grim appearance in my memory to this day.

On November 4, 1932, Mamma gave birth to my brother Andrea. Mamma really had her hands full by then. I was four and half years old, Pierino two, and here was another baby. All of Mamma's family was in Bari, and in Rome, Zio Amedeo, his wife Bianca, and their three children lived quite far from us. We saw them only for the holy days. On Mamma alone fell the task of tending to the chores of raising a family and running the household.

Babbo's hours were long, and he had to commute a half-hour each way to get to his job. He left for work at seven A.M. and came back for the midday meal and siesta at one P.M. It was the custom in Italy, and is to this day, to split the workday. Office workers went home, and all stores and shops, big and small, closed their doors. All activity came to a screeching halt, turning the big city into a ghost town. Offices, stores, and shops reopened at five and closed again at nine P.M. Babbo then returned to the office and spent an extra hour once again on the commutes.

This was Babbo's routine five days a week, and on Saturdays, he worked until two P.M. With this schedule, Babbo was of little help to Mamma, yet his salary was not large enough to cover the expense of hiring a maid even part-time.

Here another snapshot, a picture of where we lived, pops out of my album. The apartment we lived in was on the fourth floor in a building attached to several others that made up a city block. It was in a work-ing class neighborhood. The entrance to the three bedrooms, the dining room, the kitchen, and the bathroom was via a long hall. The bedrooms were on the left of the hall, and the other rooms were on the right. The rooms on the right, including the kitchen, had their windows open on the courtyard. Most buildings in Italy are built in this fashion.

With no time to shop and so many chores to attend, Mamma de-pended on the food vendors that came daily to the courtyard, skillfully maneuvering their full carts. Though slightly muffled with the passage of time, I still hear the vendors' calls as they lured potential buyers to the windows. This vibrant and noisy spectacle transformed for a few hours the calm of the courtyard into a circus-like atmosphere that we children cherished and waited for with great joy.

At about 9 A.M., the courtyard filled up with vendors and their hand-carts. Some were full of the freshest fruits and vegetables just picked from nearby fields. The milkman's cart was also full of baskets of just-laid eggs. Chickens that had been alive only a few hours before now hung motionless in the cart, still wearing their feathers. A few feet be-hind those carts, the fish vendor pushed his handcart full of aluminum bins overflowing with fish just out of the cool waters of the Adriatic Sea and still squirming on top of the ice. Not far behind him came the semi-covered handcart of the baker, full of baskets of fresh-baked loaves and rolls of various forms and shapes. The delicious aroma of the baker's cart wafted all the way to the fourth floor, making a purchase from his cart a must on Mamma's list.

To complete this circus atmosphere, two peasants mingled with the group, one playing a banged up guitar and the other a much-used mando-lin as they sang romantic songs of that era. A cute little monkey wearing red cut-up shorts and a little red hat perched on his head, completed their group. A rope attached to the monkey's pants at one side and wrapped around one of the men's wrists, kept the animal securely at the man's side. At the end of their concert, the monkey went around with a tin cup begging for money, entertaining the crowd with cartwheels and throwing kisses to everybody.

This type of exchange had a flavor all its own! Back then, this primi-tive way of purchasing the day's food was the norm. Refrigerators were not on the market, yet, so shopping for food was a daily routine. Mam-ma, as well as all the other housewives in the building who lived on the upper floors, kept a large straw basket with a sturdy handle attached to a rope long enough to reach the ground from the fourth floor. From the kitchen balcony, with great dexterity, Mamma lowered the basket and a list of products needed from each vendor scribbled on individual notes and enough money to buy what she estimated all the items would cost. The notes were passed around, and each vendor filled his own order, put it in the basket with the change, and when the orders were complete, with a twist of the wrist the last vendor yanked on the rope to signal that the basket was ready to make its journey up.

Mother then waved good-bye to the vendors and neighbors at the other balconies. She set the heavy basket on the kitchen table and arranged the merchandise in the order that it would be cooked and served. First in the lineup was the food for *il pranzo* (lunch), as it was the custom to eat the heaviest meal of the day around two P.M., and then the food for a lighter *la cena* (supper), which we enjoyed during the evening hours. After *il pranzo* came the *siesta*. It was a blessed time that alleviated the stress of the day for Babbo. He would go into his bedroom, lie down, make himself comfortable, and take a long nap.

For Mamma, though, the routine was different. Even during siesta, she juggled her time between house cleaning, changing diapers, baby feeding, and play times with Pierino and me. We were often warned to make no noise while Babbo was resting, or serious consequences would follow our disobedience. As far as I remember, most of the time we heeded her warnings.

Mamma was always busy tending the family, while Babbo took time out during the evenings to gather with friends at one of the many cafés near his office. This arrangement did not please Mamma a bit, and I remember vaguely the heated discussions they exchanged when he got home.

I could tell Mamma was jealous of her husband's freedom. As I think back to her words, I believe she knew he was fooling around. That must have hurt her because she saw Nonna's predictions slowly coming true. I guess there was little Mamma could do. She was much in love with him, and they always kissed and made up. Babbo was very affectionate to her and to us. When he was home, he spent time playing with my brother and me. He would surprise us with small presents and bags of chocolates and candies. We adored him!

Our "Roman holiday" would soon end, though. The next snapshot in my mind's album is of one of the last special times our family spent there. In so many ways, Christmas was a children's holiday. Maybe that is the way it should be, since Christ came to earth as a baby.

My last memory of Rome is of the last Christmas we spent there. In Italy, the custom of gift giving was reserved for children only, and it was on the Day of the Epiphany, January 6, when the church taught that the Magi brought gifts to the baby Jesus. On that night, Italian folklore had it that a witch called "La Befana," dressed all in black, balancing a high pointy hat on her head and riding a broom stick, quietly entered every kitchen in search of food, and when she found it, she exchanged it for the presents the children had asked for in notes left on the table. For several hours, Pierino and I (Andrea was still too young to join the fun) thought passionately of what to write on that list. Visions of sugar plums and fancy toys danced before our eyes as we promised Mamma and Babbo we would be very, very good. We knew La Befana left toys only to good children, but she left coal for the bad ones, and she knew exactly who had been good and who had been bad. So after leaving our favorite chocolates, candies, and biscotti on the kitchen table for our beloved Befana to fill her bags with, we went to bed like little angels, in the hopes of finding the next morning the toys we had wished for.

I wanted a doll so badly that I didn't care if I got anything else. When we got out of bed that morning, Pierino and I dashed to the kitchen, sure our wishes had been fulfilled. Our mouths drooped and our eyes filled with tears as we realized the table was empty. What had happened? Anxiously, we questioned Babbo as he sleepily made his way into the kitchen.

"Babbo, Babbo!" we cried in disbelief, hugging his legs. "We were good, weren't we? Why did La Befana leave nothing for us?"

I guess we made Babbo feel guilty about putting us through such torment! He motioned us to wait by the kitchen door while he made his way down the hallway. Once there, he picked up a large bundle and with a gleaming smile on his face, brought it into the kitchen and uncovered the most beautiful toys we had ever seen. Mamma was there also to catch our exuberant squeals of pure happiness!

There she was, my very first beautiful doll, dressed in satin and laces, with long, blond, shiny hair, rosy cheeks, and the most gorgeous blue eyes that opened and closed as I put her down. She was quite tall, much bigger then I had expected, and her arms and legs moved. I set her in the little chair next to a table that was part of a child's set. Other toys went unnoticed for a while, and I paid no attention to Pierino's toys, which were also just what he wanted. I had my eyes on that gorgeous doll, and I could not believe she was really mine. For many years, she was my favorite companion. She traveled with me everywhere.

La Befana had returned to her land of make-believe for another year. It was winter, and life in Rome returned to its usual routine. Mamma and we three children did not go out much in winter except to school. Our days passed in the knowledge that this splendid city was going to be our home for many years.

Or so we thought. On one sunny day in midsummer of 1933, Babbo came home with tears in his eyes. His company was failing. Many changes were being imposed to save it, and Babbo's job was being eliminated.

For days Mamma cried, not knowing what to do. Babbo searched again for a job, but there were none to be found. Then one day, another miracle happened. Unknown to us, Zio Amedeo had casually mentioned in a letter to their brother Carlo, who lived in Trieste, that Vittorio was in desperate need of a job. A few days later, a letter arrived from Zio Carlo asking Babbo if he would be willing to move to Trieste for a great job that was waiting to be filled as soon as possible.

Babbo wasted no time. He boarded the first train out of Rome and headed for Trieste alone.

CHAPTER 4

OUR NEW HOME IN SANTA CROCE DI TRIESTE

Ten days passed with no news from Babbo. Every morning, Mamma anxiously waited on the balcony for the mailman to round the corner of our street and bring us news from Babbo. She would admonish me sternly, "Emilia, I want you to mind your brothers well while I go downstairs to get the mail. The three of you will stay in this room and not leave it for any reason!"

Her voice trembled with anxiety. She did not enjoy leaving me with this responsibility. In a flash, she was gone from our sight. We heard her race down the several flights of stairs to the first floor. In no time, she was back, and with a sigh of relief, she hugged and kissed us, satisfied we had obeyed her orders.

On the tenth day, a letter did come. Instead of a letter from Babbo, a notice arrived from the landlord. The apartment had to be vacated by the end of the month or my mother had to pay the three months' rent my parents owed him. Mamma was in a panic!

Her fervent prayers were immediately answered. A knock at the door very early the next morning jolted us out of our beds. Mamma opened the door and fell into Babbo's arms with cries of joy. Laughing, he explained that he had thought it best to surprise us personally with his great news.

"We are going to Trieste!" he blurted joyfully. "Yes! It is a great place to live, and you will all enjoy it."

One by one, he picked us up, covered us with hugs and kisses, and then turned to Mamma in what I thought was an endless embrace.

As we sat down for *il pranzo*, Babbo gave us many details about the enchanted place to which we were moving. "We are going to Santa Croce di Trieste," Babbo said. "The village is about twenty miles southwest of the city of Trieste and stands on top of a high cliff on the coast of the Adriatic Sea. It has the most spectacular views and a railway line

23

that originates in Venice, crosses the town halfway down the cliff, and ends in Trieste. The trains stop at the Santa Croce station on their runs back and forth.

"I was offered the job of station master for that stop. Roberto, the present station master, has to retire due to poor health. In the back of the station, we will have our own very comfortable living quarters!"

He sounded so excited. In humble words, he expressed gratitude for answered prayers and acknowledged that only divine intervention had procured this great job during such hard times. Mother was ecstatic, too. It took her almost no time, with the help of Babbo and our neighbors, to pack crates of our movable belongings and fill suitcases with our clothes. The heavy furniture was being shipped by rail, and it would arrive about a week after we got to Santa Croce.

One bright morning, we all boarded the train bound for Trieste, and two days later, we were dropped off with other passengers in front of the Santa Croce station. On the platform Roberto, who was waiting for our arrival, met us. He escorted us to the back apartment that had been made ready for us and with excitement in every step, my brother Pierino and I went from room to room to explore our new home.

The apartment was attached to the back of the office and the large waiting room of the station. It had an anteroom, three bedrooms, a large dining and sitting area, and a very comfortable bathroom. What Mamma liked most was the large, well-equipped kitchen, the largest she had ever occupied.

We thought it a great place to live, and going to bed that night we anticipated the wonders waiting for us in the morning. Babbo was eager to show us our new surroundings, and that morning, we discovered that Santa Croce was everything he had said it would be and much, much more. I helped Mamma dress Pierino as she attended to little Andrea's needs. In no time, we were outdoors, scurrying down the ramp that led from our home to the railroad tracks. Babbo leading the way, we crossed the tracks, and a few yards over, we were at the edge of the cliff. The view was breathtaking!

From the edge, hundreds of vineyards tumbled down to the sands of a narrow beach that gently touched the blue waters of the Adriatic Sea as it stretched in a wide curve for miles in both directions. The day was clear as a bell and from where we stood the outline of the port of Trieste was vaguely visible, as were the silhouettes of the city's buildings. Their white walls covered the slopes of the famous Carso Plateau, and farther out, the spectacular backdrop of the majestic snow-capped Alps seemed to reach and blend with the clouds.

Between Trieste and our coastline, the Miramar Castle, in all its splendor, came into view at the very edge of a rocky spur that projected into the Adriatic Sea. Surrounded by luscious gardens, this castle, built in 1860 by the Archduke Ferdinand Maximilian, became the summer residence of the kings of Italy and their royal families, and it is now a well-known museum.

For almost an hour, we marveled at the view and then we walked back and around the gardens of our apartment. There, the view was more restricted. The huge cherry tree by the side of the building still had luscious cherries on its branches. To our delight, Babbo filled a couple of baskets, and later on, Mamma preserved some of them in alcohol.

Farther down, close to the fence that encircled the garden on three sides, a majestic fig tree had dozens of figs on its branches just beginning to sprout. A month later, we feasted for *colazione* (breakfast) on fresh, warm bread covered with the sweetest figs you could find anywhere.

The fourth side of the fence in the back garden was left open to join a dirt road. This road snaked its way from the direction of Trieste and continued its climb between the stand of wild cherry trees towards the west, ending up in the village of Santa Croce.

It was then that Mamma realized the town of Santa Croce was nowhere in sight.

"*Ma dove stanno I negozi?* (But where are the stores?)" Mamma inquired with astonishment.

"Sorry, Carmelina."

Babbo was slow to reply, maybe because he knew that what he was about to reveal was not such a pleasant surprise. He pointed up the hill behind us. "There are no stores down here. The village is up the hill."

"Up the hill?" Mamma sounded surprised, confused, and almost furious. "How in the world are we going to get up there and how far up the hill do we have to climb?"

Babbo looked uncomfortable. Clearing his throat, he calmly continued, "Do you see that building up there?" He pointed. "That is a hotel, and behind it there is a stairway that leads to the middle of Santa Croce, where all the stores are."

We all looked in the direction Babbo was pointing and there, a few hundred feet up the embankment behind our home, almost hidden by chestnut trees, was a beautiful white structure facing the Adriatic Sea. Its balconies overflowed with potted flowers. The hotel, Babbo explained, was a well-known stopover for tourists going to Trieste.

"Thank God there is some life here after all!" Mamma exclaimed sarcastically. "But where do we get the food?" she asked, concern in her voice. "Dove e' il mercato? *No sopra al villaggio? Ma che sei pazzo?* (Where is the market? Up in the village? But are you crazy?) How are we going to get there every morning? Did you say there is another way to get to the village?"

"Yes, there is," Babbo answered. He pointed to the dirt road we were standing on. "This road goes through that forest and ends at the village square, and as soon as I get organized, I will rent a horse and buggy and we will take a ride into town. You will like the shops a lot, Carmelina. The people are very friendly and eager to help." Looking at me, he continued, "And you will like your new school."

"Will I, really?"

I could not wait to go to school. That fall was to be my first year of elementary school, and I was very excited.

"*Va bene.* (Okay.)" I heard Mamma sigh. "I will try to adjust, but what a different place this is!" she said, shaking her head in disbelief.

"You will get used to it here in no time. You'll see!" Babbo tried hard to sound convincing, and I knew Mamma was resigning herself to a lifestyle very different from the one she had just left. In Rome, everything had been just around the corner.

"But I want to assure you, Carmelina," Babbo continued, "you will find shopping for food here at the station somewhat similar to Rome. Food vendors come here every morning with most everything you will need."

"*Veramente?* (Really?) Then I like this place already!" Mamma said, smiling and kissing Babbo on the cheek. Happily holding hands, we all made our way back to our home, and our life as the family of the station master began.

Life began to flow again. Mamma spent the mornings negotiating with food vendors to get tomatoes, onions, broccoli, and other vegetables and fruits at the best possible prices, as we kids, watching from the window, laughed at the words they exchanged. We soon discovered how good Mamma was at negotiating. She got her way most of the time. The vendors' carts were full of fresh produce and fresh baked breads. In special containers lined with ice, the vendors also offered fresh cuts of meat, fish, and dairy products. Mamma learned to give them a list of groceries she needed for the next day and the vendors were prompt to fill the orders.

Babbo learned his routine as *capo stazione* (station master) and diligently followed all the rules. Trains coming from either direction were scheduled to arrive every day at the same time, stop over on one set of tracks, let off passengers headed for Santa Croce, and pick up those headed for other cities. Ten minutes later, according to schedule and with a loud whistle, the trains continued their journey toward other cities along the coast. One of his most important duties was to make sure the railroad signals always worked perfectly. He also had to make sure all boarding passengers had their tickets and baggage ready. Babbo enjoyed his work and soon made friends with the regular passengers that worked in Trieste and commuted every day.

Once the trains left the station, silence surrounded the fairy tale place that we now called our home. The only sounds we heard were the chirping of birds nesting in the trees in our backyard and the distant whistles piercing the warm summer air as fishing boats made their way back from their catch of the day.

About a month after our arrival, curiosity brought some of our neighbors around. Of course, Pierino and I were thrilled to find that other boys and girls our age lived close by. They invited us to join in their fun, and for hours, we explored the surrounding farms. There was Sergio, who was about ten years old, his eight-year-old brother Paolo, and his six-year-old sister Giulia. Then there was eight-year-old Carlo, and Giuliano and Franca, who were both seven. One day, they all showed up at my house and asked Babbo if I could join them at the beach to watch the fishermen bring in the tuna.

"Tuna?" Babbo was startled. "Do you mean those big fishes?"

"Yes," one of the boys said, quite sure of himself. "We go and watch the fishermen at the far side of the beach when they come in with their boats full of all kinds of fish, especially tuna this time of the year."

"Is that so?" Babbo marveled at this news. "I didn't know fishing boats came down here to unload. Va bene," he said. "But be sure to not stay there too long." Then he admonished me to stay close to our friends and not get lost in that new territory. Of course, I promised Babbo that I would be very careful, and we began the descent to the beach.

My new friends were very familiar with the narrow paths that twisted between the vineyards leading to the beach. Bunches and bunches of grapes hung all over the trellises that followed each other in orderly rows. I had never before seen grapes growing on the vine, so I just trailed behind my friends, reaching now and then for a bunch to get familiar with how it felt in my hands.

Thinking that I was going to taste one of them, Sergio was quick to warn me, "Don't put it in your mouth! They are very bitter now, but in a few weeks, they will be ripe and sweet like sugar. We will be back when the pickers go in the fields, and they always give us some to take home."

That was fine with me. I followed them all the way down until we reached a secluded part of the beach that was set aside for fishermen to dock their boats and unload their catch. Usually, the boats made their way back in late morning and the fishermen skillfully maneuvered them on top of the sand, each boat taking its own space. Large and small bins were lined up there to receive nets full of squirming fish of many varieties. Pollution was unheard of at that time, and the clear waters of the North Adriatic Sea were famous for marine life that became the most exquisite and varied forms of seafood.

The air that morning was calm, and the waves of the sea rippled gently to the shore and foamed on the smooth rocks of the beach. Suddenly a boat approached, two men on each side, oars clutched firmly in their muscular hands. Yelling loudly to each other, they tugged the boat in and tilted it on a special spot of the sand. This boat was equipped with special gear to catch tuna, and on that day, it carried three of them that were still alive in its belly.

With rolled up pants and bare feet the men jumped out of the boat, and the other fishermen helped them unload those enormous fishes. Chills ran down my spine as long spears and sharp knives began to cut those massive animals into pieces right in front of my eyes! The sand underneath their bodies turned red with blood, and I felt like throwing up. I turned around and walked a few yards from where we were standing.

"Emilia, come back!" Sergio shouted when he saw me leaving. As he and our other playmates laughed, he added, "Believe me, after watching this spectacle a couple of times, you will get used to it, but if you can't take it now, go behind those bushes and wait for us."

I turned around, and covering my mouth with one hand, I ran behind the bushes, trying to think of other things. Half an hour later, the children came looking for me, and Sergio brought me a large piece of tuna wrapped in newspapers.

"Here, this is for you," he said. "And it's all cleaned. I bet your parents will love this fish."

He was right. Babbo and Mamma had never seen a piece of tuna that big. The next day, a large slice of tuna that had been grilled in our backyard enhanced our pranzo. Babbo took time to open the charcoal grill as Pierino, Mamma, and I watched him with anticipation. He set the tuna on the grill, filled a small plate with olive oil and wine vinegar, added salt and pepper, and using a bunch of fresh parsley dipped in the mixture, he sprinkled the tuna making the flames jump up the grill and spreading the fish's pungent fragrance for many feet around our backyard. And what a fragrance that was!

The month of September rolled in, and Babbo arranged for me to attend the first grade of elementary school. One sunny morning, my birth certificate in his hand, we climbed the long stairway to Santa Croce and walked to the school building a few blocks away. Parents bringing their children to register joined us as we walked down the hall and took seats next to other applicants waiting their turn. Several children standing by their parents assessed my appearance, their eyes moving quickly from my hair all the way to my shoes. I wasted no time in exchanging questions with them.

"*Come ti chiami?* (What is your name?)" I asked a girl who appeared to be my age.

"Anna," she answered. "*E tu?* (And you?)"

"*Il mio nome e' Emilia, e comincero' il primo anno* (My name is Emilia, and I am starting the first grade)," I answered.

"*Anche io!* (Me, too!)" Anna answered and turned to join other children nearby that seemed to know her. I had a very outgoing nature, and had a vocabulary and style of speaking that sounded older than six, or so my parents and their friends told me. I liked to talk and I made friends easily. I joined the group and soon we were laughing and joking as if we had known each other forever. Registration was soon over. Parting ways, we told each other we looked forward to school opening so we could spend time together again. To my delight, school opened just two weeks later.

While I waited for school to start, I spent part of my free time in the station's waiting room when it was time for trains to stop over. They were always punctual, and passengers began to trickle down to buy tickets about an hour before the trains' arrival. I enjoyed spending time with the passengers and engaged in conversations with them that sometimes revealed intimate events in our family's life. My disclosures infuriated Babbo. He often threatened to lock me up in my room if I did not stop. Of course, the passengers liked my funny stories. In their opinions, I was a very assertive child, very mature for my age, and they told Babbo they loved to have me around.

When not in the station's waiting room, I helped my mother with her chores. My brothers were growing, and I fed them, changed their clothes, taught Andrea to walk, and protected them from harm. I loved being a second mother to them. Besides helping to take care of them, I played with them to my heart's content. They must have wondered why they had *two* mothers and only one father.

School started in the middle of September, and my routine changed. I loved school. I didn't like the long climb up the stairs or the long road through the woods (it took me almost an hour every morning to reach the village), but I loved my teacher and I made many friends.

My first year in elementary school was a year of wonders. Learning to read and write, adding numbers and listening to poems astonished me to the point that I wanted to accelerate the lessons. With the help of Babbo or Mamma when they had time, I progressed rapidly and was way ahead of the class. I remember learning to hold a needle in my fingers, thread it with colored yarn, and make my first embroidery stitches around a linen handkerchief. I had an insatiable desire for learning that has never left me.

Fall began to arrive with all its beauty. The trees were aflame with color and the days grew shorter and cooler. By the middle of October, all the vineyards were heavy with tons of succulent grapes ready to be picked and squeezed for wine. This was *vendemmia*, or harvest time, and for about two weeks a year, we saw this saga unfold.

In the early mornings, dozens of women dressed in native costumes of brightly colored tops, full skirts, and flat sandals descended in groups from the village. Most were young, and they laughed and sang as they skillfully balanced large straw baskets on their heads. Skirting the station's ramp, they crossed the tracks and disappeared between the vineyards down the cliff. By noon, they were crossing back, their baskets full of grapes. When they came to the benches along the ramp, they sat down briefly, welcoming the rest before starting the long climb back to the village.

When Babbo saw all those women with their baskets overflowing with grapes, he turned to Mamma and wistfully said, "Someday, when I can afford it, I will buy enough of them to make a barrel of the best wine you have ever tasted!"

"Well," said Mamma, jokingly, "I guess we will have to wait a long time!"

It was then that an idea flashed in my mind. The ladies looked tired and sweaty after all that work in the fields. Why not bring them cool water in exchange for a bunch of grapes? I was giving birth to an entrepreneurial spirit that would bring its rewards many years later.

"Pierino!" I called from the open door. "Come over. You have to help me!"

With that, I rushed into the kitchen, grabbed a couple of glasses, and asked him to fill them with cool water. I grabbed two more glasses, filled them also with cool water, and motioned Pierino to follow me. I went down the ramp and offered one of the ladies a drink. Smiling, she showed her appreciation by giving me a bunch of grapes. The scheme worked perfectly. Pierino followed my steps, and in no time, we had our own baskets full of grapes. That was just the beginning. Every day after school, we had our pitchers full of water, ready to be poured for the ladies, and we were rewarded with bunches of grapes. When the *vendemmia* ended for that year, Babbo had enough grapes to make his barrel of wine without paying a single penny for it. Several months later, Mamma and Babbo enjoyed what they agreed was the best wine ever.

But where were all those grapes going? Mamma and Babbo were curious. The answer came in the form of an invitation for dinner. Roberto, a friend of my father's, wanted us to meet his family, and he arranged for that occasion to coincide with the beginning of the *vendemmia*, which was beginning to take place at a farm on the outskirts of Santa Croce. That afternoon, after enjoying a most delicious *pranzo* with our friends, we all climbed in Roberto's horse-drawn carriage and headed towards the part of town where the wine production was located.

As we approached, a strong and pungent odor assailed our nostrils. Rounding a curve suddenly, we stared at huge round barrels half full with grapes. In the middle of them stood three or four women, their skirts pulled together in the middle of their legs and folded to reach their waist. They were jumping up and down and squeezing the grapes with their bare feet. That was a sight to remember forever. Many years later, when I came to the States, a similar scene appeared in one of the episodes of *I Love Lucy*, and it brought to my mind happy memories of those bygone childhood days.

As fall faded, winter blew in with all its fury. The snow, unknown to us until then, covered the countryside with a white heavy blanket. We also became acquainted with *La Bora*, a strong wind that filters down from the high peaks of the Alps and unleashes its rage on the valleys below. The wind is so strong that ropes are secured by the roadsides so that people can hold onto them. Our time was spent mostly indoors during those frigid winter months, and the food vendors barely made it around twice a week. Boots and heavy coats, scarves, and gloves occupied most of the space in the anteroom. A neighbor picked me up every morning to take me to school in his sled as he made the run for the school with his own children. I enjoyed those rides, and I loved playing with snowballs in the schoolyard with my new friends.

Spring brought back the green leaves on the trees, the daffodils in the gardens, and the violets under the wild cherry trees of the forest.The chirping birds returned to fill the air with their melodious sounds as they prepared new nests. The days got longer and warmer and the eternal wonder of a new beginning captured our hopes for a better tomorrow.

As usual, the trains loaded and unloaded their passengers from cities unknown, but on one of those spring days, a horrible accident took place. As one train approached the station, an old man in the crowd lost his balance and fell over the tracks. A screech of metal on metal pierced the air as the conductor brought the train to a halt, but he could not avoid running over the man. People screamed and hid their faces in their hands. The horribly mutilated body of the old man was in plain view. Hearing the screams, I ran out after Babbo, and when I got close, I saw limbs scattered all around and blood splashed on the tracks. As fast as I could, I ran back into the house, where I fell on my bed, trembling and crying my heart out.

The incident cast a dark cloud over the station for the next few weeks. The cloud got darker when news of new railroad inspectors coming to town reached our ears. My father had not joined the Fascist Party, and he had been debating whether it would it be wise to do in order to keep his job. He must have hesitated too long. At the end of August, a notice arrived informing Babbo that his position had been terminated and given to someone else. No reason was given. In those days, no reason was necessary. The government decided how things would be, and it was in control of the situation.

There we were again! Someone popped our balloon full of hope, and all our dreams were tumbling and disappearing again in an ocean of insecurity. By mid-September, we were on a train heading back to Bari.

CHAPTER 5

BACK IN BARI

There was no one waiting for us at the station when we arrived in Bari that late afternoon in August 1934. We did have a place to stay, though. Nonna Antonia owned a small apartment towards the old part of Bari in one of the least affluent neighborhoods, and it was empty. Nonna generously offered it to us.

"You can stay in my apartment in Via Libertá as long as you want and don't worry about the rent," she assured Babbo when she heard of his job loss and our return to Bari. "Just think about finding a job and feeding your family. I will take care of the rest."

God bless Nonna Antonia! She was always there for us. When we arrived in Bari, Babbo warned us not to expect a castle, but to think of this place as a "pass over." Whatever that meant.

Grabbing the suitcases, Babbo made his way out of the railroad station and on to the piazza with all of us following him. Stationed outside along the sidewalk, rows of *carrozze* (horse and buggies) and *carrozzieri* (drivers) patiently waited to pick up passengers when trains arrived. Babbo motioned to one of the many *carrozzieri* on the line and he promptly helped us enter the carriage and settle on the comfortable seats. He then climbed up front on his high bench, and holding tight the reins with one hand, shouted, "Ghiriap!" He waved his leather whip in the air and brought it lightly down on the horse's back, sending the animal into a swift gallop. The carriage gave a jolt, then the screeching of wheels and the thump of horse's feet on the cobblestones blended in a melodious rhythm as the *carrozza* made its way to our destination.

It was almost dark when we arrived in Via Libertá. The carriage pulled into a narrow space among the carts lined along the narrow sidewalk and stopped in front of our building.

"Whew! What is this smell?" Mamma, holding little Andrea in her arms, exclaimed in disgust. One by one, we climbed out of the carriage,

33

covering our noses with our hands as our eyes swept over the new surroundings. Wide-eyed, we stared at the overflowing barrels of putrid garbage.

"*Guarda a tutta questa immondizia*! (Look at all this garbage!)" My brother Pierino shouted, closing his nostrils with his fingers.

"*Non ti preoccupare* (Don't worry)," Babbo reassured Pierino. "By tomorrow it will be all gone."

I think we were all afraid this was just the beginning of what lurked ahead. After paying the driver and sending him on his way, Babbo walked to the *portone* (heavy wooden door) that opened on a small entryway, picked up our suitcases, and made his way up the ramp of stairs in front of us. Behind the stairway, partly visible, another massive wooden door left partly ajar caught our attention.

"Babbo, Babbo!" Excitedly, Pierino and I said, "Let's go see what's behind that door."

"No, no, that is not for you to explore!" Babbo was stern. "And if I catch you—" he added, as a loud neighs of horses behind the door sent us scurrying up the stairway at great speed. Trailing closely behind Babbo, we reached the second floor and landed on a long, dimly lit corridor that stretched for about forty feet in both directions. Babbo turned to the left, passed one door, and a little farther down stopped in front of another. Putting the suitcase down, he reached for a large key in his pocket and opened the door.

"Here we are! This is going to be our home only for a very little while, I promise!"

He turned on the light switch, and disgust filled our eyes and hearts as we saw our new home for the first time. Mamma started to cry on Babbo's shoulders.

"How is this happening to us?" she sobbed, wiping her tears with the back of her hands.

"It will be just for a while," Babbo comforted her. Turning to us kids, he started making jokes about what was around us.

"Now tell me, have you ever seen anything so beautiful? Look at this shiny round table and all these chairs around it."

The table was stained and covered with scratches, and the chairs had some of their back slats broken or missing. Was Babbo seeing things we could not?

"And there, look at that magnificent *bouffet* (sideboard)!" He pointed at an old piece of furniture, broken shelves plainly visible, which would hold water glasses, dinner plates, cups and saucers, cutlery, and pots and pans. Was he kidding? Next, his finger pointed at the old discolored *divano* (sofa) that took up space at the far left of the same room. It had an old stained painting of a horse hanging above it.

"Look at this soft and comfortable *divano!*" Babbo exuberantly added, trying to make us see a brighter side of the picture. Hard as he tried, he was not succeeding. We children were ready to make a run for the front door. Mamma, realizing our fears, composed herself and joined Babbo in the merriment.

"Okay. Let's see," Babbo continued. "Is there a treasure hidden under—" He started to lift a wooden board from the top of a coal burning stove attached to the wall on the right side of the room.

Suddenly, from under the board, in an instant, dozens of black roaches of every size took off and scrambled in every direction! Even Babbo was stunned. He slammed the board down and, grabbing a broom from where it leaned against the wall, he went into attack mode. The more he crushed them the faster they ran. Screaming and stamping our feet, my brothers and I attached ourselves with all our might to Mamma's legs, afraid to take another step in any direction. What a sight! In a few seconds, the roaches were gone. They just disappeared between cracks in the walls and floors—anywhere there was a place to hide.

"What a mistake I made! Let's get out of here, fast." Babbo's voice was full of anger. He picked up the suitcases and marched towards the front door. "I should have checked this place out before bringing you here! Let's go to Zia Elisa and Zio Pierino's house and stay with them for a few days until I refurbish and clean the apartment."

Mamma did not say a word. Surely she was thinking, "How could you bring us here without seeing the apartment first?" Her disappointment was evident on her face!

We spent that night and several others at my uncle's house while Babbo got rid of the roaches. A few days later, in full daylight, we made our way back to Via Libertá, and this time Babbo took us through the whole apartment, which had been painted and decorated with new furniture. He made it a point to tell us that the roaches were gone for good, thanks to strong "medicine" that was applied in every room.

As we walked from room to room, we saw that the apartment's only toilet was nudged between the bedrooms in a small closet, and the only sink was in the kitchen next to the stove. From the back wall of an entry room that served as the kitchen, dining room, and sitting room, a door opened into a bedroom that had a bed for Mamma and Babbo and a bed for my brother Andrea. An old *armadio* (portable closet) rested against the wall. There was no window in this room. From the back wall, a door opened into another bedroom that I had to share with my brother Pierino. When we opened that door, sunshine at last filled the room. That room actually had a balcony.

We ran outside to see the view, and we were assailed by a sickening, foul smell.

"Look, Babbo! There are horses in the yard!" Pierino shouted joyfully, covering his nose with his hand. We all looked down, and in plain sight, about half a dozen stallions were being groomed and cared for by several *carrozzieri*. Those were real stables! Comparing the magnificent view of lush mountains and the fragrance of the Adriatic Sea we enjoyed only a few days before to the view we now faced, was like going from heaven into hell. The horrible stench from the stalls forced us to keep the balcony's glass doors closed. Thank God, they were glass doors. At least they were a window into the world and we could tell when it was day and when it was night.

Fall approached, and it was time again for school. I was registered for the second grade at an elementary school not far from where we lived, but my learning was soon interrupted by the measles I contracted and brought home to infect my brothers. Mamma was very patient and took good care of us while Babbo worked. He had found a small job that barely paid for our food.

As December moved in, I counted the days in anticipation of Christmas. During this time, Zio Nino and Zio Pierino put aside certain hours of the day to build *il presepio* (the crèche) in their homes. This tradition prevailed throughout Italy, and in many homes, the head of the household was in charge of the project. The churches in Bari were also erecting nativity scenes indoors as well as outdoors. The life-size figures of Mary, Joseph, angels, shepherds and sheep, oxen and donkeys, and the manger with Baby Jesus in front of backdrops recreating the town of Jesus' birth captivated the attention of passersby and mesmerized children. Christmas was a Holy Day.

It was a special time when the only gifts exchanged were the gifts of oneself, as families and friends gathered for dinner to share traditional specialties prepared *with love*, and it was a time for prayer and worship. On Christmas Eve that year, my family and all my uncles, aunts, and cousins assembled in Nonna's home in Piazza Mercantile. We gathered around the huge table in the dining area and after hearty helpings of traditional foods, especially seafood, young and old immersed themselves for hours of fun, playing *"Tombola"* and *"Mercante in Fiera."* We played until about fifteen minutes before midnight, when we all lined up with sparklers in hand, the youngest child in front holding the statue of Baby Jesus cradled in his tiny hands. In a procession, we circled through the rooms of the house, singing *"Tu scendi dalle stelle"* (You're falling from the stars), the most popular Christmas song of that era. At the stroke of twelve, the procession stopped in front of the presepio that Zio Nino had so skillfully erected in one part of the room, and the Baby Jesus was tenderly deposited in the manger where Joseph and Mary, the cow, the donkey, the lambs, and the shepherds waited in adoration.

After celebrating the birth of Jesus, we hugged and kissed and wished each other *"Buon Natale"* (Merry Christmas) and then returned to the table to end the evening munching on traditional desserts (my favorite were the *cartellate*) and sipping homemade liquors with names like *Amarena, Anisetta, and Strega* for the adults, while we kids sipped cups of steamy hot chocolate.

In those days, we had no material wealth, but we were very rich in love. Before leaving in the wee hours of the morning, Zio Nino surprised us children with several bags of candies and special chocolates to take home. We went home to sleep until Christmas morning, which was ushered in by the peel of church bells summoning people to attend Mass.

When I returned to school after the Christmas holidays, I contracted whooping cough, and as usual, both my brothers came down with it, as well. That was a miserable sickness. It lasted about a month, with daily visits to a hospital where in a special steam room permeated with sulfur we got relief from the dreadful bouts of coughing. The treatments lasted a couple of hours at a time. Going back and forth every day, Mamma had no rest that winter, but I never heard her complain. Babbo continued looking for a decent job, to no avail, as my second year of school ended.

At the end of June, schools closed for summer vacation. Mamma and Babbo were surprised at my report card, because in spite of all the time lost to measles and whooping cough, it was still full of A's and A+'s. I really enjoyed learning.

Some of my fondest snapshots from the summer of 1935 are memories of the sundrenched days we spent at the beach. We went a couple of days a week, maybe less, but they were magical days. Zio Pierino and Zia Elisa, their children, Gianni, Andrea, Vito, and Corrado the youngest; Zia Giuditta and Zio Emmanuele with their children, Lina and Bimbino; Zia Serafina and her three daughters, Nicoletta, Antonietta, and Michelina; and my entire family all headed to San Girolamo's beach for hours of carefree fun.

The golden sand that other beaches were famous for was mixed with pebbles and small rocks; only in a few places could bathers feel smooth sand. For that reason, on one side of the beach, rows of cabins attached to each other were built on stilts that sloped for several feet into the calm waters of the Adriatic Sea. Each cabin, about eight feet by eight feet, had an internal stairway leading down to the water. They were open during the summer months to bathers for daily rentals. Usually, we rented two of them, one next to the other. Zio Nino and Nonna Antonia joined us some days during *Ferragosto*, August 15, when in Italy it is the custom to take at least two weeks of vacation and most of the stores shut down till the end of the month.

We were a happy bunch and we kids played for hours, swimming and racing each other in the water or diving from the stairway of the cabin, competing to see who would resurface the farthest away. At lunchtime, we feasted on *tiella al forno,* a baked rice, potatoes, onions, and mussels casserole; *pasta al forno con polpette* (baked pasta with meatballs); focaccia stuffed with prosciutto, salami, and provolone cheese; or eggplant parmigiana—though not all at one sitting! There was always a bowl of fresh fruit in season, and never missing from Italian meals, homemade wine of the best quality for the adults and for the children plenty of iced water. Little did us kids care that the adults were often engrossed in heated conversations of war and politics.

The depression held the nation in its iron grip, and unemployment was at its peak. Rumors of war were surfacing, and the word "Ethiopia" kept popping up in conversations. I never would have guessed then the enormous impact on my life that word would make.

As the rest of Europe began to fall under the siege of Hitler's regime and his pie-in-the-sky dreams of Nazi expansion, Benito Mussolini, our famous Duce, had his own eyes set on a new Italian Empire. Speaking repeatedly with great eloquence, he set out to convince the Italian people that Italy had the "right" to expand.

He promised the people "a place in the sun," where jobs would be plentiful and opportunities opened for factories to prosper. No wonder people believed him. What he failed to tell them was that all this good fortune would be realized at someone else's expense. On the east coast of Africa, Italy already occupied Eritrea and part of Somaliland. Ethiopia, sandwiched between the two, became a prime candidate for this expansion, making it possible for Italy to unify the whole territory.

Like a bolt from the sky, one day in late August, Babbo came home and dropped in our laps a huge surprise.

"I am joining the army again," he announced, a firmness in his voice I had never heard before.

"You are doing what?" Mamma was incredulous.

"The army is recruiting again and accepting volunteers," Babbo continued. "I have an appointment for tomorrow morning at the Corpo di Armata with the recruiting staff, and I am positive they will accept me because of my background. Finally, I will have a job that will pay well again, plus all the benefits."

Mamma sounded shocked. "But they are talking of war! Do you want to risk being sent to the front lines?"

She blurted out the words in anger.

"There is that possibility, of course, and I have to take that risk. I have no choice in this matter. I cannot see us living in this hole in the ground. It may take a year, perhaps, but I have to move the children from this filthy place." His voice reached a higher pitch. "I feel sick when I see them sick." He bolted and headed for the bedroom, closing the door behind.

"You do have a point." Nodding, Mamma had to agree, tears running down her cheeks.

The next day, Babbo met with the recruiters at the Corpo di Armata and when it was over, he had the guarantee of being reinstated in the army again. They needed men with Babbo's qualifications, and his files were going to be processed immediately.

A few days later, a letter addressed to Babbo arrived with the date to report to the Corpo di Armata. On September 5, 1935, Babbo was reinstated into military service with the rank of *sergente maggiore* (sergeant major). He estimated his pay to be double the amount he was currently bringing home. He had his uniform tailored to his size and was assigned to a special job at the Corpo di Armata in Bari, a job that could change at any time. He looked handsome in his uniform, and I was so proud of him.

In October 1935, Italy declared war on Ethiopia, and suddenly there was a great movement of troops all through Italy. Men were recruited to join the army, navy, or air force. News of the occupation of Ethiopia and the advance of the Italian troops blasted from radios in homes, offices, and storefronts. Italy was at war, and with every conquest, the number of casualties mounted every day. Families lost fathers, sons, brothers, cousins, and friends. Mamma prayed that Babbo would be spared.

In a way, her prayers were answered. During that period, Babbo was needed more in Bari than on the front lines. The Ethiopian army was no match for the onslaught of the Italian forces, and the war ended on May 6, 1936. General Badoglio's army entered the capital city of Addis Ababa and Haile Selassie, Emperor of Ethiopia, took shelter in England. Ethiopia, under Italian rule, was annexed into the newly formed colony in East Africa and became known as *Africa Orientale Italiana.*

On June 10, 1936, Babbo was promoted to *"maresciallo ordinario."* The Italian government encouraged personnel and their families to settle in Ethiopia, and Babbo began considering a transfer to the new colony. Looking through this window of opportunity, Babbo decided on a course of action that would drastically change our lives and have consequences we could have never imagined in our wildest dreams.

Babbo's deployment notification finally arrived in early March 1937. His application for a transfer to Ethiopia was approved, and he and Mamma began preparing for his departure.

An aura of disbelief mixed with apprehension, sadness, and fear floated for days over our heads. Mamma would break into tears and then run into the bedroom in an effort to hide her sorrow from us kids. For days, she asked Babbo, "Do you think you made the right decision? And if something happens to you in Ethiopia? We hear strange things going on there that I don't even want to think about."

To that litany, Babbo's answer was always calm and comforting. "Carmelina, I promise you I have made the right decision. Already my pay has doubled again and now we can afford so much more for the children. Two pairs of shoes instead of one, more sweaters to keep them warm, and more food to keep them healthy." He used his persuasion and encouragement to convince her. "Do you want me to give this up? I will always be thinking of you," he would add, holding Mamma in his arms. "And for that reason, I will take good care of myself. You and the children will join me there as soon as the time for your transfer is established."

Mamma eventually gave in to his assurances, and there came a time when she looked, if not happy, at least content, and hopeful for a future full of dreams to be fulfilled. Separation from Babbo again brought a lot of pain to her heart, but her fervent prayers were a balm to her spirit. Looking back to the years that followed and all she had to endure, I realize that only her great faith in God's protection pulled us through.

On March 23, 1937, Babbo and other military personnel boarded the train headed for Naples. On the platform assigned to the families of the military, I stood with Mamma, my brothers, and my uncles among other mothers and fathers, wives and children, brothers and sisters sobbing with no restraint and waving white handkerchiefs. Together we huddled and strained our voices in a last "Ciao, *arrivederci, scrivi presto* (write soon)! *Non ti dimenticare di scrivere!* (Don't forget to write!)" There were plenty of tears in our eyes.

The whistles of trains going in and out of the station, the hustle of the *facchini* (porters) as they pushed carts full of baggage, and the shouts of "*Il Corriere*" or "*La Gazzetta del Mezzogiorno*" by newsboys eager to make a sale seemed to mock our sorrow. Were we going to see our loved ones again? I am sure that question reverberated in all the hearts of the families left behind.

Slowly, we made our way home. As we went inside, I felt an emptiness and a void that astounded me. The reality I faced made me almost numb. I was very attached to my father, and in my heart, the loss sapped my energy. It was the deep subbing of Mamma on her bed,that suddenly made me spring into action. I had to do something to relieve her pain. I jumped in bed with her, folded her arms around my shoulders, and wiped her tears with the sheets. I held her for a few moments and then softly nudged her, whispering, "Mamma, look at Pierino and Andrea. They are waiting for you."

Mamma turned and jumped out of bed. The boys were in the kitchen, sitting at the table with a bewildered look on their faces. They were too young to comprehend what was happening.

"*Venite qui,*" Mamma said softly. "Come over here. Babbo has gone away for a while, but we will join him very soon. We just have to pray, and God will make that day come very soon, do you agree?"

"Yes, yes, Mamma." Pierino and Andrea clapped their hands. Then, folding them in prayer, they repeated after Mamma her fervent petitions directed to a God that she believed always answered.

A couple of months went by, and no news came from Babbo. Tomorrow, yes, tomorrow we will get a letter, anxiously we told ourselves, hoping that tomorrow would be that day. Finally, on a warm spring morning, the much-expected letter came in the mail. With trembling hands, Mamma opened it, and we cuddled around her as she began to read. Her face lit up, and tears of joy ran down her cheeks.

"Yes, Babbo is well! Thank you, Jesus! What a relief," Mamma mumbled with gratitude as she extended her arms to embrace us. She went on to explain the particulars of his trip and said he was not able to communicate more details. He had left Naples on a military ship and for security reasons, he was not told his destination. He had crossed the Suez Canal, disembarked in Djibouti, a famous port in the French Somaliland,

41

and then traveled partly by train and partly by convoy until he arrived in Harar. In this Ethiopian city, he was assigned to an office of special operations in the Italian high command stationed there.

This was the first time the name "Harar" entered into my life, and never did I expect the magnitude of the events that soon evolved in that city. Mamma lost no time in answering, for she had something very special to tell him.

Surprise, surprise! Mamma was pregnant again. That news must have hit Babbo with the force of an earthquake. When his answer came back, it was filled with surprise, pleasure, apprehension, and suggestion, all wrapped into one mode of action. He wrote to Mamma a few days later that according to the disposition then in place, we had to leave Italy before the baby was born. By army decree, no babies under a year old were allowed to travel to Ethiopia, but it was permitted for a pregnant woman to give birth there. Mamma was three months pregnant, and that meant we had only five months, at most, to get ready. Could that be possible? Would we make it in time? How long would it take us to travel from Bari to Harar?

Documents necessary for our admission into Ethiopia piled up in record numbers. As usual, dealing with the government, filing applications, and requesting certificates meant hours of waiting in long lines. The paperwork seemed endless. At this time, Babbo also arranged for Zio Rodolfo to obtain a good paying job in Harar.

Zio Rodolfo had married Mamma's sister Serafina about a year earlier. Their story is worth telling because it gives a glimpse of the way God orchestrates our circumstances. Some twenty years before, Zio Rodolfo and Zia Serafina had met and fallen in love. For a couple of years, they saw each other often and decided to get married. Both their fathers were deceased, and when they brought their wish to their respective mothers, both denied them permission and forbade them to see each other again. About a year later, Serafina was given in marriage to Benedetto, a man she hardly knew. She gave birth to two girls, Nicoletta and Anonietta, before he moved the family to a village near Paris, France. Another girl, Michelina, was born in Paris, and after a brief illness, Zio Benedetto passed away, leaving her a widow.

Meantime in Bari, Rodolfo was despondent about his mother's decision to block his marriage. Perhaps to take revenge, he began a relationship with their maid, bringing dishonor to his family. With her, he fathered two lovely girls, Elsa and Cesarina, and he finally married her on her deathbed. His mother then raised the girls.

On a warm summer day, almost twenty years after they first met, Zia Serafina was boarding a city bus to visit a girl friend she had not seen for several months. As she waited to board, other passengers were alighting. Suddenly, she was face to face with her beloved Rodolfo coming off the bus. Moving out of the way of the passengers, they fell into each other's arms with sighs of indescribable joy, softly calling each other's name: "Serafina!" and "Rodolfo!"

Free at last to pursue their dreams, they married, hoping for many happy years together. Zio Rodolfo, like thousands of men at the time, was not able to find a decent job in the city and had been contemplating a move to Ethiopia, where the victorious Italians were occupying the country and the job outlook was better. Babbo knew of a position that fitted Zio Rodolfo's qualifications perfectly, and he helped him get the job. Italian officials moving into Harar were in need of transportation and personal drivers with experience as mechanics. Was Rodolfo willing to apply? Without hesitation, he accepted it.

Fortunately, our paperwork was ready at the same time as Zio Rodolfo's. Our departure from Bari was assigned to early October 1937, and the documents specified that our journey from Naples to Harar would take roughly twenty days. We would travel part of the way by boat, part by train, and part by truck.

By truck? That part made us all very nervous. Would Mamma make it in her condition? Mamma just shrugged away the fear with a simple remark, "We will find that out once we get there. Va bene? (Okay?)" She smiled grimly, giving us a look that assured us that nothing would stop her.

I had no idea what Mamma was risking. Years later, as I sifted through the images of that trip, I wondered how she was able to overcome all the obstacles we encountered with such patience and courage. It must have been pure faith that spurred her to take a trip of that magnitude, while expecting a baby any day. She kept insisting, "It is for all our good, and God is going to bless us." I think she said this mostly to convince herself. Still, when I think about our experiences, God did bless us in ways we would have never imagined.

The day finally arrived, and it was our turn to board the train for Naples. Most of our teary-eyed relatives huddled on the platform and waved their handkerchiefs, crying, "Arrivederci!"

I was nine years old. This very special day that I had hoped would arrive, now strangely brought to my heart sadness and joy mingled in one all-consuming emotion. What lay ahead? The doors closed, the engine groaned as the whistle blew, and we were together and yet somehow alone as each of us settled into our seats for the trip to the southern port city of Naples.

CHAPTER 6

CROSSING THE SUEZ CANAL

On our arrival in Naples that morning, a small covered army truck was waiting to take us to the port where we would board the ship that was going to take us to Africa. I do not remember the ship's name, but the snapshots from my memory remind me of how comfortable our accommodations were. I also remember how well Zio Rodolfo took care of us all. During the years that followed, when Mamma recalled that trip, she would sigh, "Thank God for Zio Rodolfo."

On our arrival at the port, our baggage was loaded on the back of a cart that immediately disappeared into the hull of the ship. With Mamma holding Andrea's hand and Zio Rodolfo's holding Pierino's and mine, we climbed the gangplank of the ship and stopped on a designated platform. Confusion and noise surrounded us, but eventually we were escorted to an exquisitely furnished cabin in second class. Zio Rodolfo was assigned to a cabin in third class, a couple of decks below ours. Our spacious cabin had one porthole from which we could see the commotion and shuffle of people on the dock. Our suitcases were brought into the cabin with a set of written instructions and the command to read every one of them. We were numb with wonder. We had never seen a passenger ship as huge as this one.

As kids in a candy store would do, we explored every nook and cranny of our new and peculiar habitat, and at each discovery, we involved Mamma in our stupefaction.

"Mamma," we would ask, "is this real? Are we really going to be in this cabin for fifteen days? Are we safe or are we going to be seasick?" Anxiety and concern floated from us to our mother. Mamma always smiled and always answered with convincing assurance.

Around three P.M., we felt the ship quiver under our feet and heard the noise of distant motors break the silence of the cabin. We ran to the porthole and realized that preparations for departure were being initiated. A knock at the door made Mamma ask with apprehension, *"Chi e? (Who is it?)"*

"*Sono Rodolfo.*"

"Oh, *vieni a vedere la cabina.* (Come and see the cabin.)" Mamma eagerly ushered him in. Zio Rodolfo stepped inside, and with a sweep of his eyes scanned the cabin. With a nod, he expressed his approval.

"*Bella cabina!* (Beautiful cabin!)" he exclaimed. Turning to us kids, he asked, "*Siete contenti?* (Are you happy?)"

"Si, si!" we shouted with joy.

"Then let us go to the upper deck," he suggested. "We will have a better view of the boat leaving the port."

We were very excited. Mamma took time to tidy our clothes and comb the boys' hair, and off we rushed after Zio Rodolfo up the stairway. On deck, confusion was everywhere. We squeezed between dozens of other passengers around us on the rails. Zio Rodolfo's eyes darted from me to Andrea and Pierino, making sure we were next to him and holding tight to the railings. We all wanted to take in the intricate maneuvers of the ship leaving port.

"*Fate attenzione!* (Be careful!)" Zio Rodolfo cautioned. "*L'aqua e' molto profonda!* (The water is very deep!)" We nodded and promised to hold tight. The smoke stacks spewed smoke high in the sky, and the ship's horns blasted the warning of its departure. Some passengers had relatives on the pier waving handkerchiefs and throwing kisses, tears running down their cheeks.

Ever so slowly, the ship made its way out of its berth and curved to-wards the sea. The city of Naples sprawled on the hillsides, and its busy harbor receded slowly from our view as the coastline disappeared from sight. The sea was calm, and from our place at the stern of the ship, we saw its wake carve a path in the blue water. The sun's rays, now halfway down the sky, transformed the foamy waves into a sea of glittering diamonds.

It was getting close to dinnertime, and when we went back to our cabin, Zio Rodolfo showed us how to reach the second-class dining room and promised to be there when the bell signaled the start of dinner. We had time to wash, change clothes, and follow Mamma's instructions:

"Let's see if you remember yesterday's lesson. What do we say when we sit at the dinner table with other people?"

"*Diciamo buona sera a tutti.* (We say good evening to everyone)," said my brother Andrea, giggling with enthusiasm.

"And when you ask for something, what do you say?" Mamma con-tinued, nodding her head.

"*Per piacere posso avere questo?* (Please may I have this?)" my brother Pierino chimed in.

"And you never forget to say what?" Mamma pressed on.

"Grazie, grazie (Thank you, thank you)," we answered in unison. "And we will always behave and show good manners. We will always say *per piacere and grazie*. (Please and thank you.)"

"Bravi!" Mamma said, satisfied. The dinner bell rang, and holding the boy's hands, she walked out of the cabin and led the way to the dining hall.

When we arrived, Zio Rodolfo was already there. A steward ushered us promptly to our assigned table. I was fascinated by all that luxury. Chandeliers gleamed from ornate ceilings, and colorful wallpaper and large paintings on the walls conveyed an air of elegance I had never seen before. The tables, well arranged around the hall, were covered with spotless white tablecloths and were graced with a vase of fresh flowers. Beautiful china, delicate crystal glasses, and a lot of flatware were at every seat. I was even more fascinated by the meal we were served— not only excellent to the palate, but also appealing to the eye. I had never seen such delicate and beautifully arranged food prepared on a plate! That snapshot has remained in my mind. Years later, when I began making meals and hors d'oeuvres for others, it was a stimulus to prepare foods that were a feast for the eyes as well as the stomach.

The steward escorted us to a round table. Zio Rodolfo had permission to stay with us as our caretaker due to Mamma's advanced pregnancy. From him, we received our first lesson in table etiquette. We learned that to the left of the plate, the smaller fork was to be used for the salad and the cute little spoon and fork at the top of the plate were for dessert.

As we took our seats, a hush fell over the big room and all eyes turned in our direction. Amazement was evident on every face; probably no one could believe that a woman as advanced in her pregnancy as Mamma dared to venture such a trip.

"*Ma cara signora* (My dear lady)," a perplexed man sitting at the table next to us whispered. "*Lei ha molto coraggio!* (You have a lot of courage.)" Mamma just smiled.

Then some people's gaze fell on Andrea, and with profound admiration they kept repeating, "*Che bel bambino! Che bel bambino!* (What a beautiful little boy!)" They were right. Andrea, almost five years old, was simply adorable. His gorgeous platinum blond hair reached his shoulders in soft curls and framed his angel's face. His black eyes were almond shaped and surrounded by dark, long lashes, and they shined brightly in a peaches and cream complexion, causing anyone passing to stop, giggle, and exclaim, "*Che bel bambino!*" In stunning contrast, my brother Pierino's hair was as black as a raven, very much like Mamma's, and he had an easy, nonchalant disposition that always attracted friends.

Compared to them, I was nothing unusual. I had brown hair and mostly straight and simple features. There was something unusual about me, though: I was always commended for my maturity. Whatever that was!

"Are you sure she is only nine years old?" people would ask Mamma with skepticism. "She sounds more like nine going on fifty."

I was like a little mamma. I matured fast because of the chores I was given, and I knew Mamma needed help, especially during the last heavy weeks of her pregnancy. Stepping in was natural for me because I was the oldest child. Helping with the boys meant feeding them, washing them, helping them dress, and amusing them while Mamma prepared the meals. I was a built-in baby sitter, and often I had to give up my own playtime with friends because there was no one to help Mamma, but I did it.

The days on board followed each other rapidly and we enjoyed every minute of the trip. After our *cena* at night, Mamma and Zio Rodolfo gathered on lounge chairs on deck exchanging points of view with other friendly passengers. All were apprehensive about what waited for us in such a strange land. Mamma was happy with her surroundings because there was no housework or cooking to do.

"It is great to be served for a change," she commented. She never complained of seasickness. Everyone on board, especially the crew, was very kind, considerate, and attentive to her needs. The Mediterranean also cooperated with her condition, remaining as smooth as a glass plate. We counted the days until we were with Babbo, but peace and contentment filled the remaining days of the voyage.

It was mid-morning, about a week later, when the ship anchored at Port Said, an Egyptian city near the northern end of the Suez Canal. Oh! Life again! Land was a welcome change after days of being surrounded by sea and sky. From our porthole, we saw the ferment and bustle of this busy port.

The Suez Canal opened operations in 1869. It is 193 kilometers (about 120 miles) in length and connects the Mediterranean Sea to the Red Sea. It separates Africa from Asia and cuts Egypt into two parts. The two most important cities at either end of the canal are Port Said at the north and Suez at the south end. The canal makes it possible for the shipping trade to drastically reduce travel time and fuel costs between the Atlantic and Indian Ocean. When we arrived, ships of various sizes from various nations were in port to begin the crossing of the canal or on their way out into the Mediterranean.

At Port Said, specialized personnel (special pilots) came aboard to navigate the route and install special searchlights at the front of the ship. During that stop, no one was allowed to leave the ship, and for two days, we watched trucks full of provisions being unloaded on the dock and transported aboard. The city itself was out of our view, the weather was very warm, and we were very anxious to resume the trip.

Two days later, around three P.M., the vibrations of the engines told us the boat was preparing to leave. We ran up on deck, Zio Rodolfo making sure we were within his reach all the time. The sun was almost touching the horizon and not a cloud was in the sky. Silently, the boat moved away from the dock and followed some cargo boats at a distance. A few miles downstream, the waters around us finally converged into the entrance of the canal.

The boat moved slowly as all representations of life disappeared from sight. When night fell, the searchlights in front of the boat pointed their wide beams at the banks of the narrow canal, directing its course while casting an eerie feeling of desolation. At daybreak, the only thing visible from our port-hole was sand and more sand, sometimes gleaming on the higher mounds. On the African side of the canal, every so often, there were signs of vegetation, but on the Asian side there was only desert. The weather, too, began to change. It was getting warmer and there was hardly any breeze.

A special feature distinguishes the Suez from any other canal. It does not have locks, and for most of its length, it is limited to a single lane of traffic with just a few passing bays occasionally on its sides. One of the largest of these bays is the Large Bitter Lake, and convoys going south or north stop at this point, clearing the way for each convoy to proceed in the direction they are headed.

Our longer stop was at this point, where a convoy headed north made way for ours to proceed south. We entered the port of the city of Suez almost twenty-four hours later, and like Port Said on the opposite end, we found it a very busy stopover for ships traveling in both directions.

Our ship anchored in a quiet bay away from commercial traffic and the water was so clear that we could see the white sand at the bottom. As soon as we stopped, we were surrounded by Arab merchants in small boats yelling in their native languages and waving their hands as they eagerly tried to sell their merchandise. And what a colorful spectacle they put on! They had armfuls of brightly colored silk kimonos, leather bags and belts adorned with ivory ornaments, Persian rugs, leather sandals, bead jewelry, sarongs in many shades, baskets and seashells of every size and shape, and exotic perfumes.

While the merchants hollered to make a sale, dozens of cute young Arab boys swimming around the boat also clamored for our attention, but we could not understand what they wanted. A crewmember used to this custom dropped a few Italian coins into the water, and the boys dived in, all the way to the bottom, skillfully retrieving them. When they surfaced again, they yelled for more coins, and passengers began to throw coins into the water while others purchased items from the merchants. As night approached, the vendors in their boats headed up the bay and the children disappeared behind the bushes on the sand. At daybreak, the boat picked up its anchor and headed for the Red Sea and Massawa, our next stop.

Massawa is a major port in Eritrea, an older Italian colony on the west bank of the Red Sea. During the 1930s, Massawa was the port of entrance for all shipments and Italian naval ships that docked in the newly occupied Ethiopia. We reached Massawa a couple of days later early in the morning. Immediately, we noticed the difference in temperature. It was *hot*—very hot—in Massawa! The ship was anchored alongside the dock, and we had strict orders not to go ashore for any reason. From our porthole, we had a marvelous view of the traffic and congestion on the pier. Suddenly, Andrea gasped and fell back, fear written all over his face.

"*Che cosa e' successo?* (What has happened?)" Mamma took him in her arms and turned to gaze where he was pointing.

"*Guarda, guarda, Mamma, c'e un uomo tutto nero!* (Look, look, Mamma, there is a man all black!)" He pointed to a local man on the pier who wore a white tunic wrapped around his waist at one end, the other end tossed over his shoulder. Scared out of his wits, Andrea threw his arms around Mamma's neck and refused to look out the porthole.

Mamma suddenly realized that Andrea was seeing a black man for the first time. He didn't even know that people with a skin color different from his existed in the world. In school, I had seen pictures of black people in textbooks, and so had Pierino. We had learned about the dark-skinned people who populated Africa, but no one had thought to tell Andrea. Mamma had to convince him that the man was just like us, only with skin of a different color.

After a short while, Andrea was convinced and rejoined us at the porthole. It didn't take long for several black men and women to flock by our porthole and point and giggle at Andrea. I am sure they had never seen a little boy with platinum, curly hair before and they genuinely admired him.

Andrea enjoyed their attention, and he laughed and waved his hands. Suddenly, a smiling young black man pushed his way through the crowds on the pier to get closer to the boat. He held a large chocolate ice cream cone in his hand, and standing on tiptoe, he reached up high enough to give it to Andrea. Flabbergasted, Andrea looked at the man, then at the ice cream, and with the broadest of smiles said:

"Grazie! Grazie! Grazie!" (Thank you! Thank you! Thank you!) He had just come away from the porthole and was about to bring the ice cream cone to his mouth when Mamma grabbed it from his hands and immediately flushed it down the toilet. Andrea screamed, and Mamma gave him one of the best explanations I have ever heard, though I didn't think so then:

"Sentitemi bene! (Hear me well!)" she sternly admonished, pointing a finger at all of us. "You don't take anything from strangers, do you hear me? Never take any food from people you don't know—no ice cream or candies or anything else. Whether these people are white, black, green, or yellow! And that is an order!"

Andrea dropped his head to his chest, stopped screaming, and quietly returned to the porthole. The heat intensified as we moved towards midday, and remembering the smooth swirls of the chocolate ice cream, I was positive Mamma had made a *big* mistake! We were pleasantly surprised when we finished *il pranzo* to discover that our dessert consisted of large scoops of chocolate and vanilla ice cream. This time, we all heartily enjoyed them.

For two long days, we waited in Massawa for provisions and equipment to be hauled on board, and around noon the third day, the engines started again. We were on our way to Djibouti, the capital of the French Somaliland and our last destination by boat. Babbo had promised he would be waiting for us there, and we began counting the hours that were separating us. Was Babbo really going to be on the pier when we arrived? Mamma prayed that nothing would hinder our arrival and we would soon embrace him.

Anticipation seemed to make the time move slowly. I felt the hour would never come, and I could tell Mamma was even more anxious. Then, in the words from *Madame Butterfly*, "*Un bel di' vedremo da lontano un fil di fumo!*" (One beautiful day, we will see from far away a thread of smoke!) We reached Djibouti, and there on the pier, Babbo was waiting for us!

Holiday Foods' Manufactoring plant in Hollywood Florida. View of front building.

Making rounds of Holiday Foods' complex on my precious golf cart!

(Above) My very special Mini Beef Wellingtons!!

(Right) Holiday Foods' front cover of the Food Service Catalog.

(Left) Linda, chef Lisa Ming, Chef Danny, Don Franza, our C.F.O. me and our office staff: Nicky, Linda, Francine, Patricia and Elenor.

(Right) A thank you note from the chief flight attendant on Air Force 1.

53

(Left) My dear friends Regina Shearns, Judy Murphy and me. (Right) My dear friends Irene and Gene Grey.

(Left) My very good friend Sam Vecchio watching me blow the candles on the special cake his wife Sally made for my birthday.

(Right) With Joyce Kelson, Josephine Martucci and on my right my very special friend Ruth Berger celebrating one of my birthdays.

(Left) With Mr. and Mrs. Sciortino, CEO Sysco Food Service, and Mr. John Chapman, the president of Union Bank, celebrating the opening of processing room #3.

(Above) With Tony Tucci and Father Dan Doyle after blessing the newly opened processing room #3 in the Holiday Foods' complex.

(Above) With Toni and Linda when I received the Small Business Pace Setters Award by the Miami Herald on November 16, 1992. (Right) Receiving the "Breaking the Glass Ceiling Award" by the Hollywood Chamber of Commerce, from Sylvia Berman (Post Haste Travel) on December 2002 at the newly reopened Diplomat Hotel.

(Right) Chef Danny tending one of the Food Shows.

(Left) Me at my very first Food Show at the Orlando Convention Center.

(Right) Linda with Steve Bruno and Eric Bruno at a food show.

(Left) Me at one of Sysco's Food Shows at the Ft. Lauderdale Convention Center.

Babbo and Mamma when they first met in 1924.

Piazza Mercantile. I was born on the second floor of the building with the green shutters.

Babbo in white uniform when he was stationed at the *Corpo di Armata* in Bari, 1924.

One day of fun at San Girolamo Beach with some of our relatives. From the top: Mamma, her cousin Bianca and Gianni in the back row. In the second row: my brother Andy and on his left our cousin Antonietta Capozzi, Zia Rosaria and my other cousin Antonietta Tullo. Bottom row: Me, Pierino and friend. 1936

My grandfather Pietro Lorusso, Consigliere of the Court of Appeals and my grandmother Emilia Vavalle Lorusso. I was named after her.

Zio Nino and Zia Rosaria with my cousin Gianni Modugno.

Nonna Antonia, Mamma, Babbo, Pierino and me on one of Nonna's visits to Rome in 1932.

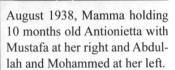

August 1938, Mamma holding 10 months old Antionietta with Mustafa at her right and Abdullah and Mohammed at her left.

Zio Pierino and Zia Elisa taking a stroll at the Lungomare in Bari.

Me and Mamma on the ship crossing the Suez Canal in October of 1937.

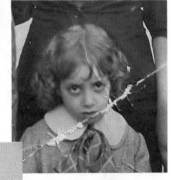

(Above) My brother Andy at 5 years old on board of the ship that brought us to Africa. 1937. (Left) All elementary students in Harar taking a picture with our Bishop. Pierino is third from the left in the front row. I am fourth from the left in the third row and next to the Bishop.

(Right) Our very first home in Harar. In the arisha were our bedrooms and in the back is the tukul that served as a kitchen and dining area. 1937.

(Above) Mamma and Babbo on the balcony of our new home in Harar. 1939

(Above) Babbo taking a break. He chose the window sill of his office in Harar, to enjoy the mysterious view of the forest stretching for miles in the distance. 1938

Mamma coming down stairway of our new apartment in Harar. The outside walls and stairway were not painted yet. 1938

(Left) Me and Ritchie taking time for a picture at the rail of the Lungomare in Bari. 1946.

Richie on leave before joining his battalion that was shipping overseas.

(Above, right, below) Richie with his buddies during maneuvers before shipping overseas.

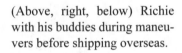

(Above) With Richie and Johnny, our delivery boy, ready to welcome customers in our grocery store. 1948.

(Above) Me and little Tommy Spada in front of his house where I was staying when I arrived in America. December of 1947.

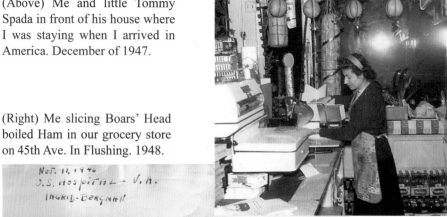

(Right) Me slicing Boars' Head boiled Ham in our grocery store on 45th Ave. In Flushing. 1948.

(Left) Richie in the V.A. Hospital on Kingsbridge Rd. in Bronx, New York in February of 1948.

(Left) My husband Richie organizing the merchandise in our grocery store in Flushing, New York, soon after we opened in 1948. (Right) Mamma and Babbo strolling in Kissena Park and taking care of Ricky and Vinny.

My brother Pete with wife Anna and daughters, Phyllis and Lina, the day Lina received First Communion.

CHAPTER 7

FROM DJIBOUTI TO HARAR

The pier in Djibouti where our boat dropped anchor was extremely busy. The port had an international flavor. Boats and cargo ships mounted with flags of red, white, blue, green, and yellow, the colors of many different nations, went in and out, their crews shouting to each other in different languages as they loaded and unloaded all sorts of materials. We had to wait our turn to get off our assigned gangplank, and when it finally arrived, we raced each other to reach Babbo first. Hugs and kisses, tears of joy and happy laughter—how can I even describe the feelings? We couldn't let him go. Babbo's eyes filled with tears as he embraced Mamma and kissed her with passion.

Her condition took first priority. Zio Rodolfo, loaded with our bags, patiently waited for Babbo to give directions. Babbo pointed to an army vehicle at the end of the long walkway.

"That truck is waiting to take us to the hotel for the night and then to the station, where we will board the train to Dire Dawa," Babbo explained. We walked towards the truck and Mamma slowly followed on Babbo's arm.

"*Coraggio*," Babbo whispered in her ear. "A few more days, and you will be fine. Just don't give birth to that baby yet. Anyway, I want you to know that the first midwife to come to Harar arrived two days ago!"

"Thank God," Mamma said, relieved. She was huge, and I could see how uncomfortable she was, exposed to a temperature reaching a high we had never known before. The baby could be born at any time, and that would have caused a huge problem. But our prayers were answered—the one we prayed together and those we prayed alone in the middle of the nights. Looking back at that trip, I believe only divine intervention kept us safe.

It took about an hour in heavy traffic to reach the hotel. We heard Babbo exchange words we did not understand with the employees at the front desk, and once in our rooms, we asked why we could not understand what he was saying. "I was speaking French," he replied. He then went on to give us a lesson in geography. "Djibouti," he said, "is the capital of the French Somaliland, an old French colony. It will be very beneficial to learn French when you guys go to high school. French is spoken all over the world."

"I like the sound of that language, and I will definitely pick it up in high school," I answered earnestly. A few years later, I chose French as the foreign language I was required to learn and received very high marks on my report cards.

After a brief rest in the hotel, it was time to eat. We were hungry by then and went to a nearby restaurant. We had a lot of fun choosing food unfamiliar to our eyes and palates, but it was very tasty. We were in awe, taking in the new, strange, and wonderful world opening before our eyes.

Early the next morning, the same army truck that had left us at the hotel was waiting to take us to the railroad station. The train was the major link between Djibouti and Addis Ababa, the capital of Ethiopia. It started operations in the early years of the century and carried passengers and cargo, stopping at several towns on the way. One of its main stops was Dire Dawa, where we were getting off to catch another truck that would take us to Harar.

The train had only two passenger cars, and they were at the very front, just behind the locomotive, with several cargo cars following behind. The seats in both cars were made of shiny wood. There was no air conditioning. We climbed into the first car, joining a few other passengers. Babbo and Zio Rodolfo procured a few pillows to help cushion our derrieres as we sat for hours on the hard seats. By ten A.M., the train was ready to go, two hours later than its schedule.

The personnel operating the line were all French. The conductor stopped to collect the tickets and, pointing to Mamma, asked some questions in French. This time, even Babbo could not understand what he was saying. Soon they were engaged in a strange pantomime that drove us kids into hysterics as we watched the curious movements of their hands and the hilarious expressions on their faces.

Finally, the "All aboard" was sounded. The conductor, holding firmly to a pole, leaned out the open door and again screamed, "All aboard"—in French, of course. The train's whistles the screech of wheels on the metal tracks announced its departure as it slowly left the station. Hanging out the windows, we waved a friendly good-bye to strangers on the platform and then settled in for the long ride to Dire Dawa that, if on schedule, would take about twenty-four hours.

The heat of the sun glaring down on the train mercilessly even in the morning hours, made us all sleepy, and that was a good thing, because there was very little exciting to look at out the windows. The terrain for several hours was mostly flat, sandy, and had little vegetation. Here and there, clumps of trees and small lakes dotted the dunes, welcomed oases, and birds large and small circled in the air and dropped into the water and onto their banks. There was nobody in sight.

Several hours later, with loud screeches, the train came to a halt in the middle of a small town that simply appeared in the center of nowhere. From our windows and both sides of the train, we saw brown mud huts lining narrow dirt roads, and young children playing where herds of cattle were being pushed by men and women, barefoot and bare-chested, with white cloths wrapped around their waists that hung down to their knees. The sweat made their black skin shine in the blistering sun. Dust was in the air and settled on everything, making it hard for us to breathe.

On one side of the train several people, some holding young children by the hands, came closer to the windows to see the people inside the train. They balanced baskets on their heads and reached toward us, showing us strange-looking fruits that they begged us to buy. We couldn't even think of eating. The hundreds of buzzing flies and the peculiar stench emanating from the vendors turned our stomachs almost to the point of vomiting.

"*Babbo, quanta puzza ce' qui! Andiamo via subito!* (Babbo, it smells so terribly here! Let's go away fast!)" little Andrea begged, holding his nose between his fingers. Leave fast? Yes, we all wanted to. We covered our noses and mouths with whatever was at hand and prayed that the train would move soon. Babbo gave coins to the children, but took nothing in return.

Finally, the train started to pull away. As the train picked up speed, we saw trees and tall shrubs off in the distance that covered the side of a ridge of green hills, a refreshing change from the arid lowlands we left behind.

As my thoughts wander back in time, the memory of that town is still vivid. How could anyone live under those conditions? I was only nine years old, but a strange feeling of pity choked me. That was my first exposure to a world so remote from the one I was brought up in, and the look in those children's eyes haunted me for years. Today, I bless those children because, without their knowledge, they planted in my heart the precious seeds of compassion that gradually shaped my character.

As the train jogged along, the views became more interesting. Mountain ridges were now visible in the distance and we encountered more vegetation and greenery. Here and there between tall trees, playful monkeys jumped from branch to branch, very much like we had seen in the movies. They kept us fascinated for hours.

The hardest part for Babbo during that trip was procuring food for us hungry kids. Luckily, he and Zio Rodolfo had earlier prepared some *panini* (sandwiches) that were kept in a special container with ice. By afternoon, the ice was melted and Babbo suggested we consume the panini before they became rancid. I believe those were the best panini we had ever had. We also indulged in some fresh fruit that Babbo bought in Djibouti, tasting for the first time a very sweet tropical fruit called *ambaruti.* They were the shape of a large egg, grayish in color, and so delicious. We also had bananas grown in Africa, which were sweet as honey and much smaller than the ones we used to buy in Italy.

"This will have to do until we reach Dire Dawa tomorrow morning," said Babbo. "But if the train stops again, we may purchase some fruit from the vendors, if there are any. Anyway, I promise you when we get to Harar we will have all the pasta you want." He said "pasta" with a twinkle in his eyes, hoping to appease us—and he did.

The hours passed steadily, and darkness descended, turning the sky into a huge black canopy. Billions of stars flickered from horizon to horizon in one of the most breathtaking spectacles I had ever seen. They seemed so close I could almost touch them.

"That is because we are much closer to the equator, and there are no electric lights to blur visibility," Babbo explained when I asked him why the sky looked different from the way it appeared in Italy. Slowly, we all fell asleep, and to our surprise, the temperature dropped to a very comfortable level as we slept.

Suddenly, the train came to a halt. An anxious voice blasted through the speakers: "Hello! Hello!" and then something that must have been garbled French. It was the conductor desperately trying to get someone's attention. Evidently, he could not proceed without confirmation that he had the all clear.

We had to sit on the track a few hours until it finally came. So we sat, and sat. Mamma had to stand up a while to give her lower back a break. My brothers and I were impatient, sticky, and sleepy. Finally, the train's shrill whistle blasted into the early morning air and the engine huffed back into action. We were moving again, and at midday, we entered the crowded station of Dire Dawa.

There, too, a small army truck waited to take us to a nearby hotel, where we would spend the night. The heat was so suffocating I thought for sure Mamma would faint. She hung on with so much tolerance, never complaining. On the contrary, she encouraged Babbo to move on, assuring him that she would make it in spite of the heat.

What an example our good hearted, sound thinking, and faith-filled Mamma set for us that day. There she was, carrying the extra weight of a child about to be born, yet cheerfully encouraging us to keep moving. "We have only a little more to go, children," she exhorted as we stared at her extausted and with heavy-lidded eyes.

"Look around. All these people and all this traffic! Cheer up. Soon we will be in the hotel; we will have lunch, rest a little, and then go for a walk. Smile, children; show Babbo that you are brave."

Under her breath, I heard her softly say, "Dear God, stay with us and help us make it till the end of this trip." Even at my young age, I recognized and deeply admired Mamma's resilience. I wanted to alleviate the discomfort she was hiding, and I was always by her side, anticipating her every need.

Babbo was also constantly nearby.

"I am sorry, Carmelina, to put you and the children under this stress. But trust me," he implored, "it will be over soon and everything will be fine." He searched her face for approval.

For a moment, she studied his face, then with a quivering sigh, she put her arms around him and whispered softly, "*Io ti amo tanto e con te vicino non ho paura di niente!* (I love you so much, and with you near me I have no fear of anything!)" He held her close to his chest until the truck came around and we all climbed in, anxious to get to the hotel.

The driver of the truck, a soldier in the Italian army, snapped into a salute for Babbo. Seeing Mamma's stomach so big, he said fearfully, "*Signora, per piacere, aspettate ad avere il bambino. Vi portero'subito all'albergo!* (Lady, please, don't have this baby yet. I will take you to the hotel as fast as I can!)" By then a crowd of onlookers had gathered around us, marveling at my mother's big belly and Andrea's platinum hair. Their concern was evident in their cautionary words: "*Fate attenzione, Signora! Fate attenzione*! (Lady, be careful! Lady, be careful!)"

Once we were all in the car, the driver carefully carved a path through the crowd. Blowing the horn, he turned onto one of the narrow streets and we took off in a cloud of dust. We reached the hotel about twenty minutes later, and it was a great relief for Mamma to lie down and rest on a real mattress underneath a huge fan that kept the air cooler and easier to breathe. Fortunately, there was also a restaurant in the hotel, which made it easier for Babbo to take us to dinner. To our delight, the food was well prepared, and yes! We had pasta at last! We were Italian children, after all, and we loved pasta in any style, shape, or form.

That night I slept peacefully, though I did wake up several times. What would Harar be like? Tomorrow, I would have the answer to that question. For now, Emilia, I told myself, sleep…

Very early the next morning, I was awakened by Babbo, his face looking apprehensive. "Emilia," he whispered, "I have to make sure the truck and the driver have arrived. You have to help Mamma with the boys. I know I can depend on you." He kissed my cheek and smiled with his usual good humor and then he turned around and was gone. I jumped out of bed and went to Mamma's side, shaking her gently from her deep sleep.

"Mamma, wake up. It is time to go. Babbo left to check on our ride."

Mamma was up in no time, and we washed and dressed the boys. We all looked forward to the delicious morning *colazione* (breakfast) waiting for us before the last leg of our journey. Babbo was soon at the door, and he and Zio Rodolfo took the suitcases to the truck while we followed Mamma to the dining room. As usual, Andrea's curls and Mamma's stomach turned all eyes in our direction and we gratefully enjoyed the accolades.

Meanwhile, in front of the hotel, a new driver, a corporal with a bigger truck, was waiting for us. When the driver saw Mamma, he dropped his face into his hands as if incredulous. His eyes went from Mamma to Babbo. He managed to mumble, "Signora, do you know what you are doing? That baby could be born on the way. I am not a midwife." Tension was in his voice and it became quickly evident that he did not want to take responsibility for driving that truck.

Babbo intervened with a brisk command: "Corporal, you were assigned to drive us to Harar. Now get behind the wheel and let's proceed. That's an order."

The corporal came to attention, clicked his heels, and gave Babbo a stiff salute with a resounding, "Yes, sir!"

I watched my brothers curling their lips, and we all cracked up in laughter. As we walked to the back of the truck, I heard Babbo say to the corporal with a smile, "At ease, Corporal, at ease. I will take responsibility for my wife's safety. You just pay attention to the road. You have a big task ahead."

With no further comment, the corporal helped us get in the back of the truck. Zio Rodolfo was there already, waiting for us. The truck was spacious, and from that height, we had a marvelous view of the sur-roundings. Mamma climbed into the front seat between the driver and Babbo, and soon we were on our way to Harar.

Little did we know as we were leaving the torrid lowlands around Dire Dawa that we were beginning one of the most terrifying experi-ences of our lives! We had no idea what Babbo was alluding to when he said to the driver, "You have a big task ahead." We began to understand what he meant about an hour later.

According to Babbo's schedule, we were supposed to reach Harar in five hours. At first the road, though dusty, was smooth and wide enough for normal two-way traffic, but as we traveled farther, it became nar-rower and bumpier. Babbo told us to hold onto the slots next to the back seats and to expect a bumpy ride for several kilometers.

The road to Harar was a winding narrow strip that hugged the side of a ridge of mountains and climbed slowly for many kilometers. On one side of the road, a sheer wall of rock seemed to hold back the moun-tains, but on the opposite side, slopes covered with tall trees and bushes plunged into deep ravines with no bottom in sight. The scenery was cap-tivating and full of charm and it mesmerized me, but at the same time, it scared us all out of our wits. Falling to our knees, we cried in fear that at any moment the truck would miss a turn and fall into the ravine.

All the assurances from Zio Rodolfo did nothing to calm our panic. We refused to look outside until we were out of danger. For about an hour, we slumped on the floor of the truck sobbing and wishing we had never made the trip. Though I couldn't see into the front cab, later Mam-ma told me she had trembled with fear. She had kept her head buried on Babbo's breast, praying to God and all the saints to protect us until we passed that treacherous part of the road.

Gradually, the mountains receded, the air became cooler and less humid, and we faced a landscape out of the pages of a storybook. The road entered a broad plateau and the highlands, where the city of Harar was located. In the distance, the tall ridge of the Chercher Mountains en-circled the wide plains that extended for miles. We passed through fields of lush vegetation and emerged into forests of fragrant eucalyptus trees and tall fields of corn. Along the road, mud huts and hints of life began to appear between the trees. Men, women, and children herding cattle peeped from behind the trees to catch a glimpse of the passing truck. Finally, we were there! Harar was finally visible.

Babbo opened the small window between the cabin and the back of the truck and announced excitedly, "There, look at your right, children.

Do you see the road that enters that gate? Do you see the wall? That wall goes all around the city of Harar. We are not going there now. We are going to stay in a temporary place until our permanent home now under construction is finished. So please, be patient. What is important is that we are all together. Yes?"

"Yes! Babbo. Yes, we are all together!"

The twilight settled over the city. After turning onto a secondary road, we skirted several unfinished buildings and mud huts and finally came to rest in front of what would be our temporary home.

CHAPTER 8

OUR ARRIVAL IN HARAR AND A NEW BABY

"What is important is that we are all together." Babbo's words rang clearly in my heart as we all saw our temporary home in Harar for the first time. We arrived on October 23, 1937. Mamma was due to have the baby at any moment, literally. Thinking back to our newly reunited family, each of us tired, dusty, and uncertain of the future, I realize now that only the strongly held notion that our togetherness was worthy of any sacrifice gave Mamma the courage to face what was staring at her. I think of the doubts that must have run through her mind. Was this really going to be our home, even just for a while?

The truck stopped in front of an ugly, grayish-colored building, box-like and rectangular, with three wooden doors evenly spaced in the front. I looked at Mamma's face as she descended from the truck and I thought she was going to break out in tears at any moment.Babbo jubilantly announced, "Here we are!"

We looked incredulously at him as he continued, "This extraordinary building is called an "*arisha*." He told us the building had been used as an office outpost until a couple of months before. "It was given to me as a favor by my commandant when he heard I was desperately looking for a place to bring my family until our own apartment was ready in the next few months."

Babbo opened the first door on the right, and he let Zio Rodolfo and the driver bring in our luggage. Mamma, her ankles swollen from sitting for so many hours, grabbed Babbo's arm as her eyes swept over the surroundings, an expression of disbelief frozen on her face. Calmly, she walked into the room, all us kids closely behind her. The slanting rays of the setting sun coming through the window on the rough back wall touched the shiny top of a round table and six chairs in the middle of the room. Underneath the window was a large *divano* (sofa), and a few feet away against the right wall a long, faded brown *bouffet* (sideboard). There was nothing else to complete the room's furnishings.

The truck driver, having brought all the suitcases indoors, snapped a salute to Babbo and drove away. Eager to show us the rest of the building, Babbo opened the door to our left and steered us into the next room.

"This is your bedroom, children." He pointed to three beds lined against one wall, a few feet of space separating each other.. A long dresser lining the opposite wall was the only other piece of furniture in the room. A glimmer of sunshine from the back window cast a strange glow on the bare cement floor.

A door led to another room, identical to the previous ones, and Babbo moved aside as he opened it and gestured to Mamma to walk in.

"This is our bedroom, Carmelina." He gave her a solemn look and added, "It is the best I could find." His eyes filled with tears. He drew her into his arms and added softly, "It is only for a little while, a few months, and our home will be completed, and we will have everything we always wanted."

Trembling a little, Mamma raised her eyes to his, and as her own tears streaked her face, she smiled back at him, nodding in agreement. The squalor of that room was not an issue with her any longer. She could endure anything as long as they were together.

"Now that you have seen these 'luxurious' rooms, let us go to the kitchen." By injecting some humor into the situation, Babbo tried to change our disappointment and fear into calm acceptance and maybe even get a smile from us.

Zio Rodolfo would sleep on the sofa until he could find a place suitable for him and Zia Serafina, who hoped to join him in six months. Picking up on Babbo's efforts, he gave several suggestions on how he would improve the environment. We went back through the rooms, and then Babbo opened another door on the right wall of the dining-living area and we were outdoors again.

About ten feet away, a strange looking and never seen before structure loomed in the shade of tall trees.

"This is very important for all of you to learn." Babbo said. He shifted into an instructive tone and jokingly began a history lesson. "Take a good look at this splendid building. You have never seen anything like this, right?" His eyes went to and fro, studying our expressions. "It's called a *tukul*. As they have for centuries, most Ethiopians in this region live in tukuls just like this one. In time, we will explore the hills around here and you will see how these people live." The tukul was a round structure with a thatched hut made by tying tree branches and tree trunks together with straw and plastering the cracks with plain mud. The cone-shaped roof, made also of dry grass, finished off the hut.

Babbo opened the door facing us and we followed him inside. "This is going to be our kitchen," he said, "and our everyday dining room."

Kitchen? I looked around and could not see a kitchen anywhere. On one side of the round wall was a primitive barbeque pit made of bricks with ashes and wood inside it. Babbo called it a cooking stove. There were shelves lining the round wall next to the pit holding a rude assortment of colored dishes, water glasses, and an assortment of spoons, forks, and knives that were remnants of diverse flatware sets, some bent and warped but still usable. Babbo tried to make light of the collection, calling it our new "one-of-a-kind flatware." Dented pots and pans sat on a bottom shelf. There was no sink, and the floor, well, was just plain earth. There was one window in the tukul, and an electric light bulb dangled from the roof over a banged-up picnic table with benches attached to it. That was it! The water faucet was outside and attached to the wall of the tukul, and it was the sole outlet for drinking, cooking, and washing water. We looked at each other in disbelief!

Zio Rodolfo walked behind us, his eyes assessing the possibilities. He was fast to reassure us that in two days, he would have a shower working behind the tukul and a sink installed inside next to the stove. We felt a little better because we knew Zio Rodolfo's hands were made of gold. He was gifted with a rare ability to see special needs and use his skills to meet them—the true embodiment of a handy man.

Then little Andrea urgently asked to go to the bathroom. Babbo hesitated and then muttered a few words we could hardly understand. I saw the apprehensiveness on his handsome face.

"Va bene, e ascoltatemi bene. (Okay, and hear me well.) I wish I had a better place for you, but this is all I could find. The bathroom, well—" He sounded as if he were in pain, and he seemed to have difficulty finding the proper words. "Please, please," he implored. "Don't be afraid, and follow me."

He grabbed a flashlight from a shelf in the tukul and took us about twenty feet behind it. He led us through a shady wooded area, and in the faint light of day we spotted a square metal box surrounded by tall trees. It was about ten feet high and had been embedded in the earth. Babbo got closer to the box and opened the metal door, which squeaked as it turned on its hinges.

Inside this box was a hole, just a hole, nothing else. Babbo turned on the flashlight and brought us in one by one to look inside the hole. He aimed the light beam at the bottom, where we saw a multitude of gray worms, each several inches long, twisting over a pile of waste that was encircled by a strip of thick white lime that absorbed most of the foul smell.

We all started to scream. We, Mamma included, wanted to turn around and run. But Babbo gently held us back and explained with his usual charm that this was necessary for us to experience in order to learn how some people live in the world.

"Someday, you will be more compassionate, more giving, and much more able to face anything in life. For now, here, let me see. Are you ready to show courage? Let me hear a loud yes! And give me a big smile! We are all together, right?"

How could we resist such charm? We gave him a loud "Sì!" and walked out of that box, happy for the moment and trusting in his belief that our love for each other was really all that mattered.

Zio Rodolfo quickly added that he and Babbo would build a seat to fit over the top of the hole. His promise took away our fear of falling in. We were so relieved that we all clapped hands.

We returned to our bedrooms in the next building and began unpacking the baggage. As we were putting our clothes away, a knock at the door startled us, and Babbo cautiously asked, "*Chi e'?* (Who is it?)"

"*Sono Franco e ti ho portato la cena!* (I am Franco and I brought your dinner!)"

Babbo smiled as he opened the door. Franco walked in with a box full of prepared food, enough to feed an army. Babbo introduced him first to Mamma and then to all of us. Franco, he said, was the office manager where Babbo worked, and he had the rank of *maresciallo capo*. "He's one of my closest friends," Babbo said.

After the usual formalities, Franco shook everyone's hand.

"*Buon appetito e arrivederci al presto!* (Have a good appetite and see you soon!)" he said as he left. Mamma commented on the blessing God bestowed on us that evening, and we all agreed. We ate our first meal in our new home, and then, dinner over, we realized we were exhausted from the long ride. So we undressed, jumped in our beds, and went to sleep…

Until a couple of hours later, when a strange sound behind the door woke me with a jolt. The boys were sound asleep and the door to my parent's bedroom was closed. The sound increased in volume, and it resembled the howling of animals on a hunt. My heart beat fast in my chest and a wave of terror swept over me. I jumped out of bed and dashed towards Babbo's bedroom at the same time he was opening the door.

"*Calmati, calmati*! (Relax, relax!)" he said, while I fell sobbing into his arms.

"*Ho paura, Babbo*! (I am afraid, Babbo!)" I blurted between sobs. The boys had been awakened by the noise I was making and so had Mamma. The loud howling that now seemed to be almost behind our door, brought Pierino and Andrea scurrying around Babbo's legs, shaking with fear. Mamma was still in bed. She sleepily implored us to be quiet and listen to Babbo's explanation.

"The animals outside," Babbo began calmly, "are called *hyenas* and they look much like German Shepherd dogs, so they are quite big. At night, and only at night, they come down from the hills in search of food. They usually travel in packs and devour all the garbage and dead animals around the city. We live just outside the city, and as they pass by, they scavenge in our garbage cans and clean them out!"

We hung onto Babbo's words, our fear mixed with curiosity. Even Zio Rodolfo, who had joined our frightened little group, was curious to learn more about the hyenas yelping outside.

"These hyenas do *not*," Babbo emphasized, "attack people, and they are afraid of the light, so it is wise to carry an open flashlight in your hand if you venture outdoors at night. I always do. Let me assure you that they will never break down the door and come in, but after dark, you kids had better be indoors and out of their way. Is that a promise?"

Rubbing our eyes, convinced we were safe, we scrambled back to bed and fell asleep again. . .

The next morning the rustle of leaves against the window woke me from a sound sleep again. I had no idea what time it was. Andrea was sound asleep in the bed next to mine and so was Pierino on the bed next to Andrea's. I walked around the beds and stopped to look at the view from the only window in the room. A strong breeze swayed the branches of tall trees several feet from our building and branches from the bushes behind the window rubbed against the glass. Because the window faced west, I saw the golden rays of the sunrise that weaved between the leaves of the distant trees. I became aware of the chirping of many birds, a little faint at first, then gradually louder, as if saluting the light of the rising sun. It was a beautiful morning, and I couldn't wait to go outside and explore our new neighborhood.

I changed into my day clothes and knocked at Babbo's door. Mamma answered and asked me to come in. I ran to her bed, put my arms around her neck, and kissed her many times.

Babbo was already gone, she said, to do some pressing errands. I asked if she needed help getting out of bed, and she thanked me. Smiling, she said "No."

I ran to wake the boys and then heard Babbo and Zio Rodolfo's voices outside the room. I opened the front door and joined them. Zio Rodolfo had already found enough material to bring an extension of the water pipe indoors and was working with Babbo to install a semblance of a shower on the back wall of the tukul.

Suddenly, I heard a voice I did not recognize behind me. I turned and saw a black man wearing a strange-looking uniform standing just a few feet away trying to get Babbo's attention. Startled, I ran towards Babbo and hid behind him, hugging his legs.

"Emilia, this is Mustafa." Babbo pulled me in front of him and motioning to the black man to come closer, he introduced the man to Zio Rodolfo and me.

"Now shake hands with him," Babbo encouraged. I put my hand in Mustafa's and he gently touched mine. I looked him straight in his eyes, and he gave me one of the warmest smiles I have ever seen. Mustafa was slender and of medium height. His eyes shone like bright stars in a face as black as the night sky. His wide smile uncovered a set of the whitest teeth I had ever seen. He wore a khaki jacket and khaki knee-high pants. A wide red band with a fringe wrapped around his waist and on his head sat a red fez (a round, tall felt hat with a flat top) with a tassel on one side that flipped every time he moved his head.

By this time, Mamma, Pierino, and Andrea had joined us, and they, too, hesitantly shook Mustafa's hand. Mustafa looked completely dumbstruck as his eyes fell on Mamma first and then on Andrea's platinum curls. I wondered ,what was he thinking?

Babbo explained that Mustafa was his personal attendant. "That means that he takes orders only from me and is in charge of everything that is mine," Babbo said. "That includes you. He is one of a native group of soldiers called *ascari* (soldier). Mustafa has been with me for over six months and is a loyal attendant. He will take very good care of you guys."

I wondered how in the world we were ever going to communicate. We'd need to use some kind of sign language for sure, at least at the beginning. Mamma started to walk away on the graveled walkway in front of the building, and Mustafa lurched towards her, grabbing her by the arm. He supported her every step until she got inside the *tukul*, and then he turned his attention toward us. I thought, "So this is what Babbo meant when he said Mustafa was going to take good care of us." It took only a short time for all of us to fall in love with Mustafa.

So went my first day in Harar. It was obvious that a very different lifestyle loomed ahead of us. Babbo received two weeks of leave in anticipation of the baby's birth and was very busy organizing everyone for when that day arrived. Zio Rodolfo's ability to fix and make things was extremely valuable, especially because he had so little to work with. He even found a way to build a rude bassinet to hold the baby.

The biggest and most immediate problems were how to provide food and what to eat, not knowing what was available. "How are we going to buy food? We are living in a forest!" Mamma's concern was real.

"As soon as the baby is born and you are able to walk, I will take you to see where all the shops are located and to the marketplace in Harar," Babbo said, reaching out and caressing her cheeks. "There is a *fornaio, a macellaio e un salumiere* (a baker, a butcher, and a delicatessen) on one of the roads to the city. Every morning, Mustafa will come here to pick up a list of items that you need for the day and the money for them. For a while, he will do the shopping alone."

Mamma gave him that subtle smile of complete agreement, and it erased from his mind the fear of her reaction to the new way of buying groceries. We kids spent most of that day and the next just poking around, helping Babbo and Zio Rodolfo with their tools and the materials, though I stayed close to Mamma, who seemed very uncomfortable.

Just three days after we arrived, I was awakened in the middle of the night by Mamma's moans as she went into labor. "Thank you, God, the day has come!" I repeated it over and aver again! I couldn't wait for that baby to be born. I was hoping and praying that a little girl would join our family. I had two lovely brothers and I loved them a lot, but, oh! How nice it would be to have a little sister at last!

At sunrise, Babbo had all us children get up, get dressed, and follow Zio Rodolfo. A day-old loaf of bread and a pitcher of milk just brought in by a native girl served as our breakfast and then we were off for a long walk around our new surroundings. Luckily, the midwife lived a couple hundred feet up our road and Zio Rodolfo summoned her to our home on our way down that street. Excited to deliver her first baby in Harar, la Signora Luisa, holding a strange looking basket on her arm, shot out of her home like a bullet.

Zio Rodolfo led us up and down the hills nearby. We went on a sort of discovery hike, with him encouraging us to find this or that or to look at this or that. Around noon, he decided to turn around so we could make our way home. The timing was perfect. While we were still a ways back, the faint cry of a baby reached our ears, and it got louder as we came closer to the house.

My heart pounded in my chest, and I ran up the driveway shouting, "*Il bambino! Il bambino*! (The baby, the baby) Mamma! Mamma!" I wanted to see the baby so badly, but my biggest concern was for Mamma. Was she all right?

She must have been hurting so much when I heard her scream during the night. "Please God, make Mamma feel better now." My prayer was simple, but He was listening, I was sure. I rushed into the bedroom as the midwife said good-bye. She had a big smile on her face.

"You have a beautiful, healthy baby sister,!" she announced as she passed me. The words were strange, but wonderful to absorb. I went near Mamma, where she lay in bed. Her face looked strained from the pain she had endured, and she was wet with perspiration. It was hard for me to believe that she still had strength to smile. Thank God, she was all right!

On the other side of the bed, Babbo picked up the tiny bundle lying next to Mamma. He told me to sit in a chair. "Here is your sister Antonietta," he said softly, leaving the bundle in my lap.

I shook as I held my little sister for the first time. She was a little doll! Her eyes were barely open and her tiny fist was desperately trying to connect to her open little mouth.

A new life had begun, and with it, a new direction for the rest of the family.

CHAPTER 9

HARAR, THE MAGIC WALLED CITY

With the baby's arrival, many changes became necessary, especially for me. Chores were added to my daily schedule, and some of them were really not to my liking. I was only nine years old, but because I was the oldest, I was expected to do and to help more. To me fell the responsibility of watching over my brothers. I was responsible for their getting up in the morning, and I had to help them wash and dress properly for whatever occasion of the day. Most important, I had to be vigilant of their moves, so they wouldn't get hurt or get into trouble on our frequent outdoor escapades. Babbo was very firm in prohibiting us from venturing more than 100 meters away from home without his supervision. He often reminded me that we lived in a very primitive part of the world where wild animals and strange people roamed the nearby hills.

A couple of days after the baby's birth, Babbo took some time one morning to accustom us to our new surroundings and give us a lesson in obedience. Holding firmly to Pierino and Andrea's hands and motioning me to hold Pierino's other hand, he brought us outdoors. We crossed the paved road in front of our home some fifty feet away and walked several feet on a rocky field towards a shallow canal. The canal stretched in both directions, with one side disappearing into the distant forest and the other side continuing in the opposite direction until it merged with canals several miles away.

The clear water rippled towards the forest, frothing around the smooth boulders and pebbles it encountered on the way. Babbo described the canal as a watering hole used by gazelles, baboons, monkeys, snakes, birds, and other wild animals that inhabited the forest. Babbo chuckled:

"Don't even think of coming near this place! The animals will have you for dinner!" That settled any notion we might have had of an adventure in that direction.

Then he went on to explain:

"The water in the canal is high at the moment because we're just coming out of the rainy season that starts in June and ends in September. This water will soon become a little trickle, and I will be able to cross the canal to get to my office. Do you see that row of white buildings on the other side of the canal? My office is in one of those buildings. Someday I will bring you to see where I do my work."

The boys were ecstatic. "Can you take us there now, Babbo, please?" they implored.

"No, we can't go there now." Babbo patiently calmed them with a promise to take us there when Mamma and the baby were strong enough to come along. Skipping and laughing, we returned home and were surprised to see an automobile parked in front of it and a lady coming out to meet us.

"*Buon giorno*, Vittorio," she greeted Babbo warmly.

"*Buon giorno*, Anna," Babbo returned the greeting and then reached for the box Anna was pointing to on the back seat. "This is Anna, Franco's wife," Babbo said as he picked up the box.

"Thank you for all this food, Anna. You are a blessing. I want you to meet my children. This is Emilia, this is Pierino, and here is Andrea. Carmelina is anxious to show you our new baby girl. Let's all go inside!"

Captivated by Andrea's platinum curls, Anna appeared genuinely friendly and eager to help until Mamma could return to her normal routine. She was a pretty, blondish woman in her mid-thirties with a kind, warm voice that made us fall in love with her immediately. Because she had no children of her own, we became her adopted children, as she often jokingly told us. Most of all, she became Mamma's best friend. God knows how badly she needed one. For days, Anna diligently prepared our meals at her own house and then brought them to us. Her help gave Mamma time to get back on her feet and regain her strength.

Mustafa was also a great help by keeping Babbo's uniforms clean and his boots shiny. He also kept the outside of the house free from fallen leaves and branches and provided the wood for the stove in the *tukul*. It was a challenge for us to adopt those crude provisions while waiting for our permanent home to be completed, and his help was welcomed exceedingly.

As soon as Mamma felt strong enough, Babbo suggested we pay a visit to the old city of Harar so we could acquaint ourselves with its surroundings. He had described the city with such arcane words I strongly welcomed that suggestion, for he had awakened in me the desire to unravel her secret attraction. Anna offered to drive us in and come back to pick us up later. A few days later, a trip to the city was arranged between Babbo and Anna. When Anna showed up with her car, we were all dressed and ready to go, including Mustafa. Mamma took her place on the front seat with my baby sister, who was wrapped in a pink blanket and peacefully sleeping in her arms. Babbo sat next to her, and I scrambled ahead of the boys to enter the car.

I was excited to take my first look at this place that Babbo often described as the "Magic City." I sat by one of the windows in the back seat, determined not to miss any part of the fabulous landscape before peeking at this strange new world into which God had catapulted us.

On the two-lane highway, Anna steered slowly between cars, bicycles, and workmen crowding the road. Massive silhouettes of distant mountains competed for the attention of the commotion generated by the birth of the new city passing me by. On both sides of the highway, heavy construction was in full swing as men and machinery contended for space and time. Babbo pointed to the first Catholic church, almost completed on one side of the street, and to a row of several houses a short way over that were complete with verandas, lush gardens, and white picket fences, almost ready to be occupied. These homes, Babbo explained, were reserved for the families of higher officials. Farther down the same highway, he turned our attention to the construction of a cluster of office buildings soon to be occupied by private companies establishing branches in the "New Harar" that was being built outside the walls of the old city.

Construction of new streets, new highways, and new buildings on the opposite side stretched as far as my eyes could see. Babbo pointed to a large building, telling us that it was our new school. Down further, more homes, office buildings, and a brand new state-of-the-art hospital were being completed in record time. Viewing this impressive panorama, Mamma seemed encouraged and a lot more receptive to our own radical changes while Babbo assured us that once we were over our immediate sacrifices, a better way of life loomed on our horizon.

After a wide curve to our left, the mysterious walled city of Harar appeared in the distance. In his long letters to us in Italy, Babbo had described Harar in such captivating words I could hardly wait to see it myself. He had depicted it as a tiny city, only one square kilometer in size, on the slopes of the Chercher Mountain chain at its southern edge, and next to Mount Hakim on its west side. Gracefully perched on a plateau at an altitude of about 7000 feet above sea level, the city overlooked the surrounding lowlands for miles around, giving it all year round one of the balmiest climates in the world.

Even more interesting was Babbo's description of the walled city's history. In one long letter to us, he had described Harar as an ancient city steeped in religion and well known as a center of Islamic learning, with almost one hundred mosques and shrines scattered along the maze of its narrow and twisted alleyways. For centuries, Harar was at the crossroads of commerce and the center of a prosperous caravan trade. The wall surrounding the city added ambiguity to the outsider about the kind of life it contained within. The wall, pierced by five gates, was built in the sixteenth century by the Amir Nur Ibn-Mujhid for protection against invading tribes. Each gate had its own name and provided entry and exit to merchants and caravans crossing the country.

When Anna dropped us off in front of the impressive Harari Gate, I had to admit that Babbo had given us an accurate description. Looking at the gate and that enigmatic wall, I imagined standing in front of a castle built in the Middle Ages. The environment emanated an air of mystery and intrigue that seemed to entice visitors to search the secrets concealed within.

By the gate, a multitude of black Harari men, women, and children gathered around carts laden with all sorts of merchandise and pulled by docile donkeys. Some of the people were struggling to get inside the gate and some to get outside. I was fascinated by the way Harari people-dressed so differently from us. The women wore mostly white, wrap-around gauzy stoles with colorful borders over long white dresses, and the men wore the same gauzy stoles over white jodhpur-like breeches. They called out to each other in languages I did not understand, and I felt I was entering a world where time stood still. Harar seemed to pop right out of the pages of the Bible, and I felt as if I was floating in a time and space foreign to my senses. The people were friendly. They smiled and waved at us as we passed through the gate and entered the main commercial road in front of us.

Pierino and Andrea held tight to Babbo's hands while I clung to Mamma's skirt. Mustafa, walking just behind us, carefully held the baby in his arms. He was so happy and proud of his charge that he would let no one get even within a foot of my little sister.

"Don't you get near me, and don't touch this baby!" Mustafa would bark in his native tongue with such a menacing expression on his face that it scared anyone attempting to look at her. He had so much devotion and love for us that he became almost part of our family.

As we walked farther down the road to the main market, the strong odor of freshly brewed coffee perked up our nostrils. It emanated from the crowded bars lining the street.

"What a pleasant aroma," Mamma commented, sniffing the air.

Smiling, Babbo explained, "Ethiopian coffee is well known all over the world, but Harar produces the best in the country." (That is still true. Today, Harar coffee is on the shelves in many gourmet shops in America.)

Along the way, shops and shopkeepers on both sides of the street displayed all sorts of merchandise on timeworn tables outside their doors as well as on indoor shelves plainly visible from the outside. Exquisite silk kimonos with colorful floral patterns hung from rods, while beautiful anklets, necklaces, bangles, armbands, earrings, and silver chains competed with brightly colored shawls, stoles, and tunics for space on the tabletops. Other shops seemed to overflow with dozens of baskets, hand woven masterpieces in bright colors and many sizes.

Soon we were in sight of the famous open-air market located in a square at the center of the city. When we arrived, we met other Italian citizens mingling in the crowd of local buyers and that made us feel less conspicuous. In fact, Babbo met a few of his friends and their families, and we were thrilled to make new friends. The market had a flavor all its own. A semicircular wall approximately three feet high in the middle of the square served as a counter top for merchants assembled there from early morning, and what an assembly they made!

Fruits and produce overflowed from large baskets that teetered on top of the wall, taking up almost half of its length. Men and women traders behind the wall shouting in their peculiar languages pointed at the baskets full of beautiful large, ripe tomatoes, white-as-snow cauliflowers, green and red peppers, golden ears of corn, sugar cane, and vegetables we had never seen before. Further along the wall, other loud-mouthed vendors gesticulated over heaping baskets of oranges, bunches of small ripe bananas, pineapples, ambaruti, yellow-skinned papayas, ruby red prickly pears just ripe and ready to eat, and other fruits new to us. Hoping to make a sale, they offered free samples of anything we wanted. The fruits had a sweetness and flavor that surprised us, even though we were used to freshly farmed products in Italy. Later, we found out that the combination of the fertile, pristine soil and the temperate climate of the region gave that perfect flavor to the fruits and vegetables. Babbo bought some fruit and vegetables, filling a burlap bag he had brought from home.

When we reached the other half of the wall, I could not believe my eyes. A menagerie of live animals scrambled noisily behind the wall. Hundreds of flies buzzing all around us were a great nuisance as we patiently tried to shoo them off our faces. Chickens and roosters flapped their wings and scurried in many directions, kicking up dust as they tried to escape the hands of the vendors. Lambs and sheep also milled around and chased each other while others placidly napped on the earth floor.

Was this for real? What grabbed our attention the most was that these animals were being sold alive! Sadness gripped my heart at seeing chickens with ropes tied around their legs, crowing in protest and perhaps anticipating their gloomy demise as they were tossed over the shoulders of satisfied buyers.

Farther down the wall, we saw baskets full of eggs dangling from its top, accidents ready to happen! Between the animals and rotten food, a rancid odor became more prevalent as the hot midday sun bathed the square, wilting everything under the heat of its rays. Local inhabitants, men, women, and children walking barefoot, entered the small area in droves, crossing the cobbled narrow lanes that radiated from the five gates of the city all the way to this square, where all the activity was daily generated.

Sweaty and overwhelmed, we had had enough. The smell chased us away.

"Babbo, please, let's go home. This smell is making us sick," Pierino implored, and so did Mamma.

"Yes, let us go back now," Babbo replied. "Next time, we'll come early in the morning before the sun gets real hot." We all agreed. We turned back on the main road and reached the Harari Gate, where Anna was waiting to take us back.

When we arrived home, a surprise in the form of a young woman was waiting for us. Mustafa, the woman, and Babbo engaged in a lively conversation, and when that was over, we were elevated to the high position of maintaining a maid. Mamma couldn't have been more pleased! With four young children to tend to, it was nice to have serious help around the house.

And so we met Chelam. She was medium height and slender, with brown velvet skin and beautiful black eyes in a very pretty face. She said she was about twenty-two years old, but she looked older. Harari men and women, used to living outdoors, aged much faster because of their long exposure to sunlight. Chelam was a friendly, full-of-fun young lady and we enjoyed having her around. She was very patient with the baby and that became important when I had to start school with the boys and Mamma was alone in the house.

Time seemed to be flying, and there were many things to tend to before Babbo returned to work. The most important was registration at our new school. Luckily, the school building on the opposite side of the city had been completed and opened two months before our arrival. School had started at the beginning of October and we were already at the beginning of November. We had lost a month of lessons, but I was sure I could catch up in no time. I loved school and could not wait to join the new class, the fourth year of elementary school. My brother Pierino was going into the second grade and little Andrea was entering the *asilo* (kindergarten). All three of us were eager to meet other children at last. It became a challenge when we began looking for school supplies and ordering new uniforms, because everything had to be accomplished before Babbo returned to work.

The day we had to register, Anna picked us up and drove us to school. When we walked in with Babbo, I was in awe! The school, a two-story building, was painted white. The entrance opened onto a long corridor with several teachers' offices on both sides. The shiny tile floor and colorful paintings on the walls gave it a warm and peaceful atmosphere. At the end of registration, the school's secretary told us to us peek inside a few of the classrooms that were still empty. The rows of brand new desks inside the rooms made me wish I could stay for the day.

The following Monday, Anna picked us up with her car and dropped us in front of the school. Mamma came along to make sure Andrea was ready for his big day. For days, all of us had told him about all the fun he would have playing with the new toys and other boys and girls. We must have succeeded, because Andrea marched straight into his classroom and happily disappeared among the toys and several other children.

When I entered my classroom, the teacher, a tall, middle-aged man with grayish, wavy hair and a bright smile, introduced me to the class. The classroom was divided in two and all the seats on both sides were occupied by boys and girls, except for one seat in the front row next to the window. The teacher explained that he had to divide the room in half because the school was short on teachers. It was easier to have fourth-grade students on one side and fifth-grade on the other. The teacher directed me to the only empty seat by the fourth-graders while I struggled to hide the butterflies fluttering in my chest. I smiled at the teacher and my new friends and went silently to my seat to begin the first day of a new school year.

School was just what I needed! I wanted to learn as much as possible, and I had a great time following the lessons of the fourth and fifth-graders—so much so that at the end of the year the teacher allowed me to take the same tests given to the fifth graders, thus skipping a year of school. If promoted, I would be eligible to enter the first year of the *Ginnasio Classico*.

At the end of the final tests in June 1938, the results were posted on the wall of the corridor outside our classroom. Proud parents and friends had the opportunity to match grades and see who had the smartest kids. This time, Zio Rodolfo drove Babbo, Mamma, and me to school the day the results were been posted. At the bulletin board, other parents and our friends crowded around us, congratulating Babbo and Mamma. I had achieved the highest marks on the tests, even though I had skipped the fifth grade. My biggest pleasure was seeing Mamma and Babbo so happy and proud of me.

In March 1938, another change took place. Babbo came home one night with some difficult news. "Construction of our new home has been temporarily delayed," he said.

Completion was not expected before the end of the year. He had come across the opportunity, though, to rent a much larger *tukul* and adjacent *arisha* that were in much better condition than the one we were living in. It was complete with furniture and very close to our house still in construction. In fact, from that location, we could keep an eye on the progress being made. The arisha had also a room for Zio Rodolfo, giving him the privacy he needed. Zio had obtained a very good job as the driver for a high Italian official and was preparing the necessary papers to call Zia Serafina, who was waiting in Italy.

Mamma made up her mind quickly. Soon we were packing and moving again!

CHAPTER 10

LIFE WITH CHICKENS AND GAZELLES

We moved to our new *arisha* one sunny morning in the month of March. It was roomier and a lot more pleasant, with better-built walls, running water, and electricity, and it was well shaded by tall, magnificent trees. Located on a high plateau, it offered us a marvelous view for miles around. About fifty feet away from the front of the *arisha* the land dropped fifteen feet to a lower meadow that stretched for several feet in both directions and was wide enough to double as a small soccer field. That was the best part of the move for my brothers. They loved to play soccer with their friends. Zio Rodolfo had his own private room at last and was happy to have some peace and quiet away from his active niece and nephews.

One day, Mustafa brought home a basket full of large fresh eggs given to him by a friend. Mamma used some to make a frittata for our *pranzo*, then washed the remaining eggs in cold water and put them back in the basket. Our kitchen was in the tukul, and after dinner, Mamma decided to set the basket of eggs on the windowsill and keep the window open during the night. In Harar, the temperature dropped considerably during the night and we always slept with blankets, so the windowsill seemed the only logical place to store the basket of eggs.

The next morning, returning to the kitchen to prepare our *colazione*, Mamma decided to make *zabaione*, a light and fluffy Italian custard made with fresh eggs. Yum! What a treat that was going to be. Gingerly, she went to the windowsill and grabbed the basket of eggs. To her surprise, the basket felt very light. How could that be? The eggs were all there. She brought the basket to the table and found that the eggs were empty. They were not broken—just empty. Amazed and scared, she yelled for Babbo and Zio Rodolfo to come quickly into the kitchen. Of course, we all ran to see what was happening, and after examining the eggs, we all broke into hysterical laughter!

The only explanation Babbo could give was that some night animal, maybe a weasel, had climbed to the windowsill during the night and, making a tiny hole in the eggs, was able to suck the inside without breaking the shells. What a feat—and what a lesson. Mamma never again left the kitchen window open at night.

A few weeks later, Zio Rodolfo came up with a bright new idea brought on by that incident.

"Let's make a chicken coop in the back of the *arisha* and fill it with a dozen chickens and maybe one rooster," he suggested. "This way, we can have zabaione and frittata a lot more often."

What a good idea! We all agreed that with everyone pitching in, we could make it happen. And it did. It took about a week to assemble something that looked like a decent chicken coop. The back and two side walls were made of corrugated iron sheets and so was the slanting roof. The front wall was made of a thick iron mesh with a swinging gate in the center. It was about ten feet long by four feet wide, and we attached several rods on the inside at different levels to give the chickens a place to sleep at night. We left the floor the way it was, plain earth with layers of straw on top, to protect the eggs when they fell. Zio Rodolfo also built a tall fence around our property in the back yard and made a wide space for the chickens to roam around in when we would let them out during the day. The fence was finished in record time. We bought twelve laying hens and a rooster at the market in Harar and brought them back to their new home.

That day, an unexpected surprise was waiting for us when we returned. Chelam had brought home a young boy by the name of Abdullah. His emaciated body was covered with dirty, smelly rags, and dust covered him from head to toe. He had large, bright, fearful eyes that scrutinized everything around him with wonder. It was apparent from his expression that he had never seen certain items before, and clinging to Chelam's skirt, he seemed afraid to make a move. Through Mustafa, Chelam explained that her family and the boy's family belonged to the same tribe and she had known him since he was born. He was fifteen years old and had a little brother eight years old. They had recently lost their mother and father and were living with their very poor old grandmother some ten miles out of the city.

The boy had never traveled far from his parent's *tukul*, and he was the sole provider for their family. He tended sheep and raised meager crops of fruits and vegetables by himself because his father had been sick for several years. Could we let him stay with us? He would do any work we needed done in exchange for food and a place to sleep.

Mamma and Babbo immediately consented. It was impossible not to be overwhelmed with compassion for the boy. With Mustafa's help, Zio

Rodolfo took him behind the house, hosed him down, and scrubbed him with soap and water. Mustafa took a clean white tunic out of his bag of clothes and pulled it over the boy's body. By this time, Abdullah had a bright smile on his face and seemed to enjoy our company. With eagerness and fervor, he joined Babbo, Zio Rodolfo, and Mustafa in bringing the chickens out of the truck and into the chicken coop. Abdullah knew just how to handle them.

Everything went smoothly until we joined Mamma in the kitchen, where she had prepared a delicious dinner. Twilight was settling over the city and the tall trees surrounding our property cast long shadows around the *tukul*. Even the kitchen was slowly slipping into darkness as we all took our places at the table. Mustafa, Chelam, and Abdullah shared a table closer to the wall. Mamma had all the food already on the table, and Babbo, the last to come in, instinctively turned on the light switch by the door. The two bulbs hanging from the ceiling illuminated the darkened room with a bright light, sending poor Abdullah into a state of terror. With a loud scream, he jumped out of his chair, throwing the table with everything on it in the air, and shot out of the kitchen like a bullet. He was still screaming in panic as he disappeared behind the trees. Abdullah had never seen electricity before, and a couple of hours later Babbo, Zio Rodolfo, and Mustafa found him crouched shivering and terrorized under a tree. Mustafa calmed him down and explained what electricity was and what it was used for. He urged him not to believe that a devil was going to appear and take him away, as he had imagined. Poor Abdullah! That episode still brings a smile to my face.

For several days, we all got along just fine. We provided a mattress and a blanket in a corner of the *tukul* for Abdullah to sleep on, and he had proved to be a great help all around, especially with taking care of the chicken coop. He knew just what to do with the chickens, and feeding them became one of his daily chores. He was happy and got along nicely with Pierino and Andrea, even joining them in their soccer games.

One night, we were all awakened from a deep sleep by the uproarious clucking of the chickens. They sounded like someone was chasing them. Babbo grabbed the gun he stored in his night table drawer and rushed outside, cautiously looking around. I stayed inside with Mamma and my brothers, afraid of what was happening outdoors. Zio Rodolfo joined Babbo, and they carefully approached the chicken coop, both still in their striped pajamas, Babbo with the gun in his hand and Zio Rodolfo with two flashlights in his. When they looked inside, many of the chickens were already dead. Some were covered with blood, but still fluttering, while others were wobbling around the floor as if they were drunk. The poor rooster was half-dead on the straw, covered with blood.

Looking at a mound of earth on the ground, Babbo discovered a gaping hole that ran like a tunnel under the mesh wall of the coop from the outside and exited on the inside. Only wild animals, like possums, could have been the culprits. They had left a long trail all the way to the fence, and chicken feathers were scattered all over the yard. These smart animals, known to dig holes to get to their prey, had found the right spot to satisfy their appetites. Considering all the work involved in adding a metal floor to the coop, Babbo and Zio Rodolfo gave up on the idea of raising chickens. Besides, that darn rooster had been waking us much too early in the morning.

For several days, Mamma prepared chickens for dinner until they were all gone, and her cooking them led us to another discovery. We noticed that Abdullah would not eat any part of a chicken that had been killed by Mustafa, and Mustafa would not eat chicken killed by Abdullah. When it was Abdullah's turn to kill the chicken, one method was used, and when it was Mustafa's, he used another one. Abdullah killed the bird by rapidly twisting its head, while Mustafa cut its head off with a very sharp knife. The reason they did things so differently? Mustafa was of the Ethiopian Christian Orthodox religion, while Abdullah, like Chelam, was of the Islamic religion. Both men followed their religion's rules on how to kill animals scrupulously.

The days passed peacefully, and a school friend introduced me to a new pleasure. She let me read magazines she called *fiumetti* (comic books), and I fell in love with them immediately. Mystery and intrigue filled their pages, and their brightly colored pictures left me day dreaming of places and people you meet only in fairy tales. I spent hours under the covers at night, flashlight in hand, reading the adventures of *Il Principe Azzurro* (The Blue Prince), *il Corriere dei Piccoli, il Topolino* (Mickey Mouse) and other stories that continued in the following issues. Babbo began to bring some home, and I waited anxiously every Wednesday until he handed them to me.

I was very happy with the school's curriculum and loved my teacher. Pierino and Andrea were also progressing nicely, and we had plenty of activities both in school and out to keep busy. We made many friends and loved to gather in the meadow by my house and enjoy the simple games children played in the era before TV, Nintendo, and computer games began to keep them indoors. In the balmy weather of Harar, with its toasty warm afternoons and cool nights, I spent many hours outdoors playing hide-and-go-seek with my girl friends, while my brothers played soccer with theirs.

One afternoon, while we were happily engaged in our games down in the meadow, an uninvited guest appeared from behind the bushes. This guest had a light brown, furry body with four skinny legs, a pair of majestic, long, pointed horns protruding from an elongated head, and shiny eyes full of wonder. We immediately recognized it—it was a gazelle. Petrified, we stopped in our tracks, afraid to move, our mouths open in disbelief. The gazelle slowly advanced, and not to join us in our games. In panic we all screamed at the top of our lungs and scrambled at full speed towards the slopes leading up to my house.

I ran as fast as I could, but thinking about my brother's safety, I slowed a little and looked back. The terrain in that spot was full of rocks, and I tripped and fell flat on my face. My knees were bleeding, rocks were embedded under my skin, and my hands were badly scratched trying to prevent my face from hitting the earth. As I rolled over to get back on my feet, I caught sight of the gazelle leaping towards me and heard Mamma scream in horror as the beast aimed straight for my body!

The gazelle leaped across my face, scraping my nose and cheeks with her hoofs. I lifted my head, thinking I could run for the slopes, when I saw her come to a screeching halt, turn around, and aim towards me again. Terror ran through my veins and paralyzed me.

The gazelle charged, her head bent and her horns ready to penetrate whatever came first. I covered my face, and like lightning, she struck, her long horn penetrating my upper leg above the knee as she jumped over my body. By then, several men had joined Mamma and the neighbors at the top of the cliff. They ran to my rescue and chased the gazelle from the field. I saw her disappear into the forest behind our home.

I was rushed to the hospital bleeding and hurting, where I received several stitches. I was bandaged and sent home to rest. From then on, we were a lot more cautious when we played in the meadow. We had known that sometimes gazelles and other wild animals ventured from the surrounding forests into populated areas in search of food, but we never imagined they would come that close—and certainly not in the daytime.

The injury kept me from school for several days. I returned just in time to join my class on a field outing. I was so glad to be able to make the trip! The destination was a plantation some ten miles south of Harar that had been owned for many years by an Armenian family. The plantation was famous for growing rare species of roses that were shipped to many parts of the world.

When we reached our destination, we descended from the bus in an orderly manner and formed a long line. The owner and his wife greeted us warmly and for over an hour took us on a tour of the plantation. The roses were magnificent. They were arranged in flowerbeds of many sizes, shapes, and colors. Their colors were so vivid and their fragrance is impossible to describe.

At the end of the tour, we were treated to a delicious lunch. On a table in one of their verandas, the family had assembled large plates of Armenian bread spread with butter and marmalade, plates of Armenian sweet cakes, and plates of bananas, slices of papaya and pineapple, and pitchers of iced juices. For many days that outing and its details was the subject of conversation at our dinner table.

Summer 1938 arrived and with it a most welcome event, especially for Zio Rodolfo. One day in August, Zia Serafina finally joined us. We all waited with Zio Rodolfo, Babbo, and Anna at the station. The bus finally arrived after more than an hour's delay, and she was the only passenger who got off in Harar. In spite of her long journey, she looked great. Our cries of happiness filled the air and tears of joy streaked our faces as we hugged and kissed each other for a while. What jubilation to see her again! Zio Rodolfo placed her suitcase, the only possession she had brought with her, in the trunk of the car. He let Mamma and Zia Serafina sit in front with him, while the rest of us scrambled to take our seats in the back. Somehow, we all fitted in one car. My mother kept hugging her sister and repeating, *"Finalmente sei arrivata* (Finally, you are here)," while my aunt repeated, *"Non ci posso credere!* (I can't believe it!)"

In fifteen minutes, we were in front of a whitewashed structure that looked like an elongated igloo, made of mud and rough stones. Zio Rodolfo had also applied for a new home near ours and construction was just under way, so for now this would have to do. Zio Rodolfo hesitantly opened the door, and the bare interiors came into view as he turned on the only light in the large room. A long curtain divided the bedroom from the kitchen. Zia Serafina's eyes swept the interior from wall to wall: the burning pit with an iron grate on top, a table, some chairs, a low cabinet, and a metal sink with a running water contraption Zio Rodolfo had put together. I am sure she was stunned to see the squalor, but she did not show any displeasure. She walked bravely into the room and, hugging Zio Rodolfo, she broke into a loud laugh, saying, *"Come e' tutto bello!* (How beautiful everything is!) As long as I am with you I have everything!" Tears flowed down her cheeks. Quietly, we slipped outside, got in Anna's car, and headed to our home. Zia Serafina and Uncle Rodolfo never heard us leave!

October and the start of a new school year was soon upon us, and we welcomed the news of the completion of our new residence with open arms. The apartment was the first of three on the second floor of a two-story rectangular building. Three apartments were also on the first floor, and all six were the same. The outside was painted a warm beige color and a stairway wrapped around the corner from the side wall, stopping at a landing first and continuing up to form a balcony that stretched trough the whole front of the building.

New furniture had been kept in storage for several months. As soon as it arrived, we moved in. What a time for celebration! I felt I was living in a castle.

The apartment had three bedrooms, a living-dining room, and a large kitchen. Finally, we had a *real* bathroom with a *normal* toilet, a large sink, and an honest-to-goodness *shower*. The first few days Pierino, Andrea, and I fought over trying to be first to enter the bathroom because we wanted to be the first to use the shower. We would stay in it so long that the next one to use it always ran out of hot water.

The kitchen was also a delight for Mamma and Zia Serafina, who often joined us for dinner with Zio Rodolfo. Mamma now had a real stove with many burners, an oven, and a grill, all fueled with charcoal where she and her sister could prepare their delicious dinners. A large sink and many well-placed cabinets made it easy to move around and enjoy the work.

From the large window, we had a marvelous view of the surrounding landscape. On one side in the distance, about five hundred feet away, an army base and ammunition depot were partially hidden by tall eucalyptus trees. The repair shop for heavy equipment attached to the complex seemed steeped in activity. The parking lots were full of army trucks entering and exiting the base, loading and unloading materials from the early hours of the morning until sunset. Army personnel moved busily everywhere in the compound. On the other side, I saw the outer rim of a huge eucalyptus forest, home of the most spectacular variety of birds I had ever seen. I used to go there with friends just to hear their songs and watch their bright, multicolored feathers swish through the high branches, and nest there.

Our front view made us more aware of the expansion projects the city of Harar was undertaking. The main road that led to Giggiga was visible for several miles and so was all the traffic that left and entered

Harar. In the distance, the Chercher Mountains with their backdrop of the blue sky raised their peaks through the white puffy clouds that shimmered under the golden rays of the sun. On the valley below, the silhouettes of office buildings and homes under construction dotted the wide landscape. Closer to us, a newly paved road from the eastern part of the city joined another that circled a large pond and merged into the highway that led to the Harari Gate.

Life was good! Calm was in the air, and we had plenty of everything: food, clothes, friends, kind neighbors, and a comfortable home. A peaceful atmosphere reigned in Harar, and we got along very well with the natives. We sincerely hoped that somehow, in the near future, they, too, would benefit from our undertakings, especially the opportunity for good jobs and the possibility for a higher standard of living. Even different tribes that for years had fought each other now lived side by side in apparent tolerance, respecting each other's beliefs. Christians and Moslems had their own houses of worship and practiced their faiths in peace.

The rumors of war circulating in Europe at the time were not our concern. After all, we were many thousands of miles away in Ethiopia, the historic land of the Queen of Sheba, the ruler described in the Old Testament who visited King Solomon. Today, we are happy and free, we believed. Tomorrow will take care of itself. That was our prayer.

CHAPTER 11

THE FIRST TIME THE BOMBS FELL

By the end of November 1938, our building was fully occupied. Next door, Francesco and Maria Carini moved in with their daughter Lina a few days after us, and in the third apartment, Giulia and Carlo Toscanini moved in a week later. Giulia gave birth to a precious little boy, Alberto, three months after they arrived from Italy. Paolo and Rosa Mancini moved into the first apartment just below us, Gianni and Lucia Montana and their two-year-old Roberto and four-year-old Maria moved into the next apartment, and the last apartment was occupied by a sweet couple from Rome, Marcello and Susanna Cardoli. Many days the grownups spent entertaining each other for dinner or playing card games such as *Scopa* and *Sette Bello* while enjoying espresso or cappuccino with delicious homemade biscotti. I shared my playtime with other children, exploring the countryside, playing hide-and-go-seek in the cornfields that covered the hillsides, and catching butterflies by day and fireflies at night.

Life moved along uneventfully, except for the times Babbo and Zio Rodolfo went hunting with friends. They always came back with something exotic. Once, they brought back a huge snake. It measured almost twenty feet long and had a circumference of at least two feet. This animal was BIG! He had been shot in the head several hours before, but when the men took the snake down from the truck and put him in a cage in the back of our building, he was still squirming. All of us children were fascinated at the size and color of the spectacular animal. A friend of Mustafa, skilled in the handling of snakes, the next day skinned it with perfection. He put together a long wooden board and, stretching the skin over it, secured it with nails, and let it stand in the hot sun for several days. When the skin was finally dry, he removed it from the board and rubbed it with a special ointment. The skin became soft and pliable and its beautiful markings came alive. A shoemaker in town made some very stylish shoes for me, my family, Zio Rodolfo and Zia Serafina, and for some of our best friends—all from that one snakeskin. The shoes were fashionable, comfortable, and lasted a long time.

Often, Zia Serafina and Zio Rodolfo came over to our house for dinner, and afterward we went for rides in their car. At night, it was fun to pass the slaughterhouse on the outskirts of the city, where flocks of hyenas gathered for their meal. Zio Rodolfo would park the car far enough from the cattle stalls that we wouldn't be noticed and then pointed the light beams in their direction so we could watch their eyes shine like bright stars.

I was a year younger than most of my fellow students, having skipped a year in school. My first school year in the Ginnasio Classico was full of new discoveries. I liked my teacher and made many friends. I also received as a great gift, a brand new Balloncino bicycle that made going to school a lot more pleasant. That year, I became acquainted with the heartwarming stories by Edmondo DeAmicis in the book called *Cuore* (*Heart*), one of the best Italian classics ever published. I read every one of the stories in the book and shed many tears as I turned the pages. Those stories had deep meanings and they touched the core of my heart. They had the ability to challenge the reader to become a better, more caring, and loving person.

When I think back to those happy days, certain episodes just pop up from my memory bank and make me smile. One of those episodes involved the weekend that Babbo and his friends organized a picnic for about twenty adults and ten children. The location, cleverly decided on by Carlo Toscanini, was by a lake about three miles away, accessible only on foot. It was agreed upon by all that a good hike would be great exercise for young and old, but how was the food to be transported? Seizing on Carlo Toscanini's idea, the men decided to hire a donkey. Donkeys were beasts of burden, they concurred, and if properly equipped, a donkey could easily carry all of our provisions.

Mustafa was assigned to provide one. Early Sunday morning, everything and everyone assembled in the rear parking lot of our building, waiting for Mustafa to arrive with the donkey. A short time later, he appeared, holding by the reins a beautiful donkey with enough gear on his back to hold all our food.

The donkey was quickly loaded. We grabbed other items that were necessary to take with us and soon were on our way. We were singing and joking, full of happy laughter as we marched on in caravan style. The terrain was mostly level, but it began to show signs of sloping upward with bushes and trees in the pathway about one mile down the trail. The climb was getting more strenuous, and some in the group began grumbling as they huffed and puffed up the hill. At the same time, Mustafa, for reasons we never knew, began to have a hard time with the donkey. The animal became agitated and more and more stubborn as it tramped along, and eventually, it just refused to take another step on the rocky ground. "*Non vi preoccupate* (don't worry), the terrain will be a little rough for only a short distance ahead, and then it will be as smooth as a sandy beach!," Carlo Toscanini said, trying to encourage the children and especially the women with a few reassuring words.

"Va bene, va bene, we understand that, but will you please tell it to this darn donkey? He won't move, and he is getting Mustafa very upset,!" Zia Serafina replied as she and the other women got behind the donkey and tried to push it forward. "Maybe you should join us in pushing this beast," Zia Serafina continued, irritated.

"Okay, I'm coming. Let me see; stay back. You, too, Mustafa. Here, give me the reins. I'll show you how to handle a donkey!." As Mustafa was passing the reins to Carlo, he let them drop to the ground. In a split second, the donkey kicked its hind feet in the air, and with loud "eee-yas," it took off with all the food on its back, never to be seen again.

Another episode that still brings me much laughter is one that could have happened only in Africa. A little past midnight one night in July 1939, we were sound asleep, when our neighbor Mary's piercing screams coming from her bedroom window awakened us. Her screams were so loud that everyone in the neighborhood heard them, jumped out of their beds, and peeked from behind locked windows to see what was happening. As Mary's window was right next to my parents', they also heard the sounds of a scuffle and furniture being banged around. Something very serious was going on next door. Sleepy-eyed and frightened by the commotion, my brothers and I hurried out of our rooms and grabbed on to Mamma's nightgown.

Babbo could not wait any longer. Our friends were in trouble, and he had to do something. He took the gun from the nightstand drawer and cautiously opened the front door, commanding us to lock ourselves in the kitchen. As he stepped out on the balcony in his pajamas, a tall, fat, furry figure passed him like a bolt of lightning, leaped from the banister, and landed on the ground below on all four legs. At full speed, he disappeared behind the bend.

Stunned, Babbo called out, his gun still in his hand,

"Francesco, Maria, Lina, *venite fuori. Cosa e' successo*? (Come outside. What has happened?) Are you all right?" Dazed and still in shock, the family of three slowly came onto the balcony as other worried, anxious, and curious neighbors joined us. Francesco held Maria trembling under his arm, still unable to talk.

Mamma brought her a glass of water that helped her to calm down some and then the story began. Still shaking, Francesco told us about his adventure:

"We got home from visiting friends on the other side of town around midnight, and when we passed the bedroom window, we noticed it was ajar. We assumed one of us must have left it open. With no other thought in mind, I opened the door and each of us went our own way. Lina went to her bedroom and closed the door. Maria went to the bathroom to remove her makeup, and I went into the kitchen to get a glass of water. The kitchen was bathed in bright moonlight, and I did not have to switch the light on. I even walked to the window and for several minutes enjoyed the night view and the glow of the moonbeams on the landscape. Suddenly, I heard Maria scream at the top of her lungs. I rushed to the bedroom and in the dark, I could faintly see Maria huddled in one corner as a large figure moved around, tripping over chairs, and slamming into the wall whatever was in his way. He was also emitting strange, raucous sounds, and I knew I was dealing with someone very strange. I turned on the light and saw a huge monkey stop suddenly and stare at me, probably waiting for me to make a move.

"For a moment, I was paralyzed! Luckily, at that same moment, a strong gust of wind blew the window shutters wide open. From her corner, Maria screamed again with all her might, and the monkey, frightened, turned, leaped over the window ledge, and was gone."

The people assembled, all in pajamas and nightgowns, listened intently to the story, pleased that the animal had left without attacking anyone. There were sighs of "Oh, my dear!" "Thank God he did not attack!" "You poor people. How scared you must have been!" "How about you, Maria? You were screaming so hard. Did he do anything to you?"

"Oh! You have no idea." Passing both hands over her face, Maria began her own version of the story. "When I came out of the bathroom and saw no lights in the kitchen, I assumed Francesco had gone to bed. I undressed, put my gown on, pulled the covers to the side, and got in bed. I got closer to Francesco, so I thought, and put my arm around him, as usual. Perplexed, I felt a strange sensation, as if I were touching a fur coat and not soft cotton pajamas. I jumped to my knees and the ugly face of a huge monkey came out of the covers. Could it be possible? Was I dreaming, or was that a real monkey in bed with me?

"I screamed, and the animal jumped out of bed, startled, and began to throw chairs and other objects around. Then Francesco turned on the light and the animal froze, obviously terrified. He started to move backwards, looking for an escape route. Luckily, the wind opened the window at the right moment. The animal turned, aimed for the window, and took off in a flash. I guess he had never heard a woman scream before.!"

The story became the laugh of the neighborhood.

Life in Harar was wonderful. We had everything we needed to make us happy and comfortable—a lovely home, plenty of food, terrific friends, and a climate so perfect it gave us the illusion of being in heaven. Italy was far away, and the rumors of war in Europe were distant rumbles that did not interfere with our daily life.

That is….. until September 1939, when the first real bad news reached our lofty mountains. Germany had occupied Poland and was marching towards Belgium and France. I began to detect a certain uneasiness and anxiety in the discussions Babbo had with his army friends. "What is Mussolini going to do?" "Is Italy joining Germany?" "How can we survive here if they close down the Suez Canal?" Questions, questions, and more questions, seeking to interpret the meaning of the growing threat in Europe, floated in many conversations.

As Hitler advanced, we received news that our own government was forming an alliance with him. This was not a surprise, but it certainly confirmed our fears. Italy was preparing for war!

Babbo seemed a lot more pensive while managing our daily routines, but life moved on. I went to school every morning on my bike as usual, and in my second year of the Ginnasio, a fascinating new subject—for me, anyway—was added to the curriculum. That subject was Latin, the cradle of our own Italian language. I liked that subject so much! To my parents' delight, I always had A's and A-pluses on my tests. My brothers, meanwhile, transferred to the Catholic elementary school annexed to St. Mary's Catholic Church at the beginning of the school year. The church was now completed and opened to the public, and it was also in walking distance from our home. As good Catholics, we went to church every Sunday and on holy days, and life went on. News about Europe and other places had little influence on our life.

Antonietta was growing up, and at the ripe age of two, she was getting into everything she was not supposed to. When I was home, I was her guardian angel. I also looked after my brothers. They were passionately involved in their soccer games, and many times, I had to pull them away if they had not finished their homework. I was stricter with them than my parents were, and they did not appreciate interference from their big sister. There was a good reason for it, though. Because I liked school, I wanted them to like it, too. I already considered education a priority above anything else.

I had made many friends, and when we finished our homework, we amused ourselves with simple projects. There was no television in those days, and we had to be creative with our free time. I worked with my friends Lina and Yolanda for hours, assembling a theater made of cardboard, complete with satin curtains made from remnants of our mother's dresses. We dreamed up a play with actors, lyrics, and music, and made puppets to act the parts. Then we staged performances for our families, and they always applauded and encouraged our talents. Such happy times, but they were soon to come to a screeching end.

By May 1940, the German army had occupied all of northern France, including Paris. On June 10, 1940, the news we had dreaded finally arrived. Italy declared war on France and England. Ethiopia was cut off from all supplies coming from Italy through the Suez Canal, making us sitting ducks! All troops were mobilized, and life changed drastically as war once again raised its ugly head. Several of my father's army friends began receiving marching orders, and they were sent to join regiments preparing for battle.

Our good life was ending, and the future looked as dark as a night without stars. I saw Babbo's fears clouding his smiles as he tried to keep up a good front when he got back from work. Zio Rodolfo and Zia Serafina spent more time at our house in the evenings as we all gathered around the radio, anxious to hear the latest news.

June 24, 1940, is a day that will remain in my memory forever. On this day, Italians celebrated the feast of St. Giovanni Battista as a national holy day, and Babbo cordially invited two of his friends, both named Giovanni, for dinner at our home. Our friends were thrilled to be invited and planned to join us around two P.M. That morning after Mass, we rushed home to prepare dinner and listen to the radio. Zia Serafina and Zio Rodolfo were there already, Zia Serafina intent in the kitchen as she mixed flour and eggs on a large board, preparing the best tasting *tagliatelle all'uovo* (egg noodles) in the world, Zio Rodolfo washing his car behind the building. Mamma turned her efforts to preparing her savory tomato sauce for the *tagliatelle, il primo piatto* (first course), *le braciole* for *secondo* (second course), and a mixed salad for *contorno*. Zia Serafina had already prepared a dessert called *zuppa inglese* that was simply out of this world.

Around one P.M., I was helping Babbo set the table while my brothers were in their room amusing Antonietta with their toys, when a strange rumble of motors pierced the air. Gradually, it got louder and louder. Puzzled, I rushed to the balcony with Babbo, and when we got there, everything happened so quickly! We saw three planes coming towards us at low altitude, at the same time the air raid sirens began sounding their ominous alarms, alerting the city of danger and urging everyone to take cover.

The planes went into a dive and opened their machine guns. Babbo yelled to everyone inside the house to take cover under the beds, and then he grabbed me in his arms and fell to the floor beneath the banister, covering me with his own body as the bullets fell below us and hit the first-floor apartments. I turned my head slightly up and caught sight of the planes passing above our heads as several bombs fell from their bellies. A split second later, we heard the sound of great explosions so close to us that our building shook and most of the windows shattered in a million pieces.

The carnage was over in a few minutes, and the planes disappeared behind the hills, leaving a path of destruction behind them. The British planes had targeted the ammunition depot behind us and had succeeded in their mission. Small explosions were still going on when we flocked to the kitchen window to see how much damage the bombs had done.

In horror, we saw the full reality of the destruction that bombs are capable of inflicting. There was fire and dense smoke billowing from the ruins of the buildings, trucks and cars twisted in flames, and the mutilated bodies of soldiers scattered all over the fields. Babbo closed the window curtains and sternly told us to stay indoors and not look out of the window. We all broke down in tears as we became aware of the ugliness of the war. From this day forward, life for us would never be as it was!

In the meantime, Zio Rodolfo, still dazed and shaken after the explosions, made his way up the stairs, crunching mounds of broken glass under his feet. Relieved to see us all in one piece and in good shape, he told us that when he heard the sirens and saw the planes so close over his head, he had taken refuge behind the garbage bin behind the building, and had received no injury from the broken glass falling all around him.

For a long while, we heard ambulances blasting their horns as they raced back and forth to the depot to collect the wounded and dead. Dinner was left undone, and our guests found themselves carrying wounded comrades to the only hospital in town. From that day on, any strange sound started our run for the nearest cover—a table, a bed, or a desk if we were indoors, or under anything that would supply any protection at all if outdoors. Fear of more bombings gripped our minds and way of life.

We spent more time indoors and didn't venture far from home if we had to go out. Even schools were closed for a couple of weeks as we waited for shelters to be built underground. In less than a month, a shelter was built near our building, large enough to accommodate all the families that lived there. We ran in as soon as the air raid sirens sounded the alarm to take cover. That happened many times in the months that followed. I remember two other incidents, when in the middle of the night, airplanes struck again, more on the outskirts of the city. They used to circulate several times over us, then bomb and strafe the military targets on the outskirts. Life had assumed the ugly face of fear, and as a young girl, I suddenly had to struggle with it and learn how to survive.

While war raged in Europe, news reached us in Harar that British troops were beginning to infiltrate Eritrea in the north of Ethiopia, and South African and British troops were advancing from the south through the Italian Somaliland. Their purpose was to liberate Ethiopia from Italian occupation and restore the territory to the exiled King Haile Selassie. My parents and my friends' parents made their best efforts to continue life as normally as possible. Their foremost concern for the moment became providing food. Since all material had stopped coming from Italy, we had to do with what was at hand. All produce was farmed locally, and there was no shortage of that, but dry goods were disappearing fast, forcing local merchants to go out of business one by one.

Our relationships with neighbors deepened as dangers multiplied. The adults' conversations became somber as they planned methods to help each other in emergencies. I sat outside on the balcony steps late at night with my friend Lina as we shared our emotions openly. We talked of war and of being afraid and suspicious of our indigenous friends now that they realized how vulnerable we were. What if they attacked us? Our future was as unpredictable as wind gusts in a storm.

One night, I was sitting on top of the stairs alone, gazing at the pitch-black sky above, and marveling at the myriads of stars that hung from that black canopy. They appeared so close I could almost touch them. I had looked at that sky many times before, but this night, the stars had a different brilliance. The eerie silence around me was pierced only by a faint squawk of far away frogs frolicking in the pond behind the bend as I gazed upon the silhouettes of trees and bushes in the distance.

I felt wonder and mystery all around me as the stars twinkled in all their brilliance. A sense of awe slowly enveloped my being. Only a supernatural intelligence could have designed such a perfect tapestry too great for my mind to comprehend. Then I perceived a presence! There are no words eloquent enough to describe my certainty that someone was there who I could not touch or see in human form, but could only sense in the deepest recesses of my soul. I was filled with a peace that passed all my understanding. That night I knew: There is a God!

CHAPTER 12

A SAD GOODBYE TO ZIO RODOLFO

By September 1940, Italy, Germany, and Japan had formed the Axis alliance. Italy was now deeply involved on many fronts. In January 1941, everything began to move very rapidly. British and South African forces were advancing in great numbers from the north and south. The Italian Somaliland was completely occupied, and the enemy was almost in Giggiga, a city not too far from us. Most of the army personnel in Harar, including my father, had received orders to join their assigned battalions. By the end of February, most of the military had left Harar. Babbo was reassigned to one of the last contingents and was told he would leave by the end of March.

Meanwhile, something tragic was lurking behind our doors. Zio Rodolfo had received orders to evacuate with all other able civilian men. They were to join a special group annexed to an army division. Orders were given that only old, disabled, and diseased men were to remain in Harar. All able men had to leave. Zia Serafina had packed her most important belongings and moved in with us. One day before he was to report to his assigned squadron, Zio Rodolfo became ill, very ill. His temperature in a few hours reached 106 degrees, and he went into convulsions. Our neighbor downstairs was kind enough to help Babbo and Zia Serafina put Zio Rodolfo into a car and drop him at the hospital.

Zio Rodolfo, incoherent and delirious, was put on a stretcher, taken inside, and transferred to a special room that no one was allowed to enter. After waiting several hours and not being able to see him, Babbo and Zia Serafina returned home on foot, never suspecting the gravity of his illness. They just commented that they were almost annoyed that Zio Rodolfo had picked a bad time to get sick. Confusion and fear of the unknown was taking its toll on everybody's emotions. People moved around like zombies, drained by the misery that, like dark clouds in a thunderstorm, hung over their lives. Babbo set about cleaning up his office, following strict orders to destroy all confidential documents that might give vital information to

British Intelligence when they arrived to occupy Harar. He was waiting for his orders to arrive at any moment and join his assigned brigade.

Still in the hospital, Zio Rodolfo was not allowed to have any visitors, not even Zia Serafina, who waited each day for hours in the waiting room, hoping to see him or any doctor that could explain her husband's diagnosis. On the third day of his admission—March 7, 1941—I accompanied Zia Serafina and Babbo to the hospital in hopes of finally seeing my beloved uncle. The hospital was buzzing with ambulances and trucks unloading wounded soldiers from the front lines, now only fifty kilometers southeast of Harar. Already the Italian army had evacuated Giggiga, the other large city on the road to Somalia, and was making a brave attempt to stall the invasion of Harar.

Wounded soldiers were everywhere, many on the arms of comrades stumbling through the hospital's doors after hours of walking in the hot sun on rough terrain. Doctors scrambled to attend to as many soldiers as they could. We saw exhaustion on the doctors' faces, undoubtedly from the long hours of patching wounds and standing duty in the operating rooms.

Zia Serafina abruptly grabbed the arm of a doctor that was passing hurriedly before us. "Please! Please! What happened to my husband? For three days, I have been waiting to speak to someone, but no one even stops for one minute!" she said with so much anguish in her voice that he took pity on her.

"Let go of my arm, and I promise I will let you know. What is his name?" he asked her calmly and resolutely.

"Rodolfo Civadda," she answered in a whisper.

The doctor turned and disappeared behind a door. Fifteen minutes later, he reappeared with another doctor. They engaged in a very animated conversation with each other. Then, coming closer to Zia Serafina, he asked her gently to sit down. His eyes were red from the lack of sleep and in his countenance we saw his dread of having to announce something grave.

He looked in her eyes with great compassion and said, "Signora, your husband is dead. He died this morning at six-thirty."

At that unexpected and terrible news, Zia Serafina shook her head. Sobbing, she kept repeating, "No! No! No! No, Rodolfo! Tell me it's not true; tell me it's only a bad dream." Tears streaming down her face, she desperately searched the doctor's eyes for a more hopeful answer. He looked at her solemnly and didn't try to hide the tears beginning to well in his own eyes.

"Si, Signora, he is gone! His temperature kept going higher and we tried everything at our disposal to bring it down. I don't know what illness he had—only an autopsy could tell us now. But as you can see, it's impossible to schedule one. Every doctor in this hospital is working almost twenty-four hours a day to treat the wounded. I will sign the death certificate and mark the cause of death as 'unknown,'" he said, reaching out and touching her cheeks.

She raised her eyes to his, and letting out a deep sob, she pleaded, "Can I see him?"

The doctor nodded and answered, "Only briefly."

Then, turning to Babbo, he added softly, "We will release him tomorrow morning for burial. However, you cannot bring him to our national cemetery; his illness could have been contagious, and you are not allowed to bury him there. Bring him to the indigenous cemetery now assigned to cases like this. There is also a possibility that the whole family may be placed in quarantine. You will be contacted."

He opened a door, and Babbo and Zia Serafina followed him inside. I was not allowed to enter and was told to stay just where I was. Fifteen minutes later, the two came out, faces white as snow, anguish written deep in every line of their faces. Babbo fortunately met a friend outside the hospital who happened to be driving a car, and after he explained to him what had happened, his friend kindly drove us home.

Plans had to be made immediately for Zio Rodolfo's burial. Mustafa, still at Babbo's service, came to his aid. He knew the location of the cemetery, and with Abdullah, he left to dig the grave.

Mamma was devastated by the incredible news. What love and admiration I felt for her as she put aside her own fears for her husband's safety to console her sister.

Babbo was to leave in a few days, and rumors of convoys being attacked by indigenous tribes were now circulating all over town. Complete chaos was around us, and our lives hung by a very thin thread. Schools were closed, and I was stunned and overwhelmed by the events unfolding and our helplessness to stop them. I often escaped from our very real nightmare to the fantasy of daydreams or by helping Mamma with her housework. At thirteen years of age, the oldest of four kids, I was given more responsibility in caring for my brothers. I also helped by washing dishes, hanging clothes on the lines outside our kitchen window, and cleaning up, but most of all by watching over my little sister Antonietta.

That was not an easy task to take on. Only four years old, she could not escape the effect of growing up in such dangerous and catastrophic

times. She would whine or break out in tantrums, demanding more attention, maybe as a way to calm her own hidden fears. Watching Mamma try
to hide her tears and seeing Babbo so worried about our circumstances, I
wanted to help even more, and in my heart wished I could have traded a
few years of my life for a few years of their happiness.

There was nothing more to do regarding Zio Rodolfo's burial, only
to provide transportation to take his body to the local cemetery. Again in
need of help, Babbo contacted Franco, one of his close friends, who had
a small truck at his disposal. Together, they arranged for the burial.

Early the next morning, Babbo decided to take only Zia Serafina and
me to the cemetery with him. He thought it best for Mamma to stay
home with the kids. He told me I was old enough to give Zia Serafina
some emotional support. When Franco arrived with the truck, I helped
Zia Serafina climb in the front and I squeezed next to her, while Babbo,
Mustafa, and Abdullah climbed in the rear.

Ten minutes later, Franco parked the truck in front of the hospital,
and Babbo jumped out and handed some papers to an orderly standing
nearby. Even at that early hour, heavy trucks, many riddled by bullets
and carrying loads of bleeding soldiers moaning and crying, were stopping in front of the hospital to unload their cargo of human misery.
The wounded were placed on stretchers by fast-moving orderlies and
brought inside. In many cases, reaching help quickly was a matter of
life or death.

After a short wait, two orderlies came toward us with a stretcher
containing the body of Zio Rodolfo. It was wrapped in several layers of
burlap material, which gave it the appearance of a mummy brought up
from a distant Egyptian tomb. Slowly, they rolled the body into the back
of the truck, turned around, and jumped to the aid of a wounded soldier
coming off another truck. The noise, confusion, and screams from men
with amputated limbs sent chills along my spine, and for a moment, I
thought I was looking at a scene straight from hell.

Franco started the motor again, and we were on our way to the cemetery. The road was clear and there was no traffic to hold us back. Guided
by Mustafa, we arrived at an intersection, made a turn to the left, and
drove one hundred feet on a dusty, one-way road carved through a fragrant eucalyptus forest that stretched for miles. Mustafa signaled Franco
to stop and pointed toward the cemetery behind a row of trees. He said
there was only one way to reach it—on foot, by the path that was opening
before us. Zio Rodolfo's body was carefully taken off the truck and tied
to a tree trunk Mustafa found lying nearby. Babbo and Franco grabbed

one end of the trunk and Mustafa and Abdullah the other. With Mustafa in the lead, they started towards the cemetery as I linked arms with Zia Serafina. We followed them, slowly moving between the trees along a trail not more than six feet wide.

About one hundred feet down, as we emerged from the forest, we found ourselves on a path where tall bushes thrived on one side. On the other side ran a tall fence made of wire mesh that wrapped around a compound that I never knew existed.

Three whitewashed concrete buildings with flat roofs and high windows were now visible from our path. Surprised, I assumed they were warehouses the Italian army kept to store and conceal secret and out-of-bounds material. As I followed with Zia Serafina on my arm, her eyes fixed on that strange procession before us, her soft sobs wrenched at my heart, and I wished I could think of words to bring her comfort, but I could find none. Thinking back to that moment, I realize that no words could have brought any relief. I was learning that the finality of death could only be accepted after shedding rivers of tears and with the passing of time.

As we got closer to the bend, a horrible and unimaginable sight took my breath away! From the top of weed-covered mounds, men, women, and children with the most grotesque features were staring at us.

"Babbo, what is this?" I asked, trembling and appalled at what my eyes saw.

"This is the leprosarium, Emilia. I'm sorry. I forgot to warn you before we got here."

Watching him huff and puff as he transported Zio Rodolfo's heavy body to its grave, I couldn't resent his omission. I sure wished he had warned me, though! For as long as I live, I will never forget the faces and bodies of those disfigured lepers, especially those of the children. Huddled together in family groups in their misery, they gave us blank looks, void of emotion. Some sat alone, just staring into nothingness. I found myself staring at a boy who could not have been more than ten years old. Part of one cheek was so terribly eroded by the leprosy that his teeth were exposed and almost half of his mouth was missing.

A woman beside him, probably his mother, touched his hair with hands without fingers. Her legs were like stumps of a tree. She had open blisters in place of feet. A man sitting with them that I imagined to be his father had no nose, and no ears. Part of one shoulder and upper arm were covered with a large open sore that oozed a slimy liquid, wetting the rags on his body.

Dozens of flies buzzed around the people as they sat in silent misery, landing on their wounds and emaciated bodies. The lepers were too weak to shoo them away. They just set there, probably for hours, in a place I can describe only as hell on earth. Many more clustered inside and outside the buildings, while others still able to walk attempted to reach the fence and those with faces not yet ravaged by the disease managed to give us faint smiles. Their looks of desperation seemed to cry, "Why? Why?"

I wondered if they prayed for the angel of death to strike during the night. To this day, the memory of coming face to face to such suffering and despair is still with me. At times, it resurfaces and restrains me from complaining about anything.

We continued on the path until we reached a large, level ground that resembled a cemetery. It was partly hidden by bushes. For many years, it had been the site of burial for the indigenous population of Harar. Only a rough, uneven stone with no name or epitaph marked each grave.

Mustafa took us to the hole he had dug the day before, and after brief prayers murmured by Franco, Zio Rodolfo was lowered to rest for all eternity. Mustafa and Abdullah picked up the shovels they had left near the hole the day before and began the sober task of covering the body with earth.

Every thump seemed to hit Zia Serafina in the pit of her stomach. She began to lean forward on her knees, arms stretched towards her beloved husband. I knew she was burying a part of herself in that tomb, and in the pit of my own stomach, I felt an undefined feeling of emptiness, but I held to the belief that Zio Rodolfo's work on earth was fulfilled and his spirit had returned to the arms of his creator.

Mustafa grabbed a stone somewhere and placed it at the head of the grave, and it was all over. We turned and began the sad walk back to the truck. The sky, overcast with dark clouds, seemed to join us in our mourning, keeping the sun's rays from shining on the narrow path and following us in the truck as we returned home.

"I need to be alone for a while," Zia Serafina said. "Please don't worry.! I will be all right. I just need a little time, please."

We nodded in agreement, and exhausted emotionally and physically, she collapsed on my bed and asked me to close the door.

Meanwhile, rumors of indigenous tribes trickling down from far-away mountains became more persistent, as did rumors of their vicious attacks. We heard that after looting homes and breaking everything they put their hands on, they rounded up the occupants—men, women, and children, white and black alike—and inflicted on them the most atrocious of acts. They decapitated heads, cut off limbs, and burned their captives while they were still alive. Could that be our fate, as well, when all our troops and men evacuated and the British army was still far from us?

When the horrible stories became more prevalent, we huddled for hours, praying earnestly for the British army to hurry up and take over the town. Without doubt, their arrival would have been the least of the two evils. Babbo's outfit was the last remaining brigade still in Harar. His commanding officer, aware of the danger the civilian population faced, kept delaying their departure to deter any assaults planned by the menacing rebel tribes.

Finally, the day arrived for Babbo's departure. The British army was almost at our doorstep, and during daytime, on the road leading to Dire Dawa, Italian convoys rolled by as they retreated in disarray.

One of my most vivid and unforgettable memories of living in Ethiopia is the day Babbo left Harar, and how terribly painful our goodbyes were! In our living room, Pierino, Andrea, and Antonietta were around his legs, holding tight to his body and crying pitifully. Bending down, he picked them up one by one in his strong arms. Tears streaming down his face, he kissed them repeatedly, telling them how much he loved them. Then it was my turn to hug him and kiss him, and then Mamma's.

Between sobs, he reassured us that God would watch over us, and He would see us through this ordeal. "Don't lose hope," he kept saying. "Don't lose hope!" His voice vibrated with a simple and strong faith, and he promised he would always have us in his heart and prayers, and if God wanted to call him to heaven, he wanted us to be strong and remember that he would always, always be with us in spirit.

Then the sound of a car horn told us it was time for Babbo to go. He grabbed his cap, set it on his head, and reached for his gun belt. He wrapped it around his waist and told us to stay inside and not follow him downstairs. From the window, we saw him hug Mustafa and Abdullah, who were crying uncontrollably and shaking their heads. Then he got in the car and sped away to join other trucks on the road to Dire Dawa. As we watched, the car got smaller and smaller, and then it disappeared behind the curve.

I hugged my little sister as we all moved away from the window. Together, we dropped on the sofa, Mamma hugging the boys, and Zia Serafina hugging Antonietta and me, and we all cried and cried...until there were no more tears.

A deep silence followed all the sobbing. A long time passed. I finally stood up, and noticed in everyone's eyes and countenance that special look of surrender that comes after a person has given up everything. We were coming to terms with the fact that we had no control over our circumstances, and the only hope of survival was in the belief that God was in charge and we would survive only if that was in His will. Can a heartbreaking moment like that ever be forgotten? Never! I am eighty-two years " young", and writing about this episode, tears still well in my eyes.

Meanwhile, from the opposite side, on the road going towards Giggiga, the sounds of battle gradually became louder. The South Africans and their superior forces were advancing rapidly. The Italian army, desperately trying to make a last stand for Harar, stopped near a ridge of mountains about ten kilometers from the city and engaged the enemy's army for three long days and nights. During daytime, the sound of heavy artillery fire reached us, sometimes muffled and sometimes extremely loud, especially when carried by the wind.

Sometimes from behind our windows, we heard the tanks and the cannons' heavy mortar fire shot into the air, leaving a trail of smoke behind as the ammunition hit its targets. Bombers circling above the battlefields dropped their deadly loads, and we saw flame and smoke rise hundreds of feet into the air from the explosions. The blasts were felt as far as Harar, and sometimes we even felt our building shake and our windows tremble. Nights were not much different—maybe a little quieter—but lit up by flares and tracers by hundreds of machine guns.

Then, three days later, all fighting stopped. The battlefield fell into a ghostly silence.. On the road from Giggiga, passing through Harar, the remnants of the Italian army slowly began to appear, decimated, falling apart, and retreating towards Dire Dawa inside its battered tanks. The ragged army pulled cannons and dilapidated trucks full of soldiers who looked too exhausted to even wave a hand. I helped Mamma and other people carry pails of water to the soldiers who were marching on foot. They looked so emaciated I wondered how they were even standing, let alone walking.

The retreat lasted until late in the night.Then in the morning, absolute silence. Everyone in the neighborhood had shut their doors tightly and covered the windows with shades and old blankets. Peeking through the shades, I saw a great part of town and noticed that nothing was moving. No one was in the streets—no white people, no black people. Harar was a ghost town!

CHAPTER 13

THE BRITISH ARE COMING!
THE BRITISH ARE COMING!

That night, we went to bed, but none of us got much sleep. The boys slept with Mamma in her bed, and Antonietta shared my bed part of the night and then curled up with Zia Serafina. I had the worst nightmares I could ever remember and spent a great part of the night under the covers, waiting for daylight to arriveAt sunrise, Mamma woke us up with a project in mind.

"Come on, children. It is time to get up and get dressed. We have to be ready for anything. We have to take turns looking out of the windows for any movement. I will be at the kitchen window and will survey the back. Zia Serafina will be at the front bedroom window. Emilia, you will relieve Zia Serafina after one hour. Zia Serafina will relieve me after another hour, and so on until nighttime. Tonight, we will implement a different system. Babbo said we must have courage. Do we follow his wishes? We have nothing left to cook, so we have to ration whatever we have left that is edible. Do you agree?"

Mamma's voice was soft and stern at the same time, and I never saw my brothers obey so eagerly and so fast. Fear of an invasion by rebel tribes had all of us in its grip, and Mamma and Zia Serafina tried to mitigate that horrible feeling of fear with small doses of optimism. They demonstrated so much courage during those unforgettable days that I will forever hold them in my highest respect and admiration. The two women were all alone and saddled with the welfare of four children during a period that could not have been more alien and remote from anything they had experienced. I felt the suppressed anxiety and dismay, but they cleverly concealed their worries under loving smiles.

During that night Mamma, Zia Serafina, and I took turns, each of us standing like sentinels to guard our fort. One of us had to be always on guard until the British arrived. For more protection, we moved the heavy credenza in front of the entrance door and other heavy furniture in front of the windows, leaving just enough space to move the curtains and scan the landscape. We kept every light turned off, and used only a couple of flashlights when we had to use the bathroom. Every little noise caused by the wind blowing through the bushes and trees outside brought us to a screeching halt, holding our breath! I was thirteen years old, and I felt like a caged bird with clipped wings.

We remained inside and alone for the longest three days and nights I can remember. It felt like being in the eye of a hurricane waiting for the other part of the storm to release its fury. And then it happened! ….On the fourth day at the breaking of dawn!

"Come over here, Carmelina." The muffled voice of Zia Serafina summoned Mamma to the window, motioning her to get closer. Terror was written all over her face, as if she had just seen a ghost. Mamma rushed to her side, and her face contorted with terror at what she beheld. I heard her gasp as I squeezed between her and Zia Serafina, anxious to glimpse what was causing such panic.

Sometimes it is impossible to describe in words the experience of coming face to face with certain conditions. This was one of those times. From behind the bushes, from around the bend behind our building, and from the road to Dire Dawa, they descended in droves!

The rebels we feared were only a short distance away from us. Moving cautiously in bands of several men per group, they leaped and jumped barefoot over anything in their way. Each man was tall, slim, and naked except for a belt that tied around his waist and two slim flaps hanging from it in front and back covering his private parts. Their skin was black as the blackest ink and their faces were painted with white markings around their eyes and mouths. White stripes ran down their arms and legs and leather bands, beaded collars, and bracelets of many colors adorned their necks, ankles, arms, and wrists. With their left arms crossing their chests, they held oval metal scepters, while in their right hands they clutched long steel spears that sent shivers down my spine when I looked at their tips. They made no noise and stopped every so often, canvassing the area and suspiciously looking all around them as if in unfamiliar territory.

"When is the British army going to arrive?" Mamma murmured. "Please God, let them get here before these people do us harm."

Mamma's pathetic cry made my heart writhe in pain. I saw the anguish and terror in her and Zia Serafina's eyes, and I wanted to say something to calm them down. The words surfaced, but then stuck in my throat. I held Mamma close to my breast for a few minutes, and then she tore away from my embrace, stood, and summoning all her strength, called us all together.

"*Venite tutti qui e ascoltatemi bene.* (Everyone come here. Listen to me well.)" Her voice was composed and determined to have us follow her instructions without argument.

"We are surrounded by the rebels, and we don't know what their intentions are," she continued in a deep and steady tone. "The British should get here soon, so let's stay calm, and pray together quietly. In case the natives should break in, Pierino, Andrea, and Antonietta will hide together under the bed in my room and not make a sound. Meanwhile, Zia Serafina, Emilia, and I will take turns at the windows and keep watch over the area. *Capite bene?* (Do you understand well?)"

Trembling with fear, we nodded our heads and didn't dare say a word. As Mamma had suggested, she took watch at the front window and Zia Serafina took the back window. I collected my siblings, told them to sit on the floor with me, and began the recital of the Rosary. Repeatedly, we fervently recited the Hail Mary, the Our Father, and the Gloria, imploring our heavenly Father with all our hearts to keep us safe. It is strange how we are driven to prayer when confronted by calamity and disaster!

The hours passed slowly that unforgettable day. We expected any minute to hear our front door being smashed in and those horrible warriors grabbing us so they could whip us into oblivion. No one dared to mention food, and even Pierino and Andrea refused the few biscotti Mamma had saved in the pantry. Antonietta was too young to comprehend the danger we were in, and it took a lot of patience to keep her quiet and occupied. We took turns trying to keep her amused.

Occasionally peeking behind the curtains, I saw waves of warriors appearing from one direction and disappearing in the eucalyptus forest towards the road to Dire Dawa. I assumed they were going to hide in the forest and make their assault during the night.

But lo and behold, in late afternoon, on March 26, 1941, the first rumbles of the advancing British and South African troops reached our ears.

"State zitti, state tutti zitti! (Be quiet! Everyone be quiet!)" Zia Serafina's voice was full of excitement. Her index finger against her mouth, she ordered us to keep quiet. Immediately, we all stopped any action we were involved with, joining her in trying to identify the distant sound reaching our ears. Like the humming of a thousand bees swooping in our direction, the strange noise got gradually louder.

We jumped to our feet and clustered at the front window, facing the road from Giggiga. We remained there speechless and motionless, just staring at what was passing before our eyes. Heavy tanks, motorized artillery, and military trucks full of soldiers began to emerge from the far end of the road and head towards Dire Dawa.

"*Siamo salvi! Siamo salvi!*" (We are safe! We are safe!)" Mamma finally exploded, tears of joy running down her face. Yes, it was time to celebrate. We hugged and kissed each other, this time sobbing happily and thanking God for answering our prayers.

"We are safe! We are safe!" Mamma and Zia Serafina kept repeating, hugging each other and us.

Like waves washing over the seashore, relief washed over our souls as the reality of having escaped a horrible fate slowly sank in. We had cheated death, and gratitude was the only response. "Thank you Lord, for your protection. Thank you, Jesus, for the answer to our prayers!" We kept repeating our prayer over and over. Everyone else in the building soon shared our feelings. One by one, they removed the obstacles crammed behind the exit doors and rushed outside, crying and hugging each other, happy to be alive.

It was dusk when the first British convoy rolled in and passed close to our home. As I remember it, for three days and three nights, men and machines continued to cross Harar as they made their way from Giggiga to Dire Dawa and eventually to Addis Abeba, the capital.

Convoy after convoy moved swiftly in pursuit of our troops. Completely cut off from any news concerning our own army, we hoped and prayed that Babbo was safe. By the fourth day, South Africa's military personnel had occupied every office space left empty by our own and gradually established their headquarters in Harar. The army depot behind our home was cleared of all debris and a South African garrison took over the buildings, using them as their offices and residences. They repaired the mesh metal fence around the depot, and from our kitchen window, we had a clear view of their comings and goings. They seemed friendly and waved between chores, looking at us with as much interest as we looked at them.

After days of near starvation, food became our only concern. Our stomachs, conforming to our circumstances for all those days, now reclaimed their need for food, and hunger hit us with a vengeance. Pierino and Andrea especially were always thinking about food. Mamma rationed the few biscotti still left in the pantry. We had one in the morning and one in the evening, and only water to drink. Though they didn't know I knew, I noticed that Mamma and Zia Serafina for the last two days had taken only one biscotti to split in half between them.

"Mamma, when are you going to make us some pasta and bread? Please, Mamma, we are hungry!"

Mamma would look at Pierino and Andrea helplessly. "Soon! very soon!" she would answer, her eyes staring into a void, contemplating perhaps an imaginary bakery in the streets of Bari. We had exhausted every can of meat, every package of pasta, every ounce of flour that we had in the pantry. There was no more food in the house. Our neighbors, too, were running out of food and had nothing to spare. We were all waiting for someone to give us direction. Could we go to the market at least to buy vegetables?

As we exchanged our frustrations with Maria and Giulia, Pierino, Andrea, and a couple of friends that lived on the next street sneaked out and approached the fence of the army depot. Behind the fence, several South African soldiers, busy unloading materials from trucks, stopped their work and approached the boys at the fence. It must have been love at first sight. As Pierino recounted to us, he and Andrea immediately made friends with the men, communicating through sign language, telling them they were very hungry. It worked perfectly, because when they rushed home, their arms were full of chocolate bars, packaged rations of the kind soldiers live on in the trenches, jars of jam and jellies, canned fruits, and so on. They dropped their loot on the table and ran back for more. This time, they came back with boxes of tea sandwiches and tea crumpets that tasted so good we just ate until we were so full we could hardly move.

Well, it seemed we had solved one problem. Food was again available—enough, in fact, to share it with Maria and Giulia's families. Pierino and Andrea kept up their daily rendezvous with the soldiers at the depot and always came back with lots of goodies.

About a week after the South Africans made their entrance in Harar, a South African captain, a sergeant, and an Italian civilian interpreter who was fluent in the English language appeared at our door. As I recall, the South Africans wore khaki uniforms very similar to the British ones except for a red stripe around their shoulder straps. They first assured us we had nothing to fear, and that second, they needed to register us in order for us to be eligible for food assistance. Moreover, they were taking a census of the population of Harar. That seemed quite sensible, and frankly, Mamma thought it was about time they provided for all the women and children's needs, since we were left with no means of support.

Through the interpreter, the captain began asking dozens of questions read from a thick notebook. The sergeant wrote down the answers in another thick notebook and the questioning went on for about an hour. When it was over, the sergeant opened the briefcase he was carrying and gave Mamma a booklet of coupons. He instructed us to bring them to a designated place to receive weekly rations of food for our family. He also cautioned us to stay indoors as much as possible for at least another week, as the British army was still rounding up remnants of rebel factions that were terrorizing the indigenous population near Harar.

The interview over, the trio marched next door to Maria's apartment, and then on to Giulia's. Both the captain and the sergeant were polite, friendly, and very eager to help. They showed compassion and assured us they never meant any harm to us.

The next day, we lost no time in making a run for the warehouse where the food was being distributed so we could redeem the coupons. I joined Mamma, Maria, and Giulia while Zia Serafina babysat at home with all the children. By the time we got to the warehouse dragging a large enough cart to hold provisions for all three families, it was around seven A.M. We were astonished to see that a long line of women had formed already. We knew why: although the coupons specified that the warehouse opened at eight A.M. they, like us, had been without food for several days and wanted to be there before the supply was gone. They had run to line up very early in the morning. We heard some began to assemble as early as five A.M.

After hours and hours of waiting, we were given flour, pasta, cans of vegetables, meat, fruits, coffee, and beans—enough to last a week. So they told us, but it actually was only enough for a few days. We had to ration everything to make it stretch until the following week, but we were thankful, anyway. We were also lucky that my brothers' soldier friends kept supplying them with extra delicacies that we often shared with our very thankful neighbors.

During the next month, almost every day, convoys of British army trucks loaded with Italian prisoners of war rolled in from the direction of Dire Dawa and proceeded to Giggiga. The men were retained in concentration camps there and in due time were sent to other camps in far countries, like Kenya and South Africa. Sometimes the convoys stopped on the road near our home and I would run with Mamma from truck to truck, hoping to see Babbo in one of them. We would ask the men if they had any knowledge of Babbo's contingent. The answer was always no.

One day, we found out that because of the great influx of prisoners coming to Dire Dawa from as far away as Jimma, a great congestion always occurred while boarding the trucks heading for Giggica, where a large concentration camp served as a stopover before prisoners were shipped to other camps outside of Ethiopia. Taking advantage of the confusion, sometimes prisoners were able to escape and secretly join their families. We wished that Babbo could do the same. Daily, we waited for the convoys to appear and hoped to see Babbo, or maybe have news about him.

One night, we had an extra special surprise, more than we could have ever hoped for. Around two A.M., a subtle rap at the front bedroom window where Mamma slept with my little sister woke her up with a start.

Frightened and holding her breath, she put her hand firmly on my sister's mouth, urging her not to make a sound as she tried to distinguish the voice coming faintly through the closed window. In the silence, she finally recognized that the voice was softly calling her name and jumped out of bed. She rushed to the door, calling us to wake up.

"*Babbo sta qui! Babbo sta qui*! (Babbo is here! Babbo is here!)" She cried jubilantly as she opened the door. Babbo came in, smiling and weeping at the same time.

"Shut the door quickly," he said softly. "We must remain very quiet and in the dark. I may have been followed."

We obeyed his wishes as we covered him with hugs and kisses. We could not have enough of him, even though he smelled like hell! What a miracle to see him alive. Then we realized how exhausted he was, and yes, he promised to tell us all about his journey to Jimma and back, especially how he had managed to escape and make it to our house.

"That will have to wait until tomorrow. Tonight, I desperately need rest and sleep." He had barely taken off his dirty uniform and slipped into clean pajamas before he fell soundly asleep while Mamma curled up on the sofa.

It was mid morning when we heard him get up and rush into the shower. When he finally got out, almost half an hour later, he told us how good it felt to be in there. "Would you believe it? I have not taken a shower since I left you in March and it is now the beginning of July," he whispered, shaking his head and apologizing for smelling so bad. His unit had been the last to surrender in Jimma, the very last outpost to fall under enemy fire. For weeks, he had had to run for dear life, jumping from foxhole to foxhole and barely surviving.

Babbo made us promise to tell no one of his arrival, not even our next-door friends. Diligently, we kept it our very own treasured secret.

121

For several weeks, Babbo spent most of his time in the back bedroom. At nighttime, he would briefly venture into the kitchen, and he always took his showers in the dark. He always spoke in a whisper; he could not risk being heard by anyone passing the door or front window. It was not a pleasant way to live, but at least we were together, and that was all that mattered.

As the days passed, we began to feel more complacent. Rumors circulated that soon all women, children, old men, and the sick were to be repatriated to Italy. Evidently, the International Red Cross, the British government, and the Italian government were arranging to equip four Italian ships for transport of the thousands of Italian citizens stranded in Ethiopia. This was both good news and bad news—good because we would be going back to Italy, but bad news because once again, we would be separated from Babbo, and we had no idea for how long.

One day in mid-September, we were all sitting for breakfast at the table in the dining area, instead of in the kitchen, as we usually did. All of a sudden, we heard the outside door open and a knock at our door. My father, caught by surprise, shouted something about having to hide and ran to the bedroom. We scrambled to our feet as Mamma opened the front door. In the doorway appeared the frame of a man in a South African officer's uniform, followed by an interpreter and several other soldiers. We could not understand what was exchanged between them, but the interpreter turned to Mamma and asked directly, "*Dove sta tuo marito, il Maresciallo Maggiore Lorusso Vittorio?* (Where is your husband, Warrant Officer Lorusso Vittorio?)"

The men's eyes swept over our faces, intent on catching a reaction. Silence fell over the room like a blanket.

"This is Major Fritz," the interpreter continued. "He got word that your husband might be hiding here. If that is true, he advises him to come out immediately. No harm will be done to any of you."

We stood there motionless, not daring to say a word, until my father came out of the bedroom. He walked towards the officer, stopped in front of him, kicked his heels, and gave him the familiar military salute exchanged between army men. Major Fritz returned the salute politely and then ordered him to sit down. Several chairs were pulled around the table, all sat down, and the interrogation began.

The questions were intended to disclose the how, where, when, and why Babbo had escaped. Of course, Babbo's answers had the explicit signs of a lie, or he would say, "I don't remember."

Major Fritz always nodded, sometime with a sarcastic chuckle. The interrogation went on for approximately forty minutes, and when it was over, Major Fritz asked Babbo, "So you thought this was going to go on forever?"

Major Fritz's tone was very deep and authoritative. He was tall and chubby, probably in his forties, with straight red hair parted on one side and a reddish mustache he kept brushing with his fingers. His eyes were deep blue, and he had a kind smile that sometimes broke into loud laughter. He was well aware that this prisoner had nowhere to go, and somehow I sensed a touch of sympathy when he saw all four of us ganging around Babbo's legs, afraid he would be punished. From his slanted looks, I was certain he noticed the fear in our faces.

Babbo looked down at us and remained silent. We could not believe what we were hearing when, after several lively exchanges between his subordinates, Major Fritz turned to Babbo, and through the interpreter told him with a smile, "You are very lucky. As of tomorrow, you will report to the prison camp west of the city. I am putting you in command of a group of about twenty Italian prisoners and giving you orders to form a detail in charge of cleaning the inside and outside of the office buildings where my outfit is stationed. Be there tomorrow morning at seven A.M. and report to my office for further orders."

He scribbled the address on a piece of paper, handed it to Babbo, and then got up. He ruffled my brothers' hair, said good-bye to everyone, and walked out the door with his entourage. We waited until they reached the bottom of the stairs and then we broke into such a loud, happy laughter that it brought Maria and Lina, our next-door friends, running frantically to our apartment.

They were stunned to see Babbo with us. Between laughs, we apologetically confessed to all the secret maneuvers that had gone on behind their backs in the last few months and how they had miraculously ended that morning. Our friends were jubilant and gladly joined us in the celebration.

Even though Babbo would move out of the house and live at the concentration camp, I knew he would be easily accessible. However, like clouds chased by the wind, thoughts raced through my mind as I wondered how long this state of affairs would last. I soon found out. Not for very long.

CHAPTER 14

THE WHITE BOATS—"LE NAVI BIANCHE"

By the middle of November, Major Fritz was transferred to another city and Babbo's job was eliminated. Rumors circulated again of our return to Italy, but there were delays in equipping the boats that would take us there. Babbo was not allowed to leave the camp under any circumstance, and one day, what we had dreaded became reality. The whole concentration camp was being dismantled, and Babbo with the other prisoners was to be shipped somewhere. Their destination was top secret, and in three days, they had to be ready to ship out.

Again we were devastated. Where was Babbo to be transported? South Africa? Kenya? India? We had no idea. We said good-bye to him again on a rainy day in late November. Dozens of trucks lined the street from the camp to the road to Dire Dawa, and we were among the few who had relatives leaving on that convoy. Babbo was allowed to spend a few minutes with us, and then between many tears, he was ordered to jump on the last moving truck. I remember him waving his white handkerchief as his truck disappeared behind the bend.

Mamma waited a few more minutes, then she and Zia Serafina took us by the hand and started back home. Everything around us seemed to mirror the sadness we felt in our hearts. The sky was dark gray, a light mist was falling that wet our clothes, and the faint sound of drums beating in the forest in celebration of Ramadan had an ominous tone as it followed us home.

November was soon gone. December 7, 1941, "a day which will live in infamy," arrived with another surprise on its wings. For us living in Ethiopia, the day was already Dec 8, a very special holy day for Catholics, the celebration of the Immaculate Conception of the Blessed Virgin Mary. For Italians, December 8 is also a national holiday. I was attending mass that morning with the family. Just about the middle of the service, a priest approached Father Gianni, who was at the altar celebrating mass. He whispered something in his ear, and Father Gianni moved slightly back, a disturbed look on his face. Shaking his head slowly, he approached the microphone at the podium and with a broken voice gave us the awesome news:

"Brothers and sisters, Japanese forces have attacked Pearl Harbor in the Hawaiian Islands. The United States are joining England and France, and World War II is greatly expanding. Let us pray for the casualties, and may God bless us all!"

The muffled sounds of grief and disbelief rose from the congregation of mostly women and children, and many broke down in tears. I recognized immediately the tragedy of that notice and the magnitude of our predicament. Our world was crumbling around us, and once again, all our dreams were being swept away by the waves of another monstrous storm. Italy was doomed, and so was Germany. The United States was entering the war like a sleeping giant out of an incubator. We feared for our relatives in Italy, and we feared our own imminent journey back. All of Europe was under siege. Why go there now?

A knock at the door the next morning brought yet another surprise. Mustafa, dressed in native clothes, was standing there with a smile spanning from ear to ear, revealing the whitest set of shiny teeth.

"Mustafa!" we screamed, astonished to see him again after months of separation. Immediately, we pulled him inside and closed the door. After a few hugs, we stared and laughed at each other and managed to communicate somehow. We grasped from his broken Italian that he was happy to see us, and in words and gestures, he tried to explain what had happened to him when the British entered Harar. We understood that he ran from the city as fast as he could and traveled with relatives to join a far-away tribe where he would be safe. Now that he had returned, he wanted to know if he could do anything for us.

Thrilled and grateful for his offer, we asked if he could go to the market and bring us vegetables and fresh fruit. At once, he said yes. He would do that every day, he said, and in lieu of money, of which we had none, he explained that our transactions had to be done with objects: plates, glasses, pots and pans, rugs, trinkets, garments, shoes, bags, ornaments, and even furniture.

And so it was that in a couple of months, we had divested ourselves of many of our belongings. It did not really matter at all, , as we were waiting daily to receive orders to lock up our home and report to the detention camp. That order came in March 1942, a few days after my fourteenth birthday. A South African officer delivered the notice by hand to each family in our building. It contained a written order to check in on a specific day and time at the building that was once my high school. The notice also said we were allowed to bring with us only one suitcase per person with a maximum weight of ten kilos (almost twenty pounds).. The instructions were very firm regarding the weight. The notice also said that all residents of the building were to be ready to be picked up by a truck and taken to our destination by 8:00 A. M. In all this commotion, only one consolation remained: we were going to be with all our friends, and that meant some security, as we were used to helping each other.

The day of our departure arrived soon enough. By 7:30 A.M., we were lined up by the door along with our suitcases containing exactly the ten kilos of personal belongings we were each allowed to bring. It was amazing to see how little volume twenty pounds of personal items took in a suitcase, especially when we had to include much-needed sweaters and shoes.

Whatever was left of our furniture remained in the apartment. Zia Serafina opened the front door, and one by one, teary-eyed, we followed her outside, with Mamma the last to come out. She closed the door and softly passed her hand over the front of it, as if whispering good-bye. She inserted the key in the lock, gave it a quick turn, and locked the door. Then she turned to face us, her cheeks wet with tears.

Stopping for a few minutes on the balcony, she smiled and said softly, "This is the end of another chapter in our lives. Keep in your heart the good days we had here. Tomorrow—" She paused and looked up to the cloudless sky. With a shudder, she sighed, "God will provide. He always does!"

We trailed her down the stairs and climbed in the back of the truck that was waiting for us. Some of our friends were already there, and in a few minutes, we were all accounted for. The driver headed for the school building that had been converted into a camp. When we arrived, we were assigned to a classroom that, like all the others, had been transformed into a dormitory with rows of bunk beds all around the walls. While Pierino and Andrea thought it was cool to sleep in bunk beds, that sentiment was not shared by the rest of us, especially when we had to move around the narrow corridors that separated the rows of beds. Evidently, the British thought they had to maximize the use of space to accommodate the thousands of refugees that were going to pass through that camp and to be detained for several months at a time.

We shared this extraordinary "Grand Hotel," as Zia Serafina humorously labeled it, with our neighbors Maria and her daughter Lina, as well as Giulia and her three-year-old son Alberto. I was glad to have my friend Lina sleep in the bunk next to mine while Giulia occupied the bunk next to us on the other side, making it easy to exchange our thoughts and play silly games to pass the time indoors. It was different outdoors. A high fence of barbed wires secured the whole camp. We were prohibited to go anywhere near it for any reason. Some parts of the camp were absolutely out of bounds to the refugees.

New convoys full of women, children, and sick people arrived at the camp each day. In a few weeks, it had reached full capacity. Briefings were held almost daily, but we were never told how long our detention would last. The British kept reassuring us that the four Italian ships, each equipped to handle as many as 2500 refugees, were soon to be dispatched to the port of Mogadishu, our designated port of departure. We would be placed on one of the four: the *Saturnia* or the *Vulcania*, which were sisterships, or the *Duilio* or *Giulio Cesare*, also sister ships.

Time dragged on, and so did the long lines at the cafeteria, where we waited three times a day for our meals. Every day, there was less and less available food, and what was available was poor in quality with no protein in it. We were hungry! Many days, Mamma and Zia Serafina had to cut their meager rations to fill Pierino's, Andrea's, and Antonietta's craving stomachs.

As for me, entering teenage years and wanting to look slim and attractive, the food had less appeal. I began to notice the boys showing interest in me by the glances they projected and the way they followed me, trying to seem casual. I must have seemed older, and in some ways, I was, as I was exposed more and more to the catastrophic events that were making me quickly grow up.

Life was very boring in the camp, and the days seemed to stretch on forever, until in early May, news finally arrived of our imminent departure for the port of Mogadishu, the capital of the defunct Italian Somaliland, where the Italian boats were anchoring to take us back to Italy.

We had received no news of Babbo's whereabouts. I had visions of him slumped on a bunk in a far away concentration camp, thinking and worrying about us. Had he been informed of our departure to Italy? Was he in good health? Was I ever going to see him again? There were no answers to those questions.

I believe it was on or around May 10, 1942, that we finally were on our way to Mogadishu. It was early morning when each of us, suitcase in hand, boarded a large army truck, one of a convoy of about twenty. The British had assigned twenty to twenty-five women and children for every truck, and fortunately, we were placed with our friends Maria and Lina, Giulia, and Alberto. Maria and Giulia, like Mamma, had no knowledge of their husbands' whereabouts. By 9:00 A.M., after the soldiers had distributed rations, canteens, and newspaper sheets to everyone on board (we found out later what the newspapers were for), we were ready to leave Harar forever. The armored trucks and tanks that were to serve as escorts had taken their places in the front, middle, and back of the convoy. They were necessary to protect us in case indigenous warrior tribes that still roamed in great numbers near the border of the Somaliland ambushed us.

Waiting to say his last good-bye was Mustafa. He stood by the roadside, crying his heart out. He had come to visit us daily during our stay in camp, even though he was not allowed to come inside the fence. Tears streaming down our cheeks, we all felt we were losing a very dear member of our family. His love, loyalty, and devotion will always have a special place in my heart and will live forever in my memory.

The convoy slowly pulled away from the camp and followed the road to Giggiga, about 100 kilometers from Harar and our first stop on the way to Mogadishu. Traveling with us were other families with boys of similar age to Pierino and Andrea. As young boys usually do, they became very friendly and amused themselves by improvising new, simple, and funny games. It was not so with Antonietta. "I don't like this, Mamma!" She complained and became cranky and in need of more attention.

For a few miles, the road was smooth. It had been paved with asphalt a couple of years before and had been scheduled to be paved all the way to Giggiga, but the war had altered that project. The convoy proceeded at a comfortable speed, the day was sunny, and the canvasses that covered the top and sides of the trucks were rolled all the way up, and from my high seat, I had an unobstructed panoramic view of the surroundings. I admired the constantly changing landscape as the road turned and twisted between high and low elevations. We traveled a stretch of highway where I spotted a string of lakes that emerged from the lower edge of a ridge of mountains between tall eucalyptus trees.

A few miles further, I was amazed at the sight of giant termite mounds that rose into the air from behind low acacia and cactus shrubs. Like lonely sentinels, they seemed to shield some unseen treasure. Occasionally, a lone rugged-faced cattle herder tending his cows on the mountainside would appear briefly, wave with both arms, and fade in the distance, leaving me feeling as if I had leapt into the pages of the Bible and encountered the boy David tending his flocks.

A few hours into our journey, our ride abruptly changed. The smooth road ended, and we ran into serious problems. The dirt road ahead of us was full of rocks and holes that made the truck bump and sway, sending us flying while clouds of thick dust took our breath away. Quickly, we rolled down the canvasses and sat mostly on the floor, but the heat and dust filtering in caused us to cough a lot. We were extremely thirsty and the water we were carrying in the canteens was soon exhausted. We were on the road for four hours when the convoy stopped on a stretch of road flanked by trees and bushes several miles deep. The commanding officer at the head of the convoy gave orders to the drivers to let us dismount and go behind the bushes to relieve ourselves. We realized then what the newspapers were for.

Of all the humiliating situations I have had to endure in my life, I believe that is at the top of my list! I felt so sorry for Mamma, Zia Serafina, and all the other mothers who had to debase themselves to that extreme! Fifteen minutes later, a loud whistle brought us running back into the truck, and after filling our canteens with water, the truck drivers jumped in the trucks and the convoy was back on the dirt road, engulfed by a thick cloud of red dust.

Four hours later, we reached the Giggiga camp as the sun was splashing its last rays before dipping behind the jagged hills around the city, the largest in the Somali region. Muslims made up the majority of the population. The camp was located at its periphery, and from my observation post in the truck, the only things I could see were the roofs of the mosques that dominated the skyline.

The convoy passed through the steel gates of a large tent city surrounded by barbed wire and came to a stop near the center of the camp. A few one-story concrete buildings that housed the staff of the British Command seemed to be the only buildings similar to the homes we had all left behind. Loud whistles pierced the air, and the military personnel in charge of logistics took over the task of vacating each truck and escorting us to our designated tents.

"Mamma," Antonietta called frantically from the top of the truck. *"Io non voglio andare giu`! Voglio rimanere qua, io ho paura di questa gente!* (I don't want to go down. I want to stay here. I am afraid of these people!)"

Like all of us, Antonietta was very tired and dusty, and she was only four years old, much too young to have to endure such events. She broke into one of her tantrums, and we all huddled around her and patiently convinced her that everything was going to be okay. Mamma and Zia Serafina made every effort to stay calm as we were escorted to the entrance of one large tent. . Inside, many straw mattresses were lined in straight rows on top of heavy canvasses covering the dirt floor underneath. We were assigned to a group of mattresses in one corner, were directed to take one mattress each, and were told where the bathrooms were located. Ten minutes later, we were given a thin blanket and a cold army ration for our dinner.

We all decided to visit the bathrooms before it got dark. We had to wait patiently almost an hour for our turn. On our return, we sat on our mattresses, almost too exhausted to open our ration boxes. Antonietta, too tired to cry, slumped on her mattress and immediately fell asleep.

We were awakened very early the next morning and made a dash for the bathrooms. As on the previous night, we had to wait in line for a time that seemed to stretch for hours. The air was cool, and the dawn was just breaking with its golden hues on the east horizon. Outside the tents, the hustle and bustle associated with the departure of a large convoy was in full swing. The commotion extended to the military authorities, who were coordinating our departure for the next camp. Orders were shouted in every direction, and finally we were again escorted and ordered to climb into the trucks assigned to us and given two rations each, one for breakfast, and one for lunch, and another bunch of newspapers.

For two days, we endured the suffocating heat and the nightly stops at two more camps. The temperature became more and more intolerable as the convoy sliced through the hot sands of the desert on the only road to Mogadishu. Then it happened. As the convoy approached the port, far on the horizon, the thin line that separates sky and the Indian Ocean became more and more visible to the naked eye. Finally, we were approaching our destination where, wrapped in hope, our lives would take another mysterious turn.

We climbed on the seats and poked our heads out of the opened sides of the trucks, stretching our necks, hoping to catch a glimpse of the extraordinary *Navi Bianche* (the White Boats). As we got closer, the sight and smell of the ocean gave us the impetus to recharge our tired bodies with newfound energy. All together, we began to sing patriotic songs. We waved our arms and jumped for joy. We were finally going to be on an Italian boat, with Italian personnel and Italian food! What a blessing. Was this going to bring closure to months of deprivation? Maybe!

For a moment, I closed my eyes and imagined the Navi Bianche stretching imaginary arms over the waves, eager to embrace us and shield us in their bosoms, like mother hens protecting their brood. However, disappointment met us as soon as we were dropped off on the pier. The boats were nowhere in sight.

Then, as our eyes searched the ocean, the frames of the two large cruise ships came into view in all their glory. The *Duilio* and the *Giulio Cesare*, anchored several hundred feet away in the Indian Ocean, wore glossy white paint with two gigantic red crosses painted on each side. From their masts, long strings of bright lights hung from bow to stern. We just stared, wide-eyed, at the wonder of their size.

How were we supposed to get out there? Along the pier, several barges had been transported closer to a section with stairs that went straight into the water. Soon the barges were filled with about twenty refugees at a time.

Fear started to creep in. Zia Serafina looked at the barges, and when she realized each had only a strip of wood on three sides for people to hold onto, she began to shiver and cry in terror. We watched the rafts oscillate in all directions on the choppy waves as the wind tossed them up and down, causing many of the passengers to become seasick.

Our turn to mount a raft came swiftly with the aid of two strong British soldiers who were able to calm Zia Serafina, but not Antonietta, who had begun to cry convulsively while holding tightly to Mamma's skirt. Pierino and Andrea were fascinated by the whole scene and followed with great interest the churned-up waters foaming behind the barge. I knew my stomach was going to react at any moment to the undulations of our flat-bottomed motorboat. It didn't take long for almost everyone, including me, to lean overboard and let it out!

Our group, including Maria and Lina, Giulia, and Alberto, were all assigned to the *Duilio*. As we approached the ship, the operator of the barge skillfully aligned it with a gangplank with a wide platform at the bottom. It was positioned in a way to make our boarding a mere jump onto the platform, where Italian sailors helped us to land. Holding our bags in one hand, we clutched the sailors' hands and then the iron rail as we made it to the upper deck, where Italian was spoken fluently and smiles and warm greetings were generously given.

It seemed the whole crew was happy to see us. I felt a surge of happiness wrapping around my heart like a balmy fragrance around my body. We had made it, and even though the heat of the day was blasting without mercy and the crowd pressed on every side, it felt good to be welcomed at last!

The only challenge we had was how to calm Antonietta. Mamma tried everything she could think of, but she continued sobbing. No one could divert her. It seemed that something very deep was troubling her, and Mamma was thinking of having a doctor look at her. Unfortunately, she had to wait until we passed one more procedure—continue to our assigned accommodations—before we could seek help for Antonietta's strange ailment.

Did I say another procedure? Indeed, I did, and this time the scope of it threw me for a loop. Was there ever going to be an end to all the requirements and procedures?

CHAPTER 15

AROUND THE CAPE OF GOOD HOPE

O nce we got on board, we were funneled in groups towards a nearby
stairway. "*Andiamo, andiamo*! (Hurry up, hurry up!)" Several nurses pushed us forward. "Hurry up! You have to be sterilized before you
are given sleeping arrangements."

Sterilized? What did that mean? We looked at each other, not understanding what the word implied. Nurses in spotless white uniforms,
white caps, and large red crosses on their breasts showed us the way
toward a cluster of rooms at the first landing. A sign against a wall said
in large black letters: "OSPEDALE (Hospital)." The nurses smiled and
tried hard to dispel our fears as we entered a waiting room full of chairs.
Once we were seated, another nurse explained the process of sterilization
and why we had to go through it:

"After those concentration camps and the long trip through dust and
heat, we want to be sure we kill all the germs that might be attached to
your clothes and bodies," she explained in a matter-of-fact tone. She
pointed to a door. "One at a time, you will enter that room. Another nurse
will be there to help you undress, and you will be naked when you enter
the sterilization room. When the treatment is complete, a bell will ring,
and you will go out through the other door. Another nurse will be waiting
there to hand you your sterilized clothes and suitcase. Don't be afraid!
They're just killing the germs you carry. It won't hurt you, but it smells
terrible in there, so hold your nose with your hand."

Our turn to be sterilized arrived, and I chose to go first. I entered the
room, suitcase in hand, and a chubby older nurse took it out of my hands.
A metal door on a side wall had a large window on top, revealing a dense
fog whirling behind the door, bringing to mind the sulfur treatments we
had to endure in Bari when we came down with the whooping cough.

"*Ragazza presto, presto, togli tutti I vestiti*! (Young lady hurry, hurry!
Take all your clothes off!)" Her stern voice stunned me. I was ready to

burst into tears. "I don't like to do this, but it is mandatory for all the *profughi* (refugees) to step into that room naked and be sterilized." She paused and stared into my eyes. "We have to kill the germs that you are carrying, do you understand? *Presto, presto* (quick, quick) take off all your clothes now." I felt my heart pound in my chest as I undressed as quickly as I could. Take my clothes off in front of a stranger? Be sterilized? My mind searched for answers.

Sensing my fear and embarrassment, she snapped, laughing loudly, "*Non ti preoccupare* (Don't worry), there is nobody in that room. *Vai, vai*! (Go, go!)" With a derisive grin, she shoved me into the room and slammed the door behind me. Inside, the acrid smell grabbed my throat and my eyes began to tear. A few seconds later, a bell rang, and I bolted out of the caustic atmosphere into a room where another nurse was waiting for me with my sterilized clothes in her hands. She was very friendly, apologetic, and even embarrassed, trying to console me with soothing words while I put my clothes on as rapidly as I could. I heard her rumble something, but I hardly paid any attention to what she was saying. My mind was on the trauma that Mamma, Antonietta, and Zia Serafina were going to be exposed to. I was very worried about Antonietta. She was traumatized enough. How would she react? I was sure she would be scared to death!

Once I was through dressing, I was given back my suitcase and told to wait in another room for the rest of the family. Shortly after, Pierino and Andrea came out smiling, choking a little, and teary-eyed, but still smiling. As usual, they took even this episode in stride. It was a pure debacle, though, when Mamma came out with Antonietta, who was screaming at the top of her lungs. Other nurses stopped to help her calm down, but to no avail. Zia Serafina pitched in by improvising a series of funny impressions with her face, her hands, and even her body. Her amusing gestures were funny to my brothers and me, but did not affect Antonietta's behavior. She kept crying, sometimes very loudly, holding on to Mamma's skirt. Everyone around gave us annoyed looks, while offering all kinds of suggestions on how to keep her quiet.

Ignoring their advice, Mamma turned to the nurse. She implored her, "Please may we see a doctor? I must have a doctor examine my child." The nurse said we had to wait until we were assigned to our dormitory.

Our turn arrived about thirty minutes later. Two nurses and a sailor in a white uniform took charge of our group of twenty-five people and motioned us to follow them closely. There was no sign of Maria and Lina, Giulia, or Alberto anywhere, and I wondered how they were coping. I was concerned about little Alberto, not quite three years old. When we saw him last, he was becoming more fragile and weak each day. Were they all right? We climbed stairs and turned narrow corners until we reached two double doors. The heat below deck mixed with the thick humidity prevalent at sea level was gradually sapping our energies. Our clothes were soaked with perspiration, and I could not wait to slump on a real bed and rest for just a while.

I thought surely that they would assign us a cabin large enough to keep our family together. No words can describe the shock we felt when the double doors opened, and rows upon rows of bunk beds three bunks high loomed in front of our sweat dripping faces. Was this possible? Was this a dream or a nightmare? Squeezed on all sides by the crowds of people, Antonietta began screaming hysterically again, pulling Mamma away, and begging her to take her out of there.

"*Voglio uscire! Non posso respirare!* (I want to go out! I can't breathe!)" Antonietta's hair was soaked with sweat and she looked as if she would faint at any moment. Mamma had reached the limit of her tolerance. Her little daughter needed help, and no one was going to stop her from seeing a doctor.

"I want to see a doctor immediately," she snapped, turning to the sailor. "She has been crying for hours, and she needs something to calm her down." Then she tried begging. "Please, let me bring her to a doctor."

Even the nurses began to show concern for my sister, and after a closer look at Antonietta, one of them, a frightened expression on her face, said to the sailor, "I see signs of a heat stroke. She needs help immediately!" This was the first time I heard the term "heat stroke," and in the following ten days, I heard it repeated many times when we anchored in Mogadishu. The daily temperature in that African city reached 110 and sometimes even 115 degrees. Even standing in the shade, people overcome by the extreme heat were fainting with heat strokes.

Alarmed by the nurse's statement, the sailor ordered my family to follow him quickly. He took us back to the hospital, and a doctor soon examined Antonietta's limp body. The rest of us were told to wait in the adjacent room. One hour passed before Mamma emerged with Antonietta finally asleep in the nurse's arms. The doctor gave Mamma an envelope with some pills and a list of things to do to make her comfortable and then moved to one corner, motioning the sailor to join him. I saw them exchange a few words. Then the doctor scribbled something on a piece of paper, gave it to the sailor, and sent him on his way. The rest of us had to remain in the waiting room until his return.

The sailor was soon back and, smiling, he asked us to follow him. "You will be very pleased when you see where I am taking you now," he said, reaching out to softly touch Antonietta's cheeks.

"I just can't wait to stretch out on a soft bed," Zia Serafina mumbled, exhausted by the torridity of the atmosphere.

Mamma was quick to add, "Me, too. I feel all my strength oozing out of my skin along with the sweat! And you poor children!" Her gaze swept first over me, then Pierino, and last Andrea, stopping for a few seconds to examine each of us. Shaking her head, she barely whispered, "God bless you all. I am so proud of you. You have been so patient and strong." Her lips curved into a wry smile as she sighed. I felt the pain in her heart as she pondered the misery endured by her children, and I wanted to hold her tight and make her pain go away.

We followed the sailor along a passageway that led us to a large landing. We walked a bit farther to a ramp of stairs at least twelve feet wide, and holding the side rail, we went down the ramp and on to another landing. On both sides of the landings, long corridors were lined up with doors.

"Those are second-class cabins," said the sailor, pointing at the doors. "And they are already assigned to special people." We did not know what "special" meant. In what way were these people so privileged? We found out shortly thereafter that the "special" category meant something very different from what we had imagined.

At that moment, though, we just wanted a decent place to rest, sleep, and nurse Antonietta back to health. "We are special people, too," retorted Zia Serafina angrily, giving him a resentful look. "Can we have one of those cabins?" she asked, expecting to hear a prompt, "Yes." But the sailor just kept on going, completely ignoring her. There were women, children, and sailors everywhere, dazed and sweaty, rushing in all directions. We kept following our sailor down several sets of stairs until we reached the one before the last ramp. He looked at a pad in his hand, turned to the right, and stopped in front of a cabin with the same number written on his pad. Smiling, he unlocked the door and we filed in, speechless, with mouths open wide. The cabin was large, and it had three bunk beds and a bathroom of sorts.

"Yes." The sailor bent down to take the suitcases from our hands, set them in a corner, and continued smiling. "You are very lucky to get this cabin. It is located in the middle of the ship, and you will not feel much rolling during a storm. You can thank the doctor for requesting a cabin and not sending you back to that dormitory. Here." He handed Mamma a bunch of papers and continued. "These are the instructions you will need while on board. Please make sure you understand them. They are very important. We are still fighting a war, you know!" He gave us another smile, turned, and left with a resounding "Arrivederci!" His steps trailed off down the corridor.

The nurse placed Antonietta on one of the lower bunks and offered to fetch some cold water, because, she explained, it was very important to drink a lot to avoid dehydration. She also mentioned the dining room on the upper deck that we could access if we wanted to eat something. But the stifling heat took all our hunger away. None of us wanted to go up on deck again. We just wanted to sleep. We were very grateful when the nurse came back with two pitchers of iced water. Pierino, Andrea, and I finally took off our wet clothes, climbed the stairs to the upper bunks, and slumped onto the soft mattresses. Mamma and Zia Serafina, both exhausted, also slipped into their bunks, and I heard Mamma softly murmur, "Tomorrow, yes. Tomorrow, God will provide."

The next morning, we woke up very early and all had one thing in common. We were very hungry. It was amazing to see how a good night's sleep revived our aching bones and cast down spirits. Even Antonietta woke with a smile. The best part about having a cabin was privacy and a bathroom to ourselves. What a blessing. Especially when we heard the ship was going to be our home for forty long days. There was no port-hole to give us a view of the outside world, and we really didn't care. We quickly washed and dressed, anxious to explore our new surroundings and find the way to the dining room, determined to satisfy our ravenous hunger.

We reached the upper deck and at last the dining room, only to be greeted by hundreds of other passengers milling around. Soon we joined a small crowd waiting at the entrance. On a large board, the sitting schedule was clearly written in bold letters:

Colazione: 6:00 to 9:00 A.M.

Pranzo: 1:00 P.M. to 4:00 P.M.

Cena: 6:00 P.M. to 9:00 P.M.

While waiting in line we basked in the delicious aromas coming from the kitchen and filling the air around us. In a short time, we were seated at one of the long tables and were mesmerized to see platters full of biscotti, baskets of fresh baked *pagnotte* (rolls), bowls of fresh butter, jams and jellies of all varieties, and pitchers of milk, iced chocolate, iced tea, and steaming coffee. Our first *pranzo* and *cena* aboard the ship were equally plentiful, and since it had been months since we enjoyed a decent meal, this abundance felt like a feast! Full of glee, we dived into platters of spaghetti and meatballs, minestrone soup and *pasta e fagioli*. For the moment, life was good again.

There was no shortage of food on the ship, but the enormous discomfort from the stifling heat of that tropical region was simply unbearable. The electric fans strategically installed in key locations did little to bring relief. It was extremely hot, so hot that many collapsed with heat strokes that often turned deadly, and dysentery spread like fire among the children.

When we finally located Giulia, she was alone. Alberto had contracted the dreadful disease, and he was not expected to make it through. Heartbroken and exhausted, Giulia kept vigil by his bed in the infirmary until, five days later, little Alberto went to heaven.

Giulia was not allowed to witness her beloved little son's burial at sea. He was one of many children and adults who succumbed to the heat or disease before we left port and since the voyage would be a long one and the ship had no morgue, burials had to occur at some time or other, but we didn't know when or how. We found out later that the crew dumped the bodies overboard during the night once we reached the high seas, when most of the passengers were asleep.

There was very little we could do to console Giulia. I spent a lot of time with her, just saying nothing. Only fourteen years old, I could find no words that could have made any difference, anyway. I knew that the healing process happened only in the course of time.

Eventually, we connected with Maria and Lina. Their quarters were on the stern of the ship and they shared a playroom converted into a dormitory with twenty other refugees. Giulia was assigned a bunk bed in one of the large ballrooms, where at least three hundred people crowded together, and where we would have been, too, if not for a doctor who took pity on Antonietta and us.

Each day, we watched convoy after convoy unload its human cargo at the pier and the *Duilio* and the *Giulio Cesare*, anchored a few hundred feet from each other in the indigo waters of the Indian Ocean, received their strange assortments of derelicts climbing aboard like a herd of cattle into a barn. At times the loudspeakers blasted strict commands to fetch the life preservers kept under the beds, and then assemble on deck for drilling practices on how to put them on.

After ten suffocating days in Mogadishu, at last the time arrived to depart. Each ship had reached its limit of twenty-five hundred refugees, and each crew prepared to embark on a journey that was to last forty long days.

The day before our departure, the captain and his officers assembled on the bridge and introduced to us the British contingent of about thirty officers and enlisted men, our escort until Gibilterra (Gibraltar). More instructions and manifests were placed at certain locations, giving us a somber account of what to expect in the days ahead. On the maps, the itinerary had been clearly traced:

Partenza (Departure): Mogadishu.

Prima fermata (First stop): Port Elizabeth, South Africa.

Seconda fermata (Second stop): Las Palmas, the Canary Islands.

Terza fermata (Third stop): Gibilterra (Gibraltar) British escort disembarks ship.

Quarta fermata (Fourth stop): Napoli (Naples), Italy.

Cleverly camouflaged on these pages were the perils we might encounter on the way. Crossing the Atlantic smack in the middle of a raging war was necessary to mitigate the dangers we were facing. Between the lines we understood that although every belligerent nation had been notified of our crossing and we were traveling under the flag of the international Red Cross, the danger remained of hitting mines floating in the ocean, or of some submarine mistaking us for an enemy ship. Reading those manifests made us wish we could turn back and disappear somewhere. Of course, as was always the case, we all turned to prayers. There was a small chapel on board, but the chaplain said mass on deck several times a day to allow more people to attend. From then on, there was always a line in front of the chapel, day or night.

It was early morning when we were awakened by the loud quivering of the ship. The heart and soul of the *Duilio* were beginning to pump new life into the arteries that ran through her body. The engines throbbed, and great energy floated in the veins of her solid structure. Although every speck of luxury she had once enjoyed when she crisscrossed the Atlantic Ocean on her cruises to America had disappeared from her hold, the ship still emanated a majestic air that wrapped around her like an invisible aura.

"Let's hurry up and get dressed. I want to say good-bye to this suffocating furnace!" Mamma said, urgency in her voice.

"Andrea, *fai presto a vestirti*! (Andrea, hurry up and get dressed!)" Pierino coaxed his brother.

"*Va bene, va bene*! *Faccio presto*! (Okay, okay! I am hurrying!)" Andrea, usually slow in getting his pants on, was ready in a jiffy.

Zia Serafina warned us of the dangers if we dared get too close to the rail. "You could fall overboard and become dinner to the sharks!" We laughed, dressed quickly, and brushed away Zia Serafina's stern admonitions as we rushed on deck to see the ship pull up anchors and leave forever that forsaken place. We made it to the stairway, only to be caught in a sea of people. Everyone wanted to be part of that special moment. Somehow, we managed to stay close to each other until we reached the top and spilled out onto the deck like roaches running for cover. I still don't know how I managed to make it almost to the rail. I heard Mamma calling us and we answered loudly until everyone moved closer to me. The stifling heat even at 6:00 A.M. engulfed everything in a silvery haze that dispersed as the sun began its eternal journey from the east horizon.

Gradually, the ship's vibrations became more intense and the smoke stacks began to eject thick black smoke. A light breeze fought hard to keep it from spiraling down on top of us. The crew, sailors, and officers alike exchanged commands and instructions, following every order with care like a swarm of busy bees minding their hive. With the anchors finally up, the *Duilio's* horns began blasting her farewell and the ship began to move. In the distance, the *Giulio Cesare* picked up the tune, returned the greeting, and began to trail after us. Shouting with joy, we clapped hands for a while then scattered in all directions. The ocean was as smooth as a mirror and for a while, it felt as if we were standing still. Only the receding lines of the pier and the sandy coast assured us that we were moving. Soon they had all disappeared behind the horizon, and the *Duilio*, with its cargo of expectant dreamers, headed for deeper waters.

For several days, we skirted the coast of East Africa.

The temperature was hot during the day and cool at the night as we crossed the equator. It got gradually colder as we traveled south, approaching the winter season in the southern hemisphere. The ocean was calm and the food delicious and plentiful—though we learned quickly that the climb to the dining room on the upper deck necessitated having to pass through the area where people with mental illnesses were housed. They were the "special people" the sailor had mentioned earlier. One of the women would call out to us, trying to coax us to come to her. She looked like the Wicked Witch of the West from *The Wizard of Oz*! We were frightened of her at first until we learned to ignore her and keep moving.

The younger children during those days passed their time playing together, improvising their own fun. I met other girls about my age, and with Lina as my accomplice, we found several ways to stay busy. A lot of our time was spent reading the popular Italian magazine *Il Corriere dei Piccoli* that was made available on board.

Twelve days passed, during which we were surrounded only by the expanse of sky and ocean. Now we began to see the crest of a mountain range slowly emerging from the horizon. As we got closer, Port Elizabeth's skyline became visible at the foot of the hills and spread for miles in both directions. From the deck, distant homes and church steeples behind tall trees seemed to wink and give us a warm welcome.

The ship had to stop to be refurbished with food and other basic supplies. We were absolutely forbidden to get off the ship for any reason. By midday, the *Duilio* smoothly slipped into her berth at the pier, followed by her sister ship at a nearby berth.

Our two days in Port Elizabeth were pleasant and without incident. Everything was proceeding on schedule and soon it was time to say good-bye to this modern city vibrant with life. In the early morning of the third day, the *Duilio* pulled up her anchors, blasted her horns as usual when leaving port, and maneuvered out of the harbor, heading again for deep waters. The *Giulio Cesare* followed at close distance, both ships heading south towards the tip of the continent, poised to encircle the famous Cape of Good Hope.

We had no suspicion that this part of the ocean would declare its own kind of war on our ships or that heavy storms were converging there to embrace each other at the Cape, releasing their fury on our humble vessels. Our encounter with the weather began one morning soon after breakfast. We went out on deck searching for friends to play games with, while Mamma and Zia Serafina settled comfortably on the lounge chairs with ladies they had befriended on board. About one hour later, the waters began to get choppy and the ship began to roll over the waves. Approaching the Cape, all hell broke loose. A dense bank of cloud emerged suddenly from the horizon and barreled straight toward us and the sun disappeared behind the thick clouds, plunging everything into gloomy darkness. A strong wind unleashed its fury in all directions, and rain fell in sheets.

Sailors spilled on the decks and dragged indoors anything that was movable. Through loudspeakers, orders were given to all passengers to remain inside, keep the children under constant supervision, and to expect the storm to last at least a couple of days. Our only encouragement came from the sailors, who between their tasks reassured us that our ship was capable of beating any storm. They had been through many of them already and had always come out the winners.

For fifty hours, the ocean furiously heaved, raged, and boiled, and the ship staggered to stay afloat. The heavy rain, blasted by a merciless and obstinate wind, pelted the decks for hours. There was water everywhere. Below deck and frightened, we huddled in groups or stayed in the cabins, holding onto anything solid to avoid being hurled across the floors.

Our stomachs, revolting at such insolence, refused to hold down food. Most everyone on board got seasick. When I ventured out for a breath of fresh air and tried to make it to sickbay hoping to get some help, I was turned back by the stench of vomit all over the walkways and stairways. The crew, familiar with the fits our stomachs were having, came around several times a day to clean up the mess. I can still remember the sympathetic nurses and sailors encouraging us to eat. "You will feel better if you keep something in your stomach."

We tried to eat after a whole day of fast. Somehow, we made it to the dining room. Few passengers were there, most of them seasick and pathetic to look at. Panini filled with provolone and prosciutto was the only food available. They were easy to hold in our hands and our stomachs screamed for solid food, nothing else. All tableware was kept off the tables as the motion of the ship kept them sliding to the floor. We ate some, and we gave up some. Antonietta had the most trouble holding anything in her stomach, but thank God, she made it up with plenty of sleep.

The storm lasted three long days. On the morning of the fourth, the bright rays of a spectacular sunrise danced and shimmered on the incredibly placid expanse of the ocean. The foamy white crests that had fermented on top of the enraged waves during the storm had disappeared and the ocean was as smooth as a small lake. We came to realize that this promontory was named "Cape of Good Hope" for one good reason: You have to "hope" really hard to make it around it.

Everything returned to normal in a short time, and life on the ship resumed its monotonous routine. Great weather accompanied us all the way to Las Palmas in the Canary Islands, where again our ship stopped over to be refurbished. I remember little about Las Palmas, as the city was not visible from the pier where we were docked. I do remember seeing a ridge of mountains in the far distance covered with vegetation all the way up to their peaks.

After two days, the *Duilio* and the *Giulio Cesare*, their store's refurbished, picked up anchors, and steamed full speed towards the Straits of Gibraltar. It wasn't long before a new threat loomed in our path. One day in mid-morning, the blasts of sirens signaled approaching danger. The waters began to get rough again and the ship rolled side to side as she sliced through the waves. We scurried to our cabins and pulled the life jackets over our clothes as we were told to do. Trembling, we waited to hear the voice of the captain giving us instructions through the loud-speakers. What ugly monster was raising his head? Were there mines in the waters? Maybe a submarine was preparing to blow us off the face of the earth?

TOWARDS THE STRAIT OF GIBRALTAR AND BACK IN BARI

Looking back at my life, I know that God has never forsaken me. He was always there, more so during my darkest moments. When I had painfully surrendered all of my will,   He drew near, and in the silence of my heart, I felt the assurance of   His presence that always gave me courage to face whatever was in front of me, and courage was what we needed as the ships turned toward Gibraltar.

There were only a few lifeboats on the ship's sides, and those were reserved for a handful of people, including our British escort. Our chances of survival if a torpedo hit the ship were almost none. So again, on our knees we prayed and prayed and prayed some more. Was God ever going to listen? Could he abandon us? I could not understand why we had become the target of so many trials!

My most difficult task was to bear the fear and pain my little sister Antonietta was enduring. Innocent children should always be happy, fun loving, and full of life, shouldn't they? Not tossed around like straws on raging waves.

"*Che sta succedendo*? (What is happening?)" Antonietta trembled with fear as she looked into Mamma's eyes in search of an answer. "*Io ho paura*! (I am afraid!)" Weeping, she stretched her arms around Mamma's neck in a tight embrace. We waited fearfully to hear the voice of the captain giving us instructions through the loudspeakers. It seemed an eternity had passed when the sirens finally sounded the all clear. We took the life preservers off and rushed on deck to see if someone could explain the alarm.

We were in for quite a shock. An unidentified submarine had come close to the ship, had lifted its periscope above the waters, and followed us for over a mile. The crew warned us to expect more alarms to be sounded as we approached the strategic Straits of Gibraltar. War was raging in that part of the Atlantic, and American, British, German, and Italian ships and submarines hunted and sank each other in great numbers. On several other occasions, we ran for cover as we were approached by other submarines and airplanes flying close above our heads. Even though the *Duilio* and the *Giulio Cesare* were easily distinguished by the enormous red crosses painted in the middle of their glowing white sides and were lit night and day by thousands of bright lights, we feared that someone could make a mistake and send a torpedo our way. In earnest, we prayed that no floating mine would blow us out of the waters.

Any fun we had had before those days, was over. We constantly lived in fear and hoped each morning merely to make it through another day, until at last one blessed morning we anchored in the Port of Gibraltar. By prior arrangements with the International Red Cross, the British escort disembarked our ship and, after refurbishing, an operation that took two full days to complete, our ships were free to proceed on the last leg of our incredibly long trip. From the Atlantic Ocean, the narrow Strait of Gibraltar is the only access to the Mediterranean Sea and the multitude of countries that encircle it. In the spring of 1942, during our sojourn, the port was buzzing with battleships of every size and heavily fortified.

During our first night anchored in the port, we learned how well the British navy was fortifying the port. We went to bed early, happy to catch up on our many sleepless nights and thankful to have survived thus far, when a loud explosion shook the ship violently, tossing us around in our bunks and knocking many objects onto the floor. Terrified, we huddled together. Antonietta jumped out of her bunk and into Mamma's arms, screaming with fear. Petrified, we waited for more explosions to happen. Loud screaming and crying reached us from other cabins. What was happening? Were the Germans bombing our ship?

Finally, from the loudspeakers, we heard the explanation for the explosions. Depth bombs were being exploded under water to deter enemy submarines from sneaking through the straits while the *Navi Bianche* were anchored there. We had nothing to fear—they were only a big nuisance! We sighed with relief until the voice from the loudspeaker told us to expect the explosions to go off every few hours during the two nights of our stopover. How could they do this to us? The explosions rattled the ship and everything in its hold like ice cubes in a martini shaker. We couldn't wait to get out of there and find some peace.

On the third morning of our stay, we ran on deck, counting the minutes till our departure. The *Duilio* and the *Giulio Cesare* picked up anchor again and began the final part of the trip. With Gibraltar behind us, our eyes were set on Italy, the beautiful country that gave us birth. We spent our last days closer to Maria, Lina, and Giulia, knowing that the chances of us meeting again were very slim. The war was raging all around Italy. Who could predict the outcome? We promised to write often to each other and some day, God willing, to see each other again. So we hoped, but it was not to be. We never saw our friends again.

As we got closer to Italy's coast, we felt the excitement sweeping through the ship as we anticipated seeing relatives and friends again. Even the sea remained smooth, gleaming with pleasure to see us pass through. Like a beautiful dream after a nightmare, one sunny morning, it was finally over. One of my most vivid memories is the day we arrived in Naples on June 28, 1942.

Anticipating last minute confusion, we had packed our bags the night before and made plans to be on deck very early in the morning. Mamma hoped to stop briefly by the dining area and grab something to eat, especially for Antonietta and the boys, who seemed hungry all the time. That early morning, ready and eager to leave, we grabbed our suitcases and without any qualms filed out of the cabin that for forty days had been both our home and our prison. We rounded the landings and stumbled on the stairways among dozens of other refugees desiring the same thing: a glimpse of the hills of Naples. The disembarkation had been organized using a number system, and our turn, if everything proceeded smoothly, was scheduled to happen around 1:00 P.M.

We spilled on deck, shoved through an exuberant throng of humanity, and managed to reach a space with an almost unobstructed view of the horizon. The first light of the morning on the eastern sky gave us a hint of the approaching day, and the seagulls sweeping and diving around the ship brought evidence of land. Excitement mounted on deck, especially among those crowding the ship's rail.

"*Siamo vicino alla terra*! (We are close to land!)" many yelled from different parts of the deck. "*Presto saremo nella nostra patria*! (Soon we will be in our country!)" Eyes searched the horizon in every direction until quivery voices announced in unison,:

"*Terra! Terra! La bella Napoli si sta avvicinando!* (Land! Land! Beautiful Naples is getting closer!)"

Faintly visible against the sky, the hills of Naples emerged on the horizon and gradually appeared as they rushed to meet us. We watched, speechless at first, and then we broke into sobs. We kissed, we hugged, and we jumped for joy. Home! Home at last!

The ship got closer to land. From the top of the hills, all the way down to the busy port, the white buildings of the city of Naples spread in front of us like a picture postcard. The *Duilio* and the *Giulio Cesare* were now encircled by Italian battleships, dozens of small and large boats, barges, and sailboats. Sailors and fishermen waved their arms, blew horns, and shouted greetings welcoming us home, a comfort to the hearts of a broken piece of humanity that had almost lost all hope of a future. The White Boats had made it to Italy, and in the process, into the pages of history.

The *Duilio* was finally in port and preparing to dock. Smoothly, she settled into her berth and sailors on board threw the hawsers, while other sailors on the pier secured them to the moorings. The engines throbbed for a while then stopped completely. On the pier behind barricades, hundreds of people seemed touched by the pitiful look of the refugees, for they began yelling:

"*Benvenuti, benvenuti nella nostra patria*! (Welcome, welcome to our homeland!)" Frantically, they waved their arms. Some called loudly the names of loved ones on board. There was so much excitement and joy! In a short time, the gangplank was lowered, and the first refugees trickled down, falling amid tears of joy into the loving arms of relatives and friends.

Several hours passed as we waited patiently in line on the upper deck for our turn to disembark. We managed to get to the rails and have a better view of the people on the pier, hoping to see among them my father's sister, Zia Annettina, who lived in Naples. It had been impossible for us to contact her or any other relative from Harar, the concentration camps, or the ship. Still, we hoped that, having gotten news from radio bulletins and newspaper articles about the arrival in port of the *Navi Bianche*, she would be there to greet us. We waited on deck, patiently soaking in the warm rays of the sun, and welcomed the cool sea breeze that caressed our cheeks and ruffled our hair until it was our turn to disembark.

We filed down the gangplank, each of us—except Antonietta—holding a suitcase, and to our surprise on the pier among the crowd was Zia Annettina, looking for us. What a joy to see her after so many years! And what sadness it was to leave her just an hour later. A bus was waiting to pick us up with several other refugees and drop us at the railroad station, where we were scheduled to board the train to Bari. We shared a few precious moments and told her to telegraph Zio Nino in Bari of our arrival there the next morning.

The night on the train was tedious and uncomfortable. The only food available on board was panini and water. I slept a little, I dreamed a little, and I wandered a *lot*. During the night, the train made many stops and finally came to a screeching halt in Bari. Were we really back in Bari? In bold letters, that name was written on several boards around the station. Seeing it made me think of the many times that I had been in that station.

Once again, I was back in the city where I was born. I was only nine years old when I left. At fourteen, I felt like I had left it eons before. In that short time, I had aged far ahead of my years. My age did not matter, I told myself; what we had to contend with next, did. I felt the happiness of our return obscured by the cruel reality facing us. We had no money and no home to go to, our only decent clothes were on our backs, and our only other possessions were carefully stored in a twenty-pound suitcase we carried around.

I was certain Mamma and Zia Serafina were thinking the same thoughts and that realization gave me chills up and down my spine. Mamma had four children to support, and Zia Serafina had three daughters who were nearing their graduation dates from a Catholic orphanage and convent school. As a widow, she had to somehow provide for them all on her own. Another page was turning in the book of our lives, and I had no idea how we were going to fill the blank pages ahead. We were entering a long, dark tunnel, with not even an inkling of light at the end.

Waiting for us at the station were Zio Nino and Zia Rosaria, Zia Elisa and Zio Pierino, and Nonna Antonia. After the hugs, the kisses, the tears, and the sighs, we convened in Zio Nino's home. To our dismay, they had no news concerning Babbo. Not knowing his whereabouts dampened the joy of our return. As Zio Nino's quarters were not large enough to accommodate all six of us, we had to split. Three of us—Pierino, Andrea, and I—took residence in Zia Elisa's home. From the authority on board the ship we had received instructions on how refugees were to seek help once they arrived in their city of origin. We were to apply for assistance at the local town hall and in due time receive monetary assistance as well as room and board until we could make it on our own.

The day after our arrival in Bari, Mamma, Zia Serafina, and I went bright and early to city hall, hoping to fill out the necessary applications. Dozens of refugees were there already, and the lines kept getting longer and thicker during the day. After waiting for hours, we were told to come back the next day because they had yet to receive the funds or our temporary housing location.

Thus began three long weeks of daily visits, asking and begging for help, to the *Municipio* (city hall), then to the*Prefettura* (prefecture), and the *Corpo diArmata* (the army base), where Babbo had worked before shipping to Africa. We were assured that the government in Rome had already allocated compensation for the refugees, but because of the pro-verbial "red tape," the Bari community had yet to receive any funds. We had to have patience. Lots of patience!

We needed clothes, a place to sleep, and food. How long could we expect our relatives to support us? At last, one morning, good news was waiting for us at cCity hHall. We were to go to the hotel Moro in Via Pic-cinni, where several rooms had being set aside for the refugees. We also had access to the dining room for all our daily meals. At last something good was beginning to happen! In less than one hour, we took residence in the hotel, and for the moment, our basic needs were met.

About three months later, another change took place. Mamma began to receive a monthly stipend, and an apartment in Via Abate Gimma on the corner of Via Argiro became available for our permanent residence. The building, although centrally located in Bari, was centuries old. Our apartment on the second floor had two bedrooms and a dining/family room with an excellent view from the balconies of the busy streets be-low. Famous shops along the avenues displayed expensive merchandise in their glittering windows. In the small kitchen, a coal-burning stove and a primitive sink were the only appliances. They were on one wall and a small table was on another. A door opened onto a terrace over-looking the courtyard, where a toilet had been installed inside a closet attached to one corner of the terrace. It had no ceiling!

During the winter months, it was so cold in there that we hated to have to use it, and we used to bolt out of there shivering as soon as our business was over. There was no hot running water and no shower, ei-ther, so we bought an aluminum tub we could barely sit in, filled it with warm water, and gave ourselves sponge baths. As for furniture, we had to make do with the hand-me-downs and discarded items relatives were able to give us.

Well, we had been there before, so why complain? Even if Mamma's income for one month was only sufficient to support the whole family for half a month, we had no choice but to adjust and ration the food to ensure we had enough till the next pay day. Our biggest concern was be-ing without any news from Babbo. By October 1942, schools reopened, and I enrolled in the last year of the *ginnasio* at the Orazio Flacco. As refugees, Pierino and Andrea had been given a government grant to at-tend a maritime school run by the Italian navy in Formia, a town several miles north of Rome, and Antonietta started kindergarten.

War was all around us, but its rumbles were still too distant to affect our daily lives, until rumors circulated that the British and American armies, after their great victory in North Africa and the defeat of the powerful German general Rommell, were preparing for the invasion of Sicily. The war was moving in our direction, and fear once again took residence in our hearts. We had left one battleground behind and another one was mercilessly barreling toward our land.

CHAPTER 17

THE WAR YEARS IN ITALY AND "LITTLE PEARL HARBOR"

As was always the case, we had to adapt to whatever the good Lord put on our plate. I never was one to complain, as I always hoped for things to get better. I went to school, made many friends, and went to see an occasional movie—always paid for by my cousins—or to parties in their home. Usually, we gathered on the roof top of Zia Elisa's house for parties organized by my seventeen-year-old cousin Andrea, who was in his last year of the *magistrale*, and his friends. They made savory sandwiches, filled baskets of fruit and biscotti, and even had little presents tucked in secret places for us girls to find and to keep. A record player provided the music, and we giggled and danced to the popular tunes of that era until midnight, when each of us headed home. We were teenagers trying to have a little fun in the middle of a world that was breaking apart.

Southern Italy at that time was calm compared to the uproar the northern part of the country was enduring. The German armies were more concentrated in the north, and the Allies constantly bombarded many large cities. German troops in the south were mostly stationed on the East Coast in cities with major ports, like Bari and Taranto, and in cities with major airports, like Foggia.

All of Europe was under the onslaught of the German army, and for a while, they seemed to advance everywhere. Our radio bulletins from "Qui—Radio Bari," the only station transmitting at the time, extolled first the conquests Germany made in all of Europe, and then all the defeats, in an attempt to quench our fears with propaganda. That is, until Russia joined the Allies and the war took another direction. During those winter months, big cities like Paris, London, and Berlin were attacked and destroyed, and innocent civilians, including women and children, were killed by the thousands.

Italian partisans that had never accepted Mussolini's regime waited in mountain hideouts for the right moment to strike and end it. Meanwhile, in Southern Italy, rumors of an Allied invasion from Northern Africa grew more persistent by the month, and during the early spring of 1943, Bari received the first taste of an air raid.

It began around the time people returned from work and sat at dinner tables to enjoy the *cena*. We heard the sirens fill the air with their ominous shrills. I ran with Mamma and Antonietta down the flight of stairs with other tenants of the building, breathless and scared out of our wits. The *portinaio* (janitor), Giuseppe, waited, just as scared as all of us, on the first floor. He opened a door in the hall and shoved us down a stairway that led to the basement. Expecting an aerial attack, he had cleverly turned the basement into a shelter. He had placed several chairs and benches against the walls and a supply of bottles of water, candles, and matches in a storage cabinet. The shelter could easily hold at least thirty people.

"*Presto, Presto!*" Giuseppe shoved us down the stairs just as the rumble of planes passing above our heads was followed by an explosion that shook the ground, cutting off the electricity, knocking some of the plaster from the walls, and filling the shelter with acrid dust. Children were screaming, especially Antonietta, and everyone was crying. The sound of the sirens and the blasts of the bombs brought back to my little sister the anguish of the last days spent in Africa. I wished I had a magic wand and could make all those memories disappear!

The planes passed over again and we heard more explosions in the distance. Holding our breaths and imploring Almighty God for help, we waited until finally we heard the sirens signal the "all clear." Slowly we filed out of the shelter, afraid at first to see where and what the bombs had hit. Once on the street, we linked with a throng of people rushing toward a street behind our building, where a thick cloud of smoke billowed upwards, filling the air with ashes.

The ambulances coming from many directions blew their sirens as they sped towards the scene of the disaster. And what a disaster that was! I will never forget what loomed before my eyes as we rounded the corner of the next street.

All the buildings on that block had received a direct hit from the bombs. It looked as if a giant knife had sliced through the walls from street to street. I was looking at a picture straight from hell. From the apartment rooms, now gaping open, men, women, and children, some dead and some screaming in pain, dangled from twisted furniture and jagged walls, from the top floors all the way to the street below. Rubble from the buildings piled high on the street, and people were buried and trapped underneath. From under a pile of debris I heard a woman screaming for help and a bunch of men dug with their bare hands until they brought her and her little girl out alive. The men had bleeding hands and the woman broken bones, but they were alive!

From that night on, life became a struggle just to stay alive. We did get one great consolation—a soldier attached to Babbo's cCorpo di aArmata delivered a letter from Babbo to Mamma. Babbo was safe! He was in a concentration camp near Nairobi in Kenya. He said that he was well and he missed all of us. He was worried he could not be with us, knowing well the dangers we yet faced. We could only communicate with him by mail every few months, but at least we knew where he was.

Afraid of another bombardment and the consequences that fear had on my little sister, Mamma decided to rent out the apartment in Bari and move to Casamassima, a small town about ten miles from Bari. Antonietta was safe from the bombs there, and I could commute to school on the train that stopped daily in town on its way to Bari. Antonietta could attend a local school. With the help of friends, Mamma was able to rent a small apartment on a wide street in the old section of the town.

The building itself was centuries old and the rent very cheap. That was the only place we could afford. It had an entrance room and just a few essentials. A large table that took almost all the space in the room had several chairs around it; a cupboard, a wood-burning stove, and a small sink against the side wall were the only other items in the room. Two small rooms behind this entrance had two beds and two small dressers each.

Remembering the bathroom in that place, I feel my skin begin to crawl. It consisted of a terracotta pot in the shape of a cylinder. It had a wooden cover and was set inside an outdoor enclosure. Every morning, we had to place this pot on the front steps, and a man with a horse-drawn cart stopped at every house on the street to pick up the pots, empty the contents into the cart, rinse them, and bring them back up to the steps. That was the way life had continued for centuries in those small towns. I wonder if today in that town and on that particular street, that is still the *modus operandi*.!

Vaguely, I recall the months we spent there, but I do remember a particular incident that nearly took our breath away. In July 1943, British and American troops began the invasion of Italy. They landed first in Sicily, and by the beginning of September were in Calabria, the "toe" of

Italy. Axis forces were no match for the powerful Allied armies and were forced to retreat, some through the "boot," and some up the Adriatic coast.

Meanwhile, complete chaos was spreading in northern Italy. Oppressed for years by the fascists, partisans were ready for their revenge, and they clashed daily with the demoralized Italian army. Finally, in late July, the fascist regime was overturned. Mussolini was kicked out of power and later hanged with his mistress by his side. By early September, Italy agreed to an armistice with the Allies.

Overnight, the Germans became our enemies. Their decimated troops, retreating from the boot of Italy, were forced to pass through the streets of small towns, up the Adriatic coast toward Foggia with its strategic airport, and Bari with its very important port complex. One early morning, we were jolted by the distant rumble of motor cars. Perplexed, we ran outside as we heard a muffled sound coming from the south of town, gradually getting louder. Our neighbors, also alarmed, joined us on the street. When we came to the conclusion that a German convoy was approaching, we all ran into our homes and bolted our doors.

We were very frightened! The Germans were enemies now, and we didn't know what they could do to us. The rumble got louder, and soon the first tanks and armored cars turned onto our street, followed by trucks full of soldiers armed to their teeth. Peeping from behind the shades of the only window in the room, I saw the steel helmets on the soldiers' heads. Mamma was standing next to me, and Pierino and Andrea, back from military school in Formia, pressed against us, also hoping to catch a glimpse of the German soldiers. Antonietta, sensing the anxiety in our voices, began to cry, ran into the bedroom, and hid under the bed.

All of a sudden, the convoy stopped. Officers and soldiers waved and shouted commands to each other, then dismounted and headed for the front doors of every house on the street. My heart began beating in my chest and I saw Mamma turn pale as a sheet. The insistent knock at the door sent tremors through our veins, but we had to open it. Several soldiers walked right into the room, mumbling in German as they handed us empty canteens that we understood they wanted us to fill with water. Ignoring us completely, they pulled out the chairs, sat around the table, and began drinking from the canteens. Somber and downcast, they looked very tired and spoke little among themselves. About fifteen minutes passed, and some took their helmets off. They were young kids, maybe eighteen to twenty years old, their uniforms dirty and full of dust, and they looked like they had just been in a battle and spent long hours inside the trenches. We filled their canteens with water again, and under their breath, they muttered, *"Auf wiedersehen,"* as they exited the room. They jumped onto their trucks and in a few minutes were gone. I wondered how few would survive the carnage building in their path and how many mothers back in their country would mourn the loss of those boys.

Allied troops in Italy were advancing in every direction, and the news of their landings in Salerno gave us hope that the German army would soon be defeated. We became acquainted with the names of famous generals—Montgomery, Eisenhower, Patton, Clark, and Doolittle—and their heroic strategies that eventually did end the war. Bari, with its commercial shipping harbor and a population of about two hundred thousand at that time, was occupied by the British Eighth aArmy and by the American Fifth aArmy without any serious conflicts. Miraculously, she was spared the heavy fighting and air raids that caused so much destruction in the middle and northern parts of Italy.

Until one night in early December…

Bari received an air raid of such immense proportion that it went down in the history books as "the Little Pearl Harbor" of Italy.

Mamma had decided sometime in October to return to our apartment in Bari to be closer to her sisters and brother. I had finished the *ginnasio* and was just entering the first of three years of the *liceo classico*. I did not have to buy any books or school material, as I was the recipient of a special grant for the children of refugees that provided free admission to the school of their choice. The day that I enrolled for my first class of the *liceo* in the *Orazio Flacco* complex, nests in my memory as one of the most special days of my life. In those days, only the wealthy could afford to attend those classes, and when I was accepted, I felt my dream had come true and I was on top of the world! That is how it felt for a brief time, anyway. Then even that dream faded away……

December 2, 1943: A day that will live in infamy in the memory of every soul present that unforgettable day in the city of Bari. British and the American troops had entered Bari in September and taken possession of many government and city buildings, hotels, private homes, and the port complex. Military personnel, army jeeps, and army trucks were scattered all over the city. The port of Bari became the main supply base for the American and British armies, and on that memorable day, the port was bustling with so many British and American ships, called "Liberty Ships," that they almost touched each other. They carried in their holds cargos of ammunitions, medical supplies, cigarettes, food, replacement parts, and aviation fuel, and were in various stages of unloading. There were also Norwegian, Polish, Dutch, and Italian ships moored along the east and west jetties of the harbor and along the pier of the old port.

The city was going through its normal activities of the day, and on that Thursday afternoon, I was home doing my homework and making sure that my brothers were doing the same. The day was turning into a cold, but very clear winter night. Around 7:30 P.M., Mamma was fixing our *cena*, a simple assortment of cold cuts, cheeses, bread, and fruit. My aunts, uncles, and cousins were probably engaged in the same activities in their own homes, except Zio Nino and Zia Rosaria, who were in their shop, as busy as ever, working on their special crafts. Every store closed daily at 8:00 P.M. all over Italy. I was absorbed in a difficult Latin assignment, when a faint, ominous sound made me stop and listen intently.

"Oh, no! Oh, no!"

My heart jumped in my chest like a ping-pong ball tossed hard on the table. The ever-increasing sound resembled the aircraft hum we knew so well. I rushed to the balcony as Mamma scanned the evening sky. The boys and Antonietta followed us onto the balcony just as dozens of planes appeared in the distance, flying toward the port.

In a moment, the dark sky became as bright as daytime as flares parachuted downward, mingling with a shower of shiny tinfoil that landed like confetti on the harbor first and then on the city as dozens and dozens of planes passed over our heads. We closed the glass doors and wooden shutters of the balcony and huddled together in a corner of the hall, the safest place in the apartment and the closest to the stairway in case we had to make a run for it. At the same moment the sirens sounded the alarms and the antiaircraft guns on top of the Margherita Theater by the waterfront began firing their deadly shells, but they were no match for the multitude of planes the Germans had unleashed. They dived on the city like famished vultures.

The carnage lasted twenty minutes, as newspapers later that day would report. To us, it seemed an eternity. In those twenty minutes, explosions followed explosions and each seemed to last longer than the previous one. It became obvious that all that chaos came from the port area, where many ships were anchored in the wharves. Explosions continued long after the German planes left and long through the night into the next day. The port had received a direct hit, and just next to it, the part of Bari Vecchia closest to the port. There, homes crumbled like houses of cards, and bricks, shattered glass, and twisted steel piled in huge heaps obstructed the entrance to the main streets for days. The explosions on the ships shattered building windows deep into the new part of the city, and because we lived a short distance from the port, most of ours exploded into a million pieces.

One explosion seemed louder than all the rest. Years later, it became known that among the American Liberty ships anchored at the port that night was the ship *John Harvey*. This ship had a deadly cargo of mustard gas on board, and its presence was shrouded in top secrecy until the war ended. The gas was to be used only in retaliation, in case the Germans carried out their threats of turning to chemical warfare.

What I remember vividly is the horror we faced the next day. All work came to a standstill; the city was paralyzed by terror. Pandemonium burst out as many prepared to leave the city *en masse*. In the streets, throngs of people, some holding suitcases, some with heavy bundles on their heads, crunched over broken glass and scattered debris, and headed out of the city in a collective exodus. Men congregated on city streets in groups, confused, petrified, and struggling to think of what to do next

Scores came from the waterfront and stopped long enough to say:

"Che grande inferno! Che grande inferno! Ci sono centinaia di morti e centinaia di feriti tutti intorno! Che disastro!" (What a hell! What a hell! There are hundreds of dead and wounded bodies scattered all over! What a disaster!)

Shaking their heads, tears in their eyes, their faces white as ghosts, they described the horrible images of hundreds of burned and dismembered bodies and the heartrending cries of the wounded waiting on the piers to be picked up and taken to the hospital. They described the harbor as a hellish sight: twisted orange flames leaping on the foul scum of oil, fuel, and debris covering the water, pier, and seashore, thick smoke billowing from it, and the ships burned like cinders, many half afloat, others completely under water, silent witnesses to the magnitude of the onslaught.

Days later, news reports stated that the crews of those ships and civilians working to unload the cargo that night had suffered hundreds of casualties. All personnel who could not be accounted for were assumed to have disintegrated in the violent explosions. From our balcony, all during that day, we saw a thick pall of smoke hanging over the port, and at intervals, we saw flames shoot high into the sky as explosions continued throughout the day. The ambulances kept racing and screeching continually as they scrambled to bring the wounded to hospitals in the city and nearby towns. Casualties were so heavy that every hospital was soon overcrowded and had to use all possible spaces, even the corridors and hallways to treat the wounded. Even the Policlinic, which was under

Allied jurisdiction, our newest and largest hospital at the time, received so many casualties that it was forced to admit only American and British soldiers, turning away all Italian civilians seeking help.

The medical staff was baffled! Why were all these men brought in coughing, eyes burning, and bearing repulsive burns and toxic-looking blisters that gave out an awful smell resembling the smell of garlic? They were stunned. Moreover, they did not know how to treat the wounds, and many died that could have been saved. Years later, to their surprise, they discovered they had been dealing with the effects of mustard gas, which produces burns and raw blisters on the skin, irritates the vision and the respiratory system, and often brings agonizing death to its victims.

Later that day, we connected with all our relatives at Zio Nino's house. We were in a state of shock and wondered about our next move. Were we going to stay in Bari? If not, where could we go? We had relatives on Zia Rosaria's side of the family that lived in a town called Noci, some twenty miles from Bari. Could we all go there? Yes, we could. They owned a large plantation and hired many *contadini* (farmers) to tend their property. Surely, they would have space for us.

We soon decided to lock our homes, take a few belongings, and just go. The next day, in the early morning hours, we were on the train to Noci and twenty-five of us descended unannounced on Zia Rosaria's relatives like a human avalanche. The strain was hard for both them and us, so after two days, it was back to Bari again. After the bombardment, the port remained closed for almost a month, but eventually, the streets were cleaned and our windows repaired. The offices, schools, and shops slowly reopened, and life returned to its own peculiar rhythm, with one exception: the cost of living increased rapidly, and merchandise became very scarce in the shops.

Food, the most essential of all commodities, became so expensive that Mamma's stipend was not enough to last till the end of the month and we had no other means of support. Our meals took a complete dive: *pane, olio e sale* for breakfast (bread slightly moistened with water, covered with a slice of tomato, salt and a drop of olive oil) and for *pranzo* every day, pasta with something: pasta with lentils, pasta with chick peas, pasta *e fagioli* (beans), pasta with *cime di rape* (rapini), pasta with cauliflower, and even pasta with potatoes. For *cena* at night, we had to share the leftovers, if there were any. Many nights, we went to sleep hungry. Gone for months was meat, fresh fish, or the delicious cheeses produced in our region, all too expensive for our meager budget.

There had to be a solution somewhere! As there were no financial resources, an idea popped into my head. Why not quit school and get a job? It was painful to see the anguish on Mamma's face as she struggled to make ends meet and to see my brothers and sister grow out of the few clothes they had to wear, but where could I ever find a job?

The answer took shape one afternoon when I went to visit Zio Nino at his shop. Did you ever wonder about coincidences? Well, I used to wonder, too, until I came to see them as a work in progress. God has all under his control; He is the master arranger of all coincidences. I soon discovered how well he arranged mine!

CHAPTER 18

HAPPY DAYS ARE HERE AGAIN AND MY FIRST LOVE

As far back as I can remember, I always hoped for things to get better and tried to see that proverbial silver lining behind every cloud. I realized even at a young age that the God who is in complete control and loves me, was never going to let me down. I turned to him in prayer time and time again, and looking back, I see how every trial I endured shaped my character and changed the direction of my life. I also began to perceive how every coincidence was so well orchestrated that I renamed them "God incidences." One afternoon, deciding to visit Zio Nino and Zia Rosaria at their store before going home from school, I encountered a "God incidence."

Zia Rosaria was glad to see me and wasted no time introducing me to the gentleman waiting for his dad to be fitted for a special belt by Zio Nino in the back room. His name was Franco, and he was working in an American office as an interpreter. He went on to tell us some of his background. He had been born in New York City and went to school there, and had returned to Italy with his parents when he was fifteen years old. They moved to Alberobello, a suburb of Bari, where his parents had bought farmland. Franco had finished school in Bari and found an excellent job, but when the Americans occupied Bari, his job was eliminated. Because of his knowledge of the English language, he had secured a job as interpreter at the American U.S.O. office in one of the city's office buildings. I listened enviously, wishing I had learned English in school, instead of French.

Suddenly Franco turned towards me inquisitively. "*A proposito, signorina.* (By the way, signorina.) *Lei sa scrivere a macchina?* (Do you know how to type?)"

I felt the urgency in his voice and looking straight in his eyes I asked why he wanted to know.

"Perche` abbiamo bisogno di impiegare due dattilografe nel mio uf-ficio al piu` presto possible. Non c'e bisogno di parlare l'inglese, solo copiare in inglese e la paga e' buonissima! (We need to hire two typists in my office as soon as possible. It's not required to speak English. You just have to type in English, and the pay is very good!)"

I heard his voice trail and for a while, I was speechless, trying to fig-ure out how I could get that job. Of course, I had never pressed a finger on a typewriter, but why not? I could learn and learn fast. Zio Nino had one, a vintage Olivetti in his house. Why not ask if I could borrow it for a while? My heart raced in my chest. Then I asked Franco, *"Posso avere due settimane di tempo?* (May I have two weeks time?)"

"Yes," he replied with a smile. "And if you are eighteen years old, the job is yours. I will put in a good word for you."

On a piece of paper he scribbled the address of the office, the time to appear for the interview, and the name of the person to see—Captain Charles Stubbs—a name that has remained embedded in my memory. Zio Nino was kind enough to bring the heavy, bulky typewriter to my house. He did not approve of my decision to leave school, but he under-stood how strapped for money we were.

Mamma was also apprehensive about my decision, but I had to have my way. I convinced her that with my stipend, if I was lucky enough to get the job, we could buy more food and much-needed clothes for every-one, and I could always return to school when things got better. The next morning at school, I walked into the principal's office and informed him of my decision. He was a kind man, very approachable, displayed great sympathy for my plight, and sent me away with a blessing.

Saying good-bye to my teachers was more painful that I had thought. I heard their sincere sorrow at my leaving and their empathy for the cir-cumstances that made a brilliant student like me choose to quit. They all wished me well, and I skipped down the stairway and out into the street with tears in my eyes, clutching the books I loved so much but now had no use for. I was turning another page in my life, and the future I had envisioned only a few months before was gone. I was heading towards an unknown path, but in my heart, I felt I was making the right choice.

On my way home I stopped to pick up some English magazines and books from a friend who was studying English and rushed home to em-bark on my typing career. I converted a nightstand in my bedroom to a small desk, placed the typewriter on top and pulled a chair close to it, and then stripped a blank page from one of my notebooks. I rolled it in the machine, and I was ready to go. The going was very slow at first as my two index fingers tapped on the keys and my eyes followed the foreign words being transferred to the page. I was determined to get that job at any cost. I persisted in learning to type for as many hours as my body and eyes could tolerate. I did not understand any of the words I was typing, and I didn't care what they meant. I just wanted to put them on paper without errors and with as much speed as possible.

My two weeks were up, and I had learned enough to try my luck. It was time to apply for the job, and Mamma had to accompany me, as that was the norm at the time. It was a splendid March morning; I had just turned sixteen. The air was still cool, but I had borrowed from Zia Rosaria a dark blue coat with a small fur collar and pearl buttons down the front that kept me warm and fitted me perfectly. I was sixteen years old, but could pass for twenty-five—the poverty and hardships of the past few years had left me with a maturity beyond my age.

Mamma and I approached the office and Franco came to greet us at the door. From behind a large desk, Captain Stubbs mulled over a stack of papers. When he saw us enter the room he quickly got up from his chair and walked around the desk, extending a friendly welcome as he shook hands first with Mamma and then with me. I made every effort to look calm and poised as he held my hand in his, but on the inside, I was trembling with fear. Captain Stubbs gave me a big smile and said something in English to put me at ease, but I had no clue what he was saying. He was of medium stature, in his middle forties, and had the bluest blue eyes I had ever seen on a man. His wavy blond hair was sprinkled with gray, and it encircled a kind face. I immediately took a liking to him.

A beautiful typewriter sat idle, just waiting to be put to use. My hands trembled and my heart pounded so hard I expected it to jump out of my throat at any moment. He handed me a few sheets of paper written in English and asked me to go ahead and type.

Captain Stubbs returned to his desk and the papers piled in front of him. After a few minutes of panic, in which I wished I could run and disappear, I mustered all the courage I could find. I sat down, thinking, well, here it is. The big moment! Do you remember why you are here? Yes! I replied silently, and from deep inside, my focus shifted from the grip of fear to the firm determination to make this challenge work at any cost.

I took a deep breath and started to pound on the typewriter's keys, slowly at first, but gradually picking up speed as my confidence increased. I concentrated solely on avoiding mistakes. Mamma sat in one corner of the room, and I was sure she was praying up a storm! My concentration was so deep that I obliterated everything from my mind, concentrating only on the papers in front of me.

When I finished, Captain Stubbs looked at my papers, nodded, raised his eyes to mine, and said softly:

"Okay, Emilia, I am giving you the job, but you have to promise to work a little harder on your speed!" Franco, of course, translated this to me, and I almost jumped out of my skin. I had the job! Imagine what that meant? I was on top of the world again.

Almost in a dream, I heard Franco say:

"*Ci vediamo domani mattina alle otto! Va bene?* (I will see you tomorrow morning at eight! Okay?) *Congratulazione, signorina!* (Congratulations, young lady)," he added with a broad smile.

I was ecstatic to have such a chance. I was to begin work the next day, and a feeling of gratitude to the God who answers prayers overwhelmed me. As hard as I try, I don't remember how much my salary was, but I remember that, if spent in moderation, it was enough to make food and clothing available again to my family. When I received the first envelope with my pay in Italian currency (liras), I could not wait to go home and hand it proudly to Mamma. What a pleasure it was to see her smile, tears trickling down her face as she hugged me tight. Her thankful expression needed no words. From that first paycheck, I always turned all the money over to her. Mamma and I shared a special bond, and I wanted her to use that money any way she thought best. That bond ended only with her untimely death.

The next morning, I arrived at the office jubilant and eager to meet the other girl they had hired a couple of days before. We soon became good friends. Her name was Paola, and she was about five years older than I was. I had lied about my age, but I needed the job so bad I didn't care. I asked the good Lord for forgiveness. I justified it by convincing myself that He understood it was a matter of survival. Anyway, no one seemed surprised when I said I was eighteen years old.

The summer of 1944 finally unfolded without bombs or terror in our part of the world. The war was being fought in faraway places like Monte Cassino, France, Russia, and Japan, and life in Bari took a turn for the better as we returned slowly to a degree of normalcy. Captain Stubbs empathized greatly with our modest way of living and every week generously brought us gifts of canned foods, chocolates, coffee, cigarettes, and Coca Cola that he purchased at the P.X.

Yes, cigarettes! I am ashamed to admit it, but I acquired the horrible habit of smoking during my employment at the U.S.O. At that time, it was fashionable to smoke. All the girls wanted to emulate the glamorous movie stars of the silver screen. The U.S.O. (United Service Organization) provided entertainment to the armed forces and sponsored a variety of activities and recreation, including showing of the latest motion pictures from the United States. Captain Stubbs gave us free tickets to some of the latest movies played at the Petruzzelli Theater in Corso Cavour. Many show business personalities left the States to perform for the troops to boost their morale while far away from their homes during wartime. Working for the U.S.O., we were given the privilege of attending some of the performances featuring the biggest movie stars. Frank Sinatra, our *paesano*, was our favorite when he came to perform in Bari. We just fell in love with him! But then, didn't everyone in the world fall in love with those superstars?

I was fortunate to attend the movies at the Petruzzelli Theater and for a particular reason that theater became a special place for me, Paola, and a group of other girls employed in the American offices. The American Red Cross took over the ballroom on the second floor of the theater and opened the Enlisted Men's Club. The ballroom, once used for special functions by the aristocracy of the city, was large enough to accommodate as many as five hundred people, and the club began holding dances four times a week for the G.I.s. The schedule: Monday, Thursday, and Saturdays from 4:00 P.M. until 8:00 P.M. and on Sundays a double session: two to five in the afternoon and seven to eleven in the evening. Paola and I were part of a group of fifty girls chosen to entertain the troops at these dances. We had special passes to get in, but there was another requirement: we had to have chaperones, preferably a member of the family. You may think that absurd, but that was the way it was done in those days, and we were ecstatic to have the privilege to participate in those dances!

Usually, my chaperone was my brother Andy, who loved to mingle with the soldiers and dance the jitterbug with other female chaperones. They waited in an anteroom where tea sandwiches, warm Danish pastries, donuts, cream, coffee, and Coca Cola were set out on long buffet tables. The advantage to that arrangement was that once the dance was over, the chaperones and the girls could fill small bags of leftover sandwiches and pastry to take home. Andy always made sure he had enough for the family. While the chaperones feasted on food, the girls feasted on music. Military bands that sounded just as great as Jimmy Dorsey or Glenn Miller's bands played the sentimental songs of that era. Hundreds of G.I.s and us girls flocked to the club like moths drawn to the light.

Paola and I never missed a Saturday night or both sessions on Sundays, and sometimes we managed to sneak in an occasional weekday. We danced with the G.I.s for hours, cheek to cheek to romantic melodies like "Sentimental Journey," and we bounced, skipped, and twirled with lively steps to the upbeat rhythm of the jitterbug. How could I ever forget those handsome guys, mostly in their twenties and thirties, in their sharp uniforms? They treated us like queens and courted us as if we were the most beautiful girls in the world. They treated us with respect, as was the norm in those days. They were lonely, longing for a breath of their homeland in the whirlwind of a cruel war. How sad that many of them never made it back home.

Sometimes the club held dance contests, and one Sunday afternoon, there was to be one for the best couple dancing the jitterbug. A few weeks earlier, I had met a very handsome army corporal whom I thought to be the best dancer of them all, and I was so happy when he chose me to be his partner for that contest. His name was Joe, and he lived in Falls River, Massachusetts. He was in Bari on leave before joining the rest of his company, which was fighting in France. We danced the boogie-woogie so well together that one by one, all the other couples dropped out of the competition and we were left alone on the floor with everyone clapping and cheering at our pirouettes. What a time we had! We won the contest and the prize of two cartons of cigarettes.

After that day, I became quite popular at the club, and it seemed every G.I. wanted to dance with me. As it was the custom then to tag the couple dancing, I was constantly changing partners during a number. This procedure lasted as long as the song was played and for several weeks, I could never finish a dance with the same man I started. After all the years of fear and deprivation, finally, I was enjoying myself! A glimpse of happiness rose from the embers of despair. I was having clean fun and the time of my life! Even today, I lasso the memory of those carefree days.

As invariably happens when you are young, I fell in love with one of those boys. He was a sergeant with the Fifth Air Force, his name was Edward (Eddy), and he lived in Philadelphia. He was twenty-two years old, not much taller than me when I wore high heels, and he was very, very handsome, with straight black hair, black eyes, and a cute mustache. Somehow, he made me understand he was in love with me, too, and he began to pick me up with his Jeep when I got out of work. He was warm and charming, and one day he asked me to introduce him to Mamma and the rest of the family. When I told Mamma, she was very understanding and willing to meet him. One night when he brought me home, I made him come upstairs, and of course, every one of my family fell in love with him.

He brought chocolates for Mamma, Antonietta, and me, and for the boys he had chewing gums, candies, and a set of pens and pencils for school. Eddy stayed in Bari for a few months and visited us a couple of days a week. Occasionally, he brought a friend or two to enjoy a family atmosphere like the one they had left in the States and a delicious dish of spaghetti and meatballs.

There was something unique about Eddy: he spoke often about his widowed mother with great tenderness and respect and carried with him a carved wooden statuette of her, a thin and very light silhouette that he had always with him in one of his pockets. When he came over to my house, he would set it in front of him on the table and kid around about sending her messages through Qui—Radio Bari. He was very funny, and my brothers and sister chuckled and made fun of his attempts to speak Italian.

I was learning to speak a few words of English, like "I love you" and "think of me," or "don't go away; I will miss you." I melted in his arms when we kissed as we walked down the stairway on his way back to his post. He was the perfect lover I had envisioned in my dreams who had suddenly appeared in human form. We both felt we were living in a bubble where love was the only emotion we felt!

Then the bubble popped. He was reassigned to another post, and in less than a week, he left for France. He promised to write and that he did. For about two months, I received passionate letters that Franco translated for me.

Then silence. Heart-breaking, tear-filled silence.

I never heard from him again, nor did I ever find out if he was dead or alive, but time has a way of quenching the pains of the heart, and mine slowly began to feel new life. Like sunshine that follows the rain, I returned to reality, never regretting that experience. It is true that we never forget our first love.

Months passed, and the U.S.O. office moved to a location very near the port. Captain Stubbs was promoted to major, and occasionally, he invited Paola and me to the American Red Cross Officers' Club, headquartered in a sequestered modern villa on the outskirts of the city. The Officers' Club emanated a more sophisticated atmosphere, and I felt I could not afford the proper attire for their functions, but that was okay; it was more important to buy food for the family than to worry about clothing and dancing.

As the winter of 1944 approached, the cost of living kept increasing, and my pay and ' Mamma's stipend were barely enough to buy food. I had only one winter coat and a couple of sweaters to keep me warm. I had a long walk to reach the office every morning. That winter, my hands blistered from the cold so badly (the blisters are called *geloni* in Italian) that they bled while typing, forcing me to keep them covered with bandages.

By the beginning of 1945, the war in Europe was winding up at last, and in May, we celebrated the surrender of Germany. V.E. Day had arrived and what a celebration that was! British and American soldiers were going out in the streets, kissing and embracing everyone and each other! By September, even Japan surrendered, capitulating under the enormous destruction atomic bombs inflicted on their land.

The horrific war was over, but oh! How it had changed the whole world! We will never know why it had to begin at all, and it seemed like no one was really a winner. By the beginning of 1946, most of the troops had been shipped back to the States and the U.S.O. office again moved to another building in the city. Franco and I transferred with Major Stubbs, and Paola became engaged to an Italian fellow and left her position. She was married a few months later and moved to Milano, never to be heard from again.

In my own life, the proverbial wheel of fortune began turning again, and this time it took such a curve that in a year my whole existence went in a new, wonderful direction.

CHAPTER 19

MY ENCOUNTER WITH DESTINY

March 1946 made its entrance with one of the most wonderful surprises in its wings! One bright morning, an unexpected knock at the door brought Pierino, Andrea, Antonietta, and me scurrying for cover. Mamma cautiously approached the door, demanding loudly, *"Chi e` li`? (Who is there?)"*

There was a brief pause, and then a tearful, familiar voice replied, *"Sono io, puoi aprire la porta! (It's me, you can open the door!)"*

"Vittorio! Vittorio!" Mamma threw the door open with a joyful scream. She hugged and kissed him, not quite believing her eyes. As soon as we heard "Vittorio!" we, too, raced to the door.

"Babbo! Babbo!" we shouted, pulling him indoors, pushing and racing each other to embrace him first. Almost five years had passed since we had seen him, and he looked stunned to see how much we had all changed. Babbo kept shaking his head in disbelief at how much his children had grown while he was away. The boys and Antonietta had changed the most, and I believe Babbo was considering how much he had missed during the precious years while a senseless war kept us apart.

Gradually, even for Babbo, life returned to normal. He was discharged from the army and given a job at the *Corpo di Armata* similar to the one he had before he left. His pay scarcely covered the bare necessities, and some weeks, even less. We still had to ration the food, and I was lucky to still hold a job, but how long would that job last? Soon, the few Americans left in Bari had to "pick up their tents" and move away. What then?

God will provide! Somehow, in some mysterious way, when you least expect it, he throws a rope at you and pulls you out of the ditch. I did not suspect that on a day in early May 1946, I would grab one of those ropes and let one of those God incidences reshape the course of my future.

173

That morning, I went to work as usual at the U.S.O. and almost had to elbow my way through, dodging the crowd of service men jammed in front of my office. A few days before, the P.X. had moved in next door to us with all the supplies it carried for the military, and dozens and dozens of soldiers and officers from all the branches of service were flocking there all day long to purchase items they could find only at the P.X.

To enter into that room, they had to pass in front of my office. I could see part of the traffic going by from my desk. The offices always closed at 5:00 P.M., and around that time, I was ready to head home alone. It was a long walk home, but I enjoyed the exercise. That day in May, when I got out of work, the air had warmed considerably and the sun's rays still gleamed between the new upper leaves of the trees that lined the street. I was stepping down the wide staircase in front of the building, happy to be heading home when I heard a voice call me.

"Miss! Miss! (*Signorina, Signorina*!)" I turned, startled.

It was a man in civilian clothes telling me in English to wait, for he had a question to ask me.

"I don't speak English," I replied.

"*Va bene, allora parliamo in Italiano!* (Okay, then we will speak in Italian!)" He came closer, took me by the arm, and gallantly helped me down the stairs. He had a pleasant smile, and I was curious to know what he really wanted.

"I am confused and have lost my way," he said, searching both sides of the street. "Do you know how to get to the station where I can board the train for Conversano? I believe it is somewhere near here. Can you direct me, please?" Our conversation was in Italian, of course. I wondered why this man, who could speak Italian so well, but looked more like a foreigner, was asking me for directions.

I hesitated a few moments, searching my memory. Yes, I did remember. There was a nearby station that a friend of mine used to commute from every day. It could have been that one, I thought, and so I proceeded to give him directions.

"Yes, I believe the station is a few blocks away and a few streets behind this one. However, I am not so sure. Try going two blocks down this way, turn left, walk a couple of blocks, then turn right, and the station should be there. If you don't see it, ask someone there."

I had begun walking when he asked me again, "Thank you so much, but could we walk together? You can show me where to turn!"

He put me on the spot. I couldn't say no without being rude. Should I? I felt I had to say yes, and we started to walk together. The first thing he did was walk around me to take his place on the side of the street. I didn't think anything about it at the time, but when he did that a couple more times, as we crossed the street and turned corners, I had to ask him why he would make such a move.

"Well," he answered, "in America, a man never lets a lady walk by the side of the street. It's a kind of protection and respect."

I was impressed and amused at such a show of chivalry and jokingly said, "I wish someday I could see this wonderful America!"

This little exchange served to break the ice. To put me more at ease, he began expanding on his background. He was born in Conversano, and he had emigrated to the States years before with two of his brothers. He lived in Flushing, a suburb of New York City, and had served two years in the American army and been discharged. He came to Italy on the request of his elderly mother. She was gravely ill and wanted to see him. Unfortunately, that was never to be; she passed away a few days before his arrival.

"I have many relatives in Conversano," he continued. "I have a brother and a brother-in-law, and several nephews and nieces. My mother wanted to see me settled down, and in her letter, she had mentioned she might have a nice young lady that could make a great wife for me. You see, I am still single. She always had some young lady waiting for me whenever I visited before the war, but I never liked any of them!" He lowered his voice and turned to search my face for a reaction.

That sounded so typically Italian! Lightly, I said, "I don't think you need help in that.! You can easily find a wife on your own!" Surprising myself at my own boldness, I added, "I have relatives in Conversano, too! The Vavalle family. They are my paternal grandparents. Perhaps you have heard of them."

"Well, isn't this a coincidence?" he exclaimed, astonished. (This, as you see, was becoming another of my " God incident.")

"I know that name well! I have an appointment to see Dr. Achille Vavalle next week here in Bari. Is he a relative of yours?" he asked, incredulous that though we were complete strangers, we had something in common. I was flabbergasted, too, at the path my encounter with this man was taking.

"He is my father's cousin!" I replied, wondering what to expect next. By then, we had turned the corner and the station came into full view. I asked if he was in time to catch the train, and looking at his watch he nodded, saying he had ten minutes left. With a sigh of relief, he took the bundle from under his arm, and opening the top, showed me the six cartons of cigarettes he had bought at the P.X. for himself and his brother.

"I will be back in two days," he added, "to shop for other items at the P.X. Can I see you again? I don't know anybody in Bari, and I sure would like to spend some time with you!"

He was handsome, with a special charm. He had large, languid eyes and looked remarkably like Humphrey Bogart. Thinking about how lonely he must be in a city he hardly knew, I was touched by the tone of sadness in his voice and I heard myself say, "Okay. Where do we meet? By the way, what is your name?" I suddenly realized I was making a date with someone and I didn't even know his name. Was I out of my mind?

"My name is Domenick Richard, but they call me Richie, and my last name is Zecchino." He laughed and continued, "You know that means gold, pure gold! My name has it—the gold, I mean—but not me!" He was right. In Italian, when we want to refer to pure gold, we call it "*oro zecchino.*"

"What is your name?" he asked, looking intently into my eyes.

Trying to evade his gaze, I barely answered, "Emilia Lorusso."

Well, there it was! I had given my name to a stranger crossing my path out of the blue. And I had even made a date! Was I out of my mind? We said good-bye and promised to see each other that Saturday afternoon at 3:00 P.M. in front of the Petruzzelli Theater. I turned fast on my heels, trying to look as normal as possible, but on the inside, I felt far from normal. I searched for the reason I had agreed so quickly to see him again and tried to make sense of my stupidity. Could I ever tell my parents? They would never accept the fact that I was going to see a complete stranger.

Oh well, something will come up to stop me, I told myself. Besides, I am sure he has already forgotten our rendezvous. For two days, I kept debating whether I should drop the whole idea, but hard as I tried, a certain feeling kept creeping in and my heart beat faster.

I kept watching the clock on the mantel that Saturday afternoon, and by two, I had to decide. Something pulled at me and an urge to keep my commitment made me spring into action. I looked for my brother Andrea and bribed him into going with me on an errand and keeping it a secret. I explained our "errand" to my parents as a visit I had promised a friend who was ill. I needed Andrea's help in moving some items around her house. They had no reason to doubt my story and let me go without mistrust. I felt guilty, but I was fast to swallow it. This man just kept popping in my thoughts, and I could not escape the magnetism!

I turned the corner on Corso Cavour with my brother at my side. Although embarrassed, I was secretly hoping to see Richie waiting for me, and to my delight, he was there. I told Andrea I was meeting a good friend and not to worry. "Please don't mention this to Mamma and Babbo!"

Andrea nodded with a grin and walked with me to meet Richie. We all felt awkward at first, then Richie took Andrea to the side, slipped a dollar bill in his hand, and politely, I think, told him to get lost. Andrea, giving me a victorious smile, did just that.

We walked that afternoon, Richie and I, along the *lungomare*, Bari's beautiful waterfront boulevard. At first, we both were embarrassed and grabbed for banalities to start a conversation. We sat on a bench facing the blue waters of the Adriatic Sea and watched the fishermen's boats unload their catch at the pier and the sailboats' white sails bobbing on the light waves of the shimmering expanse of water in front of us. I felt tranquil and very comfortable next to Richie and made no resistance when he took my hand and held it tight in his. I had just met this man, and yet I felt I had known him forever. This feeling was strange—both pleasant and mysterious. Was I going out of my mind?

The surprise we had at the beginning soon changed into a desire to know more about each other and so we talked and talked about many subjects for a few hours. We were enjoying each other's company when he decided to take something off his chest.

"I have a confession to make," he said, hardly suppressing a smile. "Remember when I told you I had lost my way and asked for directions to the station? Well, that was an excuse to get to know you. I knew where the station was better than you did. I lied. Do you forgive me?"

I laughed at his candor and thought his scam was very amusing. After another hour at a café on the *lungomare*, savoring hot chocolate and biscotti, we walked towards my home and said good night just around the block, with the promise to see each other again at the same place and time three days later.

We met again, and this time, instead of watching the boats, we sailed on the sightseeing one that toured for two hours around the bay. There were no clouds in the sky and a soft breeze kept playing in my long hair. The sun's radiance sparkled on the water like thousands of shimmering diamonds, and the sound of soft music playing in the distance from an outdoor café along the lungomare gently caressed our ears.

Everything converged into such a romantic setting that the inevitable happened. While the boatman had his back toward us, Richie gently held me close, then kissed me with a mix of tenderness and passion that made me feel as if I was on the edge of the universe. Was this love again, or were my senses playing tricks? I enjoyed being in his arms, and I was glad I was capable of feeling and giving love again.

We saw each other for about a month twice a week, and he confessed one day that he had fallen in love with me the first time he saw me at my desk the day he came to the P.X.

"I cannot explain it, but I believe in love at first sight!" he said as he looked at me intently. "Of all the women I have met, I had to fall in love with you! Why? I ask this question every morning, and I keep saying to myself: let her go, you have nothing to—"

He stopped abruptly. It was evident he was struggling to cover up the perturbed tone in his voice. I had a feeling he wanted to tell me something very important, but could not find the proper words, so just as abruptly, he took my hand and wove my fingers around his, drawing me into his arms.

We had known each other not more than two months. As we sat on the bench along the lungomare that day, he asked a question that stunned me: "Will you marry me?"

Yes! I was stunned, and yet I was not surprised. The question appeared to be the only conclusion to the way we felt for each other; however, he seemed unusually serious and pensive. Before I could answer, he held his hand on my lips.

"Wait before you answer," he said. He sounded restless. I sensed he was going to tell me something grave and very important. "There are some things about me that I haven't told you yet. Before you give me an answer, you have to know first the truth about my age."

He had told me he was thirty-five years old, and I had believed him. Never had I expected him to tell me he was a "solid" forty-three. I was in shock. Wow! He was an old man! However, his shock was even greater when I told him that I had lied to him, too. I was only eighteen years old, not twenty-five, as I had told him.

What a huge surprise for both of us. We were almost twenty-five years apart in age and nobody, absolutely nobody, would approve of our marriage. What should we do?

For a long time, we had nothing to say. We just stared into the void and waited for one of us to speak. Then he dropped another bombshell in my lap.

He pulled up his sleeves and showed me patches of scaly red skin on his arms. He did not know why, but soon after he was discharged from

178

the army with chronic bronchitis, red patches began appearing on his body. He had been diagnosed with psoriasis, an unsightly skin disease for which there was no cure.

He had been to see Dr. Vavalle, he said, in hopes that as a skin specialist he would have had some remedy, but no medicine on the market could cure that condition anywhere in the world. He had been to the Veterans Hospital in the Bronx for a few months of treatment for both bronchitis and psoriasis, and had gotten so much better that he had decided to travel to Italy to see his mother. Now the psoriasis was coming back. He planned to go back to the Veterans Hospital once he was back in the States.

He was not offering me a bright future, he said, and he would understand if I chose to end the relationship. There were too many obstacles on our path; perhaps it was much better to end it then. He apologized for putting me through such pain. Surely, my parents would object, and so would his relatives.

We both wept, and wept. We parted with a sad good-bye, as if that would be the last time we saw each other. I was in pain and my mind rejected the thought of not seeing him again.

On the day we usually met, I went to the *lungomare* and walked to the bench we had sat on for hours holding hands and sometimes each other. That stretch of the *lungomare* was usually deserted when we met, and that day was no exception.

I was there only five minutes when I felt a familiar touch on my shoulder. It was Richie. He had come to the *lungomare* for the same reasons I did. From that moment on, we saw our futures converging into one single, long highway. Come what may, our hearts played one tune. I told him I would marry him.

When I got home, I told my parents all about Richie and my two months of rendezvous behind their backs. I could not explain how the circumstances taking hold of my life had set me marching to the beat of a different drum.

Babbo and Mamma were concerned, to put it mildly, about our ages, his sickness, and about me going so far away from them to America, but they consented to see him when I made it plain I was not going to budge. He was the man I was going to marry.

Richie met my parents and asked for my hand. He used all the proper words and stated all the facts, the good, the bad and the ugly, and he kept nothing from them. Richie ended the meeting cordially, intending to bring his family to meet my parents, as a gesture of acceptance and trust.

Two days later, Richie appeared at the door with his brother Antonio, his brother-in-law Mimi, and Mimi's wife Graziella. We spent a few hours in friendly conversation, at the end of which we felt very comfortable with each other. It was apparent that, as odd as it seemed at first, Richie and I were meant for each other. By August 1946, my job ended, and Richie left for the States with the promise to come back and marry me.

Mamma and I accompanied him to Naples, where we spent two days sightseeing the ruins of the nearby town of Pompei and one night at the trendy Giardino degli Aranci, a beautiful nightclub on the slopes of the Vomero. Richie stayed at a hotel, and Mamma and I were guests of my aunt Anna, Babbo's sister.

At the club, we were dancing to the melodious music of a tango Argentino when I commented on the perfection of his steps, and he confessed that dancing was his passion. While in the army, stationed at Fort Carson, Colorado, he had performed in exhibition dances with the most glamorous stars of that era. He showed me pictures and news articles of him dancing with pinup girls Rita Hayworth, Betty Grable, Jinx Falkenburg, Lana Turner, and Cyd Charisse. The articles were very impressive I had to admit, but they did nothing to alleviate the loneliness I felt when the boat that was taking him away picked up anchor and disappeared behind the horizon.

The months rolled by and we ushered in 1947 with no sign of Richie. He wrote to me every day, sometimes twice a day, from the Veterans Hospital in the Bronx. He sent me tons of pictures depicting the daily routine and life he shared with hundreds of wounded G.I.s, but there was no sign of a discharge from the hospital or a trip to Italy.

Then one day in June, a letter arrived with a proposition written that put me right back in suspense. How was I going to explain this to my parents? They would never consent. I mulled over the contents of the letter and finally mustered enough courage to approach them with this new dilemma. I began reading the letter to them:

> DearestEmilia,
>
> I may have to be in the hospital for at least another month. I have been out of work for so long and coming back to Italy will absorb a big chunk of my savings. Once out of the hospital, I am planning to open a business in Flushing. I mean, I would like to open a grocery store similar to the one I owned with my brother Nino before I went into the army. My brother wants to run the

store with his wife, and he changed his mind on a partnership with me. That is okay because I will be able to operate another store with your help. I think you will enjoy the environment around the food, and I will even teach you how to cook. For this project, I will need as much capital as I can put together.

So far, everything sounded logical. My parents were amused until I read them the next page and confronted them with the bombshell:

There is a law in effect until the end of 1947 that allows G.I.s that served in wartime to call to the States their brides and fiancés. Fiancés will have all the privileges of war brides if they marry before December 31, 1947. As my fiancé, are you willing to come to America alone? We will get married here as soon as all the papers and licenses are assembled. Until then, I can arrange for you to stay with a very lovely Italian family, my friends of many years. Please ask your parents their permission. I think this solution will help to give us a solid start to our future. Etc. Etc.

Of course, they reacted with their worst fears. They gave me dozens of reasons why I should forget the whole idea and look for a husband in our city. How could I consider going so far away alone? "Suppose…" and "Suppose…" They went on and on, and I listened and cried, and sometimes I even agreed with them.

My whole world was crumbling around me again, and I prayed earnestly for an answer. A few days later, having received a letter from Richie, Mimi and Graziella came over the house for a conference with my parents. I never found out what was exchanged between them, but when it was over, I had permission to travel alone. I was jubilant and at the same time sad, thinking that my wedding day was not going to be shared with the ones I loved the most, but the war and its consequences had already taught me that life is like a garden full of flowers. The flowers bend and droop under the pelting of heavy rain, and then they straighten up in all their glory under the warm rays of the sun. I felt like one of those flowers, and I thanked God for both the rain and the sunshine.

The next few weeks I hopped from office to office. I was being inoculated and filling out all sorts of papers. Finally, the passport arrived in the mail. I booked passage on the *Saturnia* leaving from Naples and arriving in New York on September 6, 1947.

With Mamma's help, I put together a small trousseau to take with me. I meticulously packed the very popular cookbook by Ada Boni called *Il Talismano della Felicita`*, looking forward to learning to cook with Richie's help. I still have that book stored in a plastic Ziploc bag; it's yellow and brittle, and the pages are falling apart, and I still consult it when I want to cook something that is authentic Italian.

In late August, my relatives gave me a going-away party attended by most of Richie's family from Conversano. Early the next morning, I was standing again in Bari's station, saying good-bye to Pierino, Andrea, little Antonietta, and most of my relatives. Everyone was crying. Antonietta wept inconsolably as she hung to my skirt, not wanting to let go! She considered me a second mother, and I felt her sobs like sharp thorns tearing into my heart. No soothing words could ease the pain of her losing me.

I climbed aboard, followed by Mamma and Babbo, who were accompanying me to Naples. The conductor blew his whistle and loudly sounded the "all aboard." Hanging out of the window, I waved through my tears to my brothers and sister. They huddled together and watched the train pull out of the station, pick up speed, and slowly disappear from their sight.

(Left) Easter Sunday with two-year-old Linda in my arms, Ricky, Vinny and Richie, in front of our blooming forsythia bush, in the yard of our home on Smart St. in Flushing. (Right) Linda having fun at the Worlds' Fair.

(Left) With my son Ricky when he graduated from St. Mary's School in 1964.

(Right) Celebrating in our backyard. Vinny's Graduation from St. Mary's School in Flushing, N.Y. in 1965. He is surrounded by Ricky, Linda, Toni and Richie.

183

(Left) With Vinny on his graduation from St. Mary's School in 1965.

(Below) Linda with Vinny, the day he graduated from Bishop Reilly H.S. in 1969.

(Above) Linda with Vinny the day he graduated from St. Mary's School in Flushing in 1965.

(Right) Ricky's graduation from Bishop Reilly High School with Linda and Richie at his side. 1968.

(Left) Linda practicing for one of her solo twirling competitions.

(Right) Richie and his brother Nino in front of their store in the Murray Hill section of Flushing, New York.

(Left) Lina, Phyllis, Linda and best friend, Christine, celebrating Linda's birthday.

185

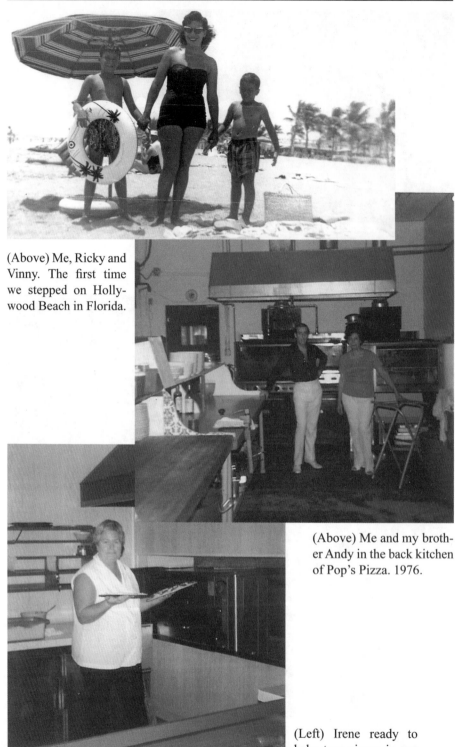

(Above) Me, Ricky and Vinny. The first time we stepped on Hollywood Beach in Florida.

(Above) Me and my brother Andy in the back kitchen of Pop's Pizza. 1976.

(Left) Irene ready to bake two pizzas in our Blodgett Ovens. 1976.

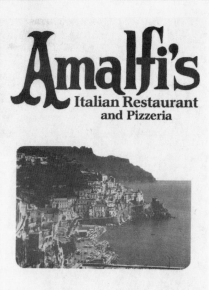

1299 E. Commercial Blvd. • Ft. Lauderdale, FL • 491-1550

(Left) Front of menu of Trevi's Italian Restaurant on Hollywood Blvd., in Hollywood. (Right) Front cover of menu of Amalfi's Italian Restuarant on Commerical Blvd. in Ft. Lauderdale.

The interior of Amalfi's Restuarant on Commercial Blvd. in Ft. Lauderdale, Florida.

(Above) Laura, me, Wilma, and my brother Andy. The girls came from Rome with their mother Edelweiss who needed a very rare eye operation.

(Above) Linda and me the day she graduated from Hollywood Hills High School.

(Above) Linda at a Food Show at the Javits Convention Center in New York City.

(Right) With Linda at the Orlando Food Show.

(Bottom) Linda and Steve at a Food Show in Boston, MA.

189

(Left) Linda, Alfred Schwan, and me on his first visit to Holiday Foods.

(Right) Alfred Schwan paying a visit to processing room #4 with chef, Lisa Ming on his left and Vahick, the quality control supervisor just behind him. In this open room the talented hands of these ladies bring to life the most elegant canapes and finger sandwiches served at some of the best hotels in the nation.

(Left) Alfred Schwan visiting processing room #2 - our meat production room.

(Below) Holiday Foods plant in Hollywood, Florida. Preparing products in processing room #1.

(Right) The ladies at the plant surprising me with flowers and praying over me, celebrating one of my birthdays.

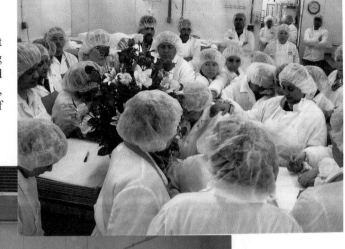

(Left) A brief pause before the beginning of production in processing room #3.

(Right) Fausto, me, and Ronny.

(Left) Holiday Foods Plant. Busy at work in processing room #2, where only raw meat products are processed.

(Left) Making the daily rounds of the plant and inspecting production at Thelma's table.

Our supervisor Fausto Melo with Linda and Jose, the receiving supervisor at the plant.

With Margaret and other employees celebrating Christmas at the plant.

(Left) A Christmas party for employees and families of Holiday Foods.

(Right) Me, Linda, Fausto and the employees of Holiday Foods celebrating the takeover by the Schwan food Company.

(Left) Dancing with Fausto at my retirement party.

(Right) Celebrating my retirement day, at the ripe old age of 78, with the music of a local Mariachi Band.

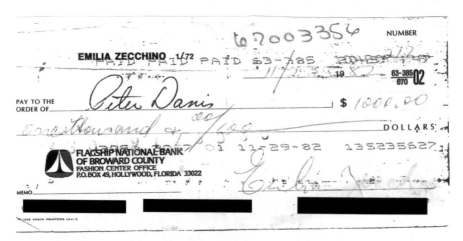

My one thousand dollar investment in the inception of Holiday Foods.

Outline of original warehouses that gave birth to Holiday Foods.

CHAPTER 20
LIFE IN AMERICA

We arrived at the Naples railroad station in the early morning hours with other trains making their entrance at the same time and couldn't escape the congestion of passengers on the platforms. Somehow, Babbo was able to find the exit, and we scrambled outside, searching for a taxi to take us to the port. It was a cloudy, gloomy morning with a fine mist settling on our clothes and wetting our faces. Babbo hailed a taxi and we headed for the port. I sat in the back seat between Babbo and Mamma as she tightly held my hand. The pain in our hearts and on our faces was evident. I struggled to find words to comfort them. I had hoped and prayed for this day to arrive and yet, now that it had, I really wished it didn't have to be this way.

"Mamma," I said softly, squeezing her hand in mine, "I promise I will be back to visit as soon as possible. I will never forget all of you, and I will write to you every day, if possible, but every week absolutely!"

"Of course." Mamma managed a smile. "Your happiness is all I want, and I will always keep you in my prayers. I will miss you terribly, Emilia, but you have my blessing, and remember, I will be always there if you need me." At that moment, I thought of her as the most precious person in my changing world.

We arrived at the port around noon and found a bigger crowd that we had anticipated. After several inquiries, we were able to locate the office I had to report to, near the berth where the *S.S. Saturnia* was anchored. I had all the documents required to enter the United States, thanks to the G.I. Fiancée's Act (Public Law 471) Congress had passed on June 29, 1946. This law allowed the alien fiancée of an American soldier who had served in World War II to enter the United States for three months. After getting married within that period, the wife could stay in the States as a war bride and a permanent resident alien.

With my papers and passport finally stamped and approved in one hand, my suitcase in the other, I stepped on the *S.S. Saturnia*'s gangplank after many hugs, kisses, and torrents of tears. The moment had arrived. The *Saturnia* was preparing to leave, and after taking my suitcase to the assigned cabin, I raced on deck and found a spot on the rail that gave me a clear view of Mamma and Babbo on the pier below. This scene still floods my mind as one of the most unforgettable and painful memories of my life.

The view of my father and mother on the pier waving white hand-kerchiefs and throwing me kisses grew smaller and smaller and then completely disappeared from my sight. The full impact of my decision hit me like a heavy brick. Alone and headed towards an unknown future in a faraway land, I couldn't help asking myself, did I do the right thing? I was only nineteen, and for the first time, I was completely alone.

I ran to the cabin I shared with three other ladies, fell heavily on my bed, and cried my heart out. As always, I found solace in prayer. Looking back now, I see how marvelously well God built in me the resilience I needed to face the bumpy road I had to travel in the years ahead.

The *Saturnia*, once transformed into one of the famous White Boats that carried refugees from Ethiopia, had been restored to its original use as a transport ship, making its rounds between Naples and New York. On board, the food was plentiful and delicious and the company quite friendly. The passengers were mostly Italians either returning to the States after a visit with relatives in Italy or were like me, making the trip for the first time. On board were several other war brides I became acquainted with, but unfortunately lost track of as the years pulled us in different directions.

The *S.S. Saturnia* had a smooth crossing and arrived in New York harbor on September 6, 1947, as scheduled. Like the departure from Naples, the arrival in New York is stored in my memory as an episode that changed my life. I closed a door on one continent and opened a new one on the continent called America. What wonder I felt when I saw the Statue of Liberty and the magic skyline of New York City for the first time! My heart jumped for joy when I saw Richie standing on the pier waving his arms. He had seen me first and was trying to catch my atten-tion as I leaned on the rail. He was engaged in a conversation with a man and a woman standing near him, and I was sure they were Rose and Tom, the couple I was going to stay with until we married.

With my suitcase in one hand and my purse bulging with the usual girl's accessories and fifty dollars in cash, my sole treasure on earth, on the other, I walked into the immigration office on board ship, had all the necessary documents stamped, and then raced down the gangplank and at last into Richie's arms. I thought I was dreaming! Rose and Tom hugged me and made me feel very much at home. I had a little problem understanding them, as they were attempting to speak in broken Italian sprinkled with Sicilian dialect. They were very funny, and we remained very good friends for many years.

Richie grabbed the suitcase, and holding me tight around my shoulders, guided me towards the exit and a parking lot, where his big army truck was parked. He said good-bye to Tom and Rose with the promise that he would take me home as soon as he gave me a tour of the city. Rose and Tom left in their car, and Richie helped me climb into the front of the truck.

I was amused and surprised at his mode of transportation. When he decided to drive into the middle of the city and show me the sights, I was filled with wonder and excitement. From the high seat of the truck, I had a wide view of the surroundings. Everything seemed so big! The sidewalks, the streets, the buildings, and the traffic around Broadway, Fifth Avenue, and Times Square just boggled my mind.

A couple of hours later, we arrived on Murray Street in Flushing, Long Island, where Tom and Rose lived, and where I was going to stay until new arrangements could be made. That first night, Rose prepared so much food for dinner I could hardly believe my eyes. Rose assured me that as long as I stayed there I was to share my meals with them, and to this day, I'm grateful that they accepted me as one of their family.

After dinner, Rose escorted me to my bedroom. By then I was really tired and it didn't bother me much when she took me up three flights of steps to the second-floor landing, where a door opened on another stairway that led to an unfinished attic. Well, that was not what I had envisioned for my temporary quarters. However, Richie had written how difficult it was at that time, just after the war, to find an apartment anywhere. I told myself that if I had survived the concentration camps, I would survive even this temporary inconvenience. We hoped that soon things would change and we could find a decent apartment nearby.

What amazed me the most waking up the day after I arrived was the lifestyle this family seemed to enjoy. Rose was a stay-at-home mom minding three-year-old Tommy Jr. and two older boys, ages twelve and fourteen. The whole family was already sitting at the table when I came downstairs to join them for breakfast. They all kissed me and welcomed me with profuse gestures of "Good morning" and "Welcome to America." I felt overwhelmed with thankfulness. God had provided me with a home away from home, and it just seemed too good to be true.

As I took my place at the table, an exquisite odor filled my nostrils, and for the first time I heard mentioned the word "bacon," with other novelties like French toast, pancakes with maple syrup, and Wheaties being served simultaneously. I marveled at the abundance. When I thought of my family back in Bari struggling to buy a small loaf of bread, a lump formed in my throat and I wanted to cry. I felt almost guilty that I had so much food in front of me. For the first time, the words "God bless America" I had heard so many American soldiers in Italy utter with nostalgia made sense to me, and I thanked God for bringing me to this land.

Moreover, I was flabbergasted when Tom opened the back door and brought inside two bottles of fresh milk and a loaf of fresh bread left on the steps behind their door by the milkman and the bread man. Could it be possible? Who ever heard of food being left outside the door? That could have never happened anywhere else, yet I learned that was the American way!

Astonished, I soon had a bigger surprise. Two days later, on a Saturday morning, Rose took me food shopping at Amoruso's Market, a grocery store on Parson's Boulevard a few blocks around the corner from their house. We walked there in mid-morning, Rose pushing little Tommy in the stroller. The stalls inside and outside the market overflowed with fresh fruits and vegetables. I was in awe at the cans and boxes of all sizes on the shelves of the market. Such abundance shocked me. When Rose filled her basket with enough merchandise to last a week (they had a large refrigerator, the likes of which I had never seen) she placed everything on the counter, paid for it, and then asked the clerk to have it delivered, as usual, to her house. I was in for a big surprise when I heard her say to have the delivery boy open the unlocked front door and put all the merchandise on the kitchen table.

"Did we leave the house without closing or bolting the front door?" I dared to ask if I had understood her directions to the clerk.

"Yes," Rose nodded nonchalantly. "We leave our front doors open all the time here. We have nothing to fear." It was hard to believe the reality of this blessed way of life! (What a pity that today in our homes we have to install alarm systems to keep us safe.)

At the market, Rose introduced me to many of her friends, who were also shopping at Amoruso's, and everyone welcomed me with open arms. My fears of not being accepted in this new country disappeared as all these wonderful people made me feel at home. Many were Italian immigrants of years gone by, eager to support and aid me in whatever I needed. What a wonderful feeling.

There was no sign of Richie's brother Nino or his wife Ann, not that day, and not for several weeks. That puzzled me for a while. I had to ask Richie why. He was hesitant at first, but then told me a story that I did not expect. Ann had known a girl for many years, and when she transferred to New York from Detroit, they had a very strong relationship. She decided, with Nino's approval, to introduce her to Richie, hoping they would fall in love and someday get married.

According to Richie, he had met this woman, gone on a date with her, and decided she was not his type. He had refused to see her again. They felt hurt by Richie's decision, and when they heard he was bringing back a bride from Italy, they thought it was a mistake and even a bigger mistake when they heard about the difference in our ages. They thought he had completely lost his mind. The attitude of my future in-laws did not sit well with me, especially his brother's lack of support after what Richie had gone through in the war and his struggle against the psoriasis that was flaring up again.

Richie stood his ground against his brother's objections and set the date of our wedding for December 1, 1947. Rose volunteered to take me to Macy's to buy my wedding dress. I was struck again with wonder when I traveled the subway for the first time on the way to New York City and when we entered Macy's in all its grandeur! There were floors and floors of splendid merchandise, from mink coats to pots and pans. I had never seen a store that big in my life.

I fell in love with a simple, off-white woolen dress that reached my knees and a beige winter coat with a fur collar. I also bought gloves, boots, scarves, and sweaters, as I had brought no winter clothes from Italy.

The temperature on our wedding day was below freezing. In St. Mary's Church, Tom and Rose served as best man and maid of honor and witnesses. Nino and Ann came and stayed until the vows were exchanged, then wished us a few brusque congratulations before returning to their daily routine.

Also absent from our wedding was Richie's older brother Mike and his family. Richie told me that they had not talked to each other for a couple of years, because of finances. Whatever the reason, I thought it would be best to reconcile. Eventually, they did. Ours was indeed a very small wedding, but for Richie and me, it was perfect. We felt the love of God blessing two lives that deeply needed each other.

After a few days spent in a hotel in New York City for our honeymoon, visiting the fabulous Radio City Music Hall, an experience that was like visiting Dreamland, we returned to Rose and Tom's attic in Flushing. Richie kept looking for an apartment and an empty store where he could open a food market, but to no avail.

Christmas arrived. We celebrated it with our adopted family, and for me it was a time of great wonder and nostalgia. The Christmas decorations on the homes and storefronts in the city and suburbs left me stupefied. At the same time, my heart yearned for the more intimate and pious celebrations in Italy. Christmas trees and the many gifts underneath were fascinating, and so was the fat Santa Claus dressed in red that supposedly brought the gifts for everybody, not only the kids. I thought of our Christmases in Italy, when La Befana brought gifts on January 6 for the children. Everything was so different here, and everything was beautiful and interesting.

The day after Christmas 1947, New York City and all of Long Island were hit by the biggest snowstorm ever recorded. The snow began falling around noon, softly at first. It gradually turned heavy, whipped by a strong wind that pushed it in drifts several feet high. It snowed for two days, and when it was over, even the majestic New York City was paralyzed. Nothing moved for a couple of days, and no one ventured outside their homes to break the ominous silence. It looked like heaven had dropped a gigantic white blanket over the landscape and just said, "Stop!" By the third day, we heard the welcome rumble of snowplows and the city and suburbs began digging out from under the snow, piling it up into icy mountains on driveways and sidewalks. The noisy rhythm of life returned to break the silence that Mother Nature had imposed in a few hours of fury.

For Richie, these days were a lot more worrisome than we had imagined. The psoriasis had appeared on his forehead, and he needed to go back in the hospital. Early in January 1948, he was admitted again to the Veteran's Hospital on Kingsbridge Road in the Bronx. I went along with him for support and also to learn how to get there. We had to change three buses to get to the Bronx, and I jotted the bus numbers on a piece of paper so I would remember when I had to make the trip alone.

We arrived at the hospital in mid-morning, sliding through snow that had turned to dirty slush. It was so cold and windy, Richie aimed for the first entrance into the enormous building, and we found ourselves at the beginning of a wide, long corridor that went all the way down to the end, to Ward F for patients with skin disorders, where Richie had to report.

On our way down the corridor, Richie stopped by other wards on both sides to greet patients he had met during his previous stay, and he introduced me to them. The hospital was full of wounded and injured veterans. We arrived at Ward F, where Richie was to meet the doctor.

In just a few minutes, the army doctor appeared with a couple of nurses. He was very cordial, thoroughly examined Richie, gave him some papers to sign, and assigned him to a bed in the ward with the promise to be back shortly with a new ointment he wanted to try on him. During this procedure, I remained an observant and silent spectator, wishing I had a better knowledge of the English language.

Richie had to remain in the hospital, and the length of his recovery was completely in the hands of God. Time for me to leave arrived soon enough, and with great care, I looked for the buses and connections I had to make. With great relief, I reached my home in Flushing, praying all the while for a miracle. For almost three months, I went back and forth to the Bronx twice a week when visiting hours were allowed, and during that time, Richie took me around the many floors and wards, visiting friends he had made during his previous stay.

The sights I beheld took my breath away. My heart surged with compassion when I was confronted by the stark reality of the consequences the war had inflicted on this young segment of humanity. I can still see in my mind's eye the maimed bodies of hundreds of young men without arms or legs, some blind, and the paraplegics in wheelchairs. The burn patients, strapped in their beds or hanging from complicated tractions, often crying in pain, were the ones I most wanted to reach out to and comfort. Sometimes I wished I could have given a few years of my own life in exchange for their cures.

One of the most unforgettable wards we visited was the one where the "basket cases" made their home. It was incredible to watch how these men had adapted to the hospital environment. Some had been there since World War I. These men had lost both arms and both legs, and the hospital was the only place they could get the treatments they needed to survive. The staff called them "basket cases" because that was what they were: their torsos were placed in baskets set on wooden legs of normal height, where they observed life passing them by, year after year. Because they could do nothing for themselves, they were at the mercies of the nurses or anyone near them to bring them water or food or whatever they needed. That was a pathetic sight!

As we visited wards, Richie often commented on how wonderfully the government provided for the treatment of its soldiers, making available to them the best medical and surgical procedures and equipment of that time. Even the U.S.O. provided some of the best entertainment for the men who had given so much for their homeland, and I could not help admiring the patriotic spirit that prevailed in my new country.

Three months later, Richie came out of the hospital with complete remission of his psoriasis and with the news of having found a location to open the grocery store he was hoping for. Sometimes, dreams do come true.

Richie wanted to start a business that would provide us a good income and someday give us enough capital to buy a house and raise a family. That is what actually happened. It took about a month to have everything in place and the licenses ready to be hung on the wall. The sign at the top of the entrance of our new store on Forty-Fifth Avenue in Flushing declared it to be, in bold letters, "Zecchino's Market." In the window, a neon sign blinked "OPEN" in red letters.

On opening day, we both were up at three in the morning and were in the store by four. Richie had many things to attend to, and I was amazed at his ability in keep so many projects under control. Our first helper arrived at six, and by seven, they had neatly arranged against one wall numerous stalls with fresh fruits and vegetables boasting both color and variety. They had also lined up outside and against the large window several bushels and baskets filled with more fresh fruits and vegetables, every one of them advertising a "special" price to entice curious homemakers searching for bargains. On the opposite wall inside the store, a large refrigerated showcase displayed all the cold cuts and cheeses, and another displayed the milk and cream and many varieties of canned and bottled beers and sodas.

I was discovering something new every hour of every day that followed the first opening. Most of all, I was busy taking care of customers of all nationalities and trying hard to learn the English names of all this merchandise. Was that easy? Certainly not! Was it frustrating? Absolutely! Especially when some nice lady would ask for eggs and I would bring her an eggplant, or ask for oatmeal and I would bring her a bottle of milk. I was also quickly learning a unique and useful sign language, in which I had only to follow a finger pointed at the item the customer wanted.

Overall, I had a lot of fun learning to speak the language, insisting that even Richie speak English to me all the time and refusing to listen to the Italian radio station until I had learned enough English to understand what was going on around me. I had so much support from our customers that many of them became very close friends and are still friends to this day, sixty years later.

Life moved on, and I fell in love more and more with this country and all the opportunities it offered. Did I miss Italy? Of course, I did, especially my family, but now I felt a window opening on my future, and I saw a rainbow encircling a blue clear sky and a green meadow below, where a field of rosebuds was ready to open into marvelous dreams.

CHAPTER 21

My New York Years

I never expected business to bloom so well. We weren't making a lot of money, but we made a very decent living. Gradually, I learned to cook. In the kitchen we had organized behind our store, I diligently watched Richie flip omelets, roast vegetables, or make baked *ziti* with meat sauce. I brought in my treasured cookbook *Il Talismano della Felicitá* and found it easy to follow many recipes because I had almost all the ingredients needed right there at the tips of my fingers.

The fragrant smells of the food cooking behind the store had the added advantage of increasing our sales, as customers in search of new ideas would ask for the recipes of whatever we were cooking in our kitchen. Many times, the conversation would go something like this with a customer like Mary:

"My goodness, Richie, it smells so good in here! What are you cooking today?"

Richie would say, smiling, "Well, at the moment I am cooking a vegetable *frittata*. It will come out of the oven in about five minutes. Would you like a taste?"

"Would I? Absolutely!" Mary would wait patiently until Richie retrieved the aromatic dish from the oven and carefully placed the pan on the counter to cool off a little. Once cooled, he cut the frittata into tiny squares, skewered a toothpick in each square, and served the pieces on a dainty tray to Mary and the other curious ladies gathered around. This tactic never failed to please them.

"It's so delicious!" they would chime like a choir singing in unison and remark that they had solved the dilemma of what they were going to cook for dinner that night. It was, as they say, a win-win situation: the ladies usually bought all the ingredients they needed to cook a frittata, and Richie was happy to have sold pounds of onions, zucchinis, green and red peppers, garlic, olives, eggs, and lots of parmesan cheese!

At times, he would sell a whole, readymade dinner to one lucky customer who happened to come in at the right time, and he would make a sale at a very profitable price. The ladies loved to go home and set on their table a delicious dinner already prepared. I believe Richie was one of the first to sell carryout dinners. He was an astute and clever businessman. I watched Richie weave that magic thread that runs through all successful businesses, and years later, I used the skills I learned at his side with great success when I ventured into my own manufacturing business.

By the end of 1948, we moved to a bigger, finished attic apartment in a two-story house owned by Richie's older brother. At first, I missed the company of Rose and Tom, especially their children. I missed joining the older boys at night as they intently followed on the radio the creepy sounds and stories of the *Inner Sanctum* series, or the joyful laughter of the much loved Burns and Allen comedy show, even though I didn't understand much of what they were saying.

We were still searching for a two-bedroom apartment in our neighborhood, but there were none to be found. Our business was going well, and I was making many friends. One of my best was Ruth Berger, the owner of the building where our store was located and the building next to ours, where she operated a prosperous dry goods business with her brothers Eli and Sol Sachs. She also took care of Shirley, her twenty-five-year-old sister, who was born with Down's syndrome. I will always keep this family in high esteem for the way they lavished Shirley with love, patience, and understanding.

Ruth was an exceptional person. I admired her ability to run a household and her business. Her husband owned a kosher butcher shop a couple of miles from us, and they had two children, Enid and Charles. She also found time to help her brothers and sister. We remained best friends until she passed away a few years ago, and because of her deep understanding of what true friendship really meant, she made it possible for me to advance in my own business years later.

Other businesses on our block fitted well together: there was Teperman's Drug Store, Mr. Loukas' candy store with its popular soda fountains and colorful jukebox, Pagano's Liquor Store, Clemente's Italian Bakery, Tyrone's Beauty Parlor, Macari's Butcher Shop on one corner, and a popular bar on the other corner. We all knew each other, helped each other, and respected each other's faiths and colors. I found in that part of Flushing the lifestyle that economic depression in Italy and later a cruel world war had kept from me since my birth.

"God Bless America" was a song that hit the right chord in the heart of a simple immigrant like me. Yes, there were many reasons for me to say "God bless America," and one of them was the possibility of having my whole family join me here. Could I dream such a dream? By law, I had to reside five years in the States to become a citizen, and then I could call for them. Richie was all in favor of it, and I began working on the necessary papers required for their entrance into America.

As time went on, my first son, Domenick Richard, was born in Flushing Hospital. By that time, we had moved into a two-bedroom apartment on Bowne Street just a few blocks from our grocery store. Two years later, my second son, Vincent Edgard, joined our family, and two weeks after his birth, in January 1952, Babbo, Mamma, and Antonietta arrived from Italy.

It is impossible to define the emotion that surrounded our reunion, or their elation at embracing their grandchildren Ricky and Vinny, as they had been nicknamed by Johnny, Clirio, Joe, and Mike, the delivery boys we employed part-time after school.

Antonietta, ten years old when I left was now a tall young lady of almost sixteen. My brothers Pierino and Andrea joined the rest of the family a year or so later, and we were all together again, in another country and on another continent, but together. The rosebuds I had seen through the window were blooming into magnificent dreams, and I heard a voice in my heart gently whisper, "Thank you, Lord, and God bless America!"

Babbo found a job as a janitor in St. Mary's school. Pierino and Andrea also found jobs around town once they arrived, and Antonietta entered Flushing High School. We secured a three-bedroom apartment on Bowne Street for them, and gradually, everyone settled down. The young ones eagerly learned the English language to improve their positions and apply for better jobs, while Mamma and Babbo found it more challenging.

Our lives finally became calm and full of sunshine, until a black cloud on the horizon covered the sun and dropped a shocking tragedy at our doorsteps.

One morning, I left the boys in Mamma's care on my way to join Richie in our grocery store, and she complained about back pains. I sensed concern in her voice, though she tried to make light of the matter, hoping to keep me from worrying. She had struggled with ovarian cancer in Italy about three years before coming to America, and after a successful operation, the doctors there assured her they had removed all the cancerous tissues. She would be completely cured if in five years the cancer had not reappeared.

Mamma was not even fifty years old, and I couldn't imagine, looking at her young and beautiful face, how that dreadful disease could lurk inside her body. Nonetheless, I made sure during the next weeks she visited several doctors in different specialties, got all the possible X-rays, and heard from all of them the same reassuring statement:

"We cannot find any cancer anywhere!" We were all relieved by their diagnosis.

However, Mamma's pains grew worse each day. One morning, about two months later, she began hemorrhaging, and we had to call an ambulance to take her to Flushing Hospital.

Several doctors examined her there, and after many X-rays, the diagnosis was in. One of them gave it to me in a cold, matter-of-fact way: "Your mother has cancer in the kidneys, and we have to operate immediately! However—"

The doctor paused, fidgeting with the papers he held in his hands. "There is no guarantee." He coughed and took a deep breath. "The cancer has spread. Just hope that we got it in time." His voice trailed off, as if he was trying to convince himself that there was still hope. Without hesitation, Babbo and I consented to the operation.

A few hours later, the surgeon joined us in the waiting room where we had huddled together, praying fervently for her recovery. The somber expression on his face mirrored his internal struggle, and he tried to find soothing words to buffer the news.

"I am deeply sorry," he whispered, as if he was anxious to ameliorate the horrid news, "but the cancer has spread too deep and into other organs, too. We could not operate. The best we can do is to make her comfortable."

No! I was in shocked disbelief. This could not be true. Panic struck me with the force of a sledgehammer, and I felt myself buckle under the force of that blow. How could this happen? Mamma was too dear and too much a part of my life. I could not imagine what life without her would be like.

For a few days, I functioned as if I were inside an airless vacuum, barely able to breathe. Finally, after turning to deep prayer, acceptance and courage resurfaced to put me back on the right track. I asked God for strength, and I received just enough each day to carry on as a wife, a mother, a daughter, and a sister. We concentrated on giving Mamma the best care and making her as comfortable as possible. We had to accept the fact that God gives and God takes away.

To fulfill one of her wishes, I arranged for her and Toni (Antonietta preferred the Americanized name) to fly to London to visit her sister Serafina, who had moved there with her daughters, then to proceed by train to Lourdes, stay there a few days, and finally go on to Bari to visit the rest of the family. The trip was tiring for Mamma, but she was grateful to have had the chance to visit Lourdes and say good-bye to her brother and sisters in Italy.

Mamma held her own very well, and I noticed on her return a great transformation in the way she resigned herself to a fate that appeared unjust and cruel. She gave us the courage to accept with faith the unfathomable will of our God. For a couple of months, we watched helplessly as daily she diminished, like a candle burning slowly out.

One morning, after dropping Ricky and Vinny at my friend Sarah's house, I rushed to give Mamma her morning injection of morphine. I had a strange feeling that the end was approaching. Around midday, Mamma's eyes opened, and she gave us a long, loving gaze. Then her eyes closed forever!

On September 20, 1956, Mamma went to be with God and her loved ones in heaven. Even though we expected her demise, our hearts were crushed with sorrow when that dreadful time arrived. Babbo was devastated, and so was Toni. For days, Toni had been diligently tending Mamma's needs and had been at her bedside day and night. Pierino and Andrea were summoned home from their jobs, and after rivers of tears, together we found solace in the knowledge that her excruciating pains were finally over.

Our lives returned to the normal beat that healing brings in the folds of time. Ricky and Vinny went through the stages of growing up. They had First Communion, Confirmation, and the added sprinkling of graduations in between.

Our dream of owning a house came true. We bought a two-family house on Smart Street, just around the corner from our grocery store. It sat on a large lot, had large rooms on both floors, and a two-car garage with a shed attached to it that at one time had served as stables for the horses and buggies owned by the original owners. In the backyard, there was a built-in barbeque pit and a large kiosk-like structure all paved and surrounded by two glorious vines of climbing roses, one red and one white. At the beginning of May, the roses bloomed and hugged the kiosk on both sides, filling the air with an exquisite fragrance.

On one side of the house, a huge, rare weeping beech tree spread its branches to bring welcome shade to the swings we installed underneath for the children to play on. On the opposite side of the house, a reddish Japanese maple and a gorgeous forsythia tree competed for attention, especially when the forsythia branches exploded with their bright yellow flowers to greet the coming spring.

The property was fenced and safe for children to play in, and many of them from the neighborhood and school joined my children in our back yard. I remember with nostalgia the summer days with our friends from next door and across the street, sipping iced tea, lemonade, refreshing drinks, or an occasional ice-cold beer while chitchatting on the front steps or in the backyard kiosk. People seemed friendlier in those days, and we always found time to spend with each other.

Life was great again, and I acquired the skills of party giving and entertaining. For the boys' Confirmations and graduations from St. Mary's Elementary and later from Bishop Reilly High School in Fresh Meadows, I busied myself by first making attractive ornaments around the kiosk in their schools' team colors, then setting up festive wares on buffet tables to blend with the decorations. Last, I brought out the most important element of the party: food that with its mouth-watering aromas and plentiful quantities always received the greatest of compliments. Everyone was eager to be invited to my parties, and I was always finding a reason to celebrate something. I enjoyed the excitement of the festivities and the pleasure they gave my guests, both visually and on their plates.

I knew that the preparation of food was an art. My hands were the "paintbrushes" used to create my masterpieces. As the painter chooses first the picture he wants to paint, puts the colors he needs on a palette, then dips his brushes in the colors and with bold strokes brings them to the canvas, making the picture come alive, so it is with the passionate cook. He or she first chooses a recipe, collects all the ingredients, cuts, slices, mixes them inside pots and pans, and then arranges everything on a plate, bringing to life the culinary work of art.

I became passionate about food. I was always complimented on how delicious my cooking tasted. The funny thing was, when people asked for a recipe, I could never give them the proper quantities of the ingredients. I usually added "a little of this" and "a handful of that," but the main ingredient, I was quick to add, was always *love*. I still cook the same way, and I still get great results.

As the years marched on, my relatives increased. My brothers "Pete" and "Andy," as they were now nicknamed, met two lovely girls, Anna and Lucy, and they got married. Pete and Anna moved to Brooklyn near Anna's family, and in time became the parents of two lovely girls, Lina and Phyllis. My brother Andy, who moved into the second-floor apartment of my house, also became the father of a sweet little girl, Andrea.

In October 1961 a blessed event fulfilled a dream I had nourished for years, but neither Richie nor I had imagined would ever happen. I gave birth to the most beautiful girl in the world. Nine years had passed since Vinny's birth, and when Linda made her debut, I was so overwhelmed with joy I could not sleep for a couple of nights. What a miracle! I had wanted a girl so badly I had bought several little girls' dresses and hidden them in my closet, and when she was born, I felt my prayers had been answered.

About a year later, Richie began having bouts with bronchitis and psoriasis that kept reappearing, and he had to enter the hospital for treatments. We decided then to sell the grocery store, and fortunately, we sold it in a month's time. Richie began working with his brother Nino again, and I was happy to be a stay-at-home mom, giving all my attention to Linda and the boys.

It was a new pleasure to see Linda grow up, go to school, and make many friends. This time around, I was wrapping dolls, miniature stoves, little tea sets, and all the dainty toys little girls play with and expect to find under the Christmas tree, instead of the cowboy gear the boys were fond of. When Linda started elementary school at St. Mary's, she joined a twirling club that a teenager named Patty was teaching after school, and I enjoyed driving with other mothers and sharing the pleasures and frustrations of seeing them compete against other schools. Linda was quite good with her baton and received many trophies performing as a single, as well as with St. Mary's team.

Long established in my memory are the fun days I enjoyed with the family visiting the breathtaking pavilions at the New York World's Fair that opened in 1964 in Fresh Meadows and closed at the end of 1965. We learned to sing Walt Disney's catchy tune "It's a Small World" while gliding silently on small boats as they zigzagged through narrow canals, encountering at every turn enchanting scenes that enraptured the young and the young at heart. We feasted there for the first time on the huge and yummy Belgian waffles topped with juicy strawberries and fluffy whipped cream that were making their debut at the fair.

We were happy and fun loving, until another tragic blow hit us with the force of a hurricane. My brother Peter began having pains in his left leg. When he was examined at the hospital, doctors diagnosed him with advanced bone cancer caused by the radiation treatments he had undergone two years earlier for a mild case of prostate cancer. Evidently, the radiation he had received had been too strong. There was still a kernel of hope, the doctors said, if he could be operated on to have his leg amputated up to the hip, but even then they did not guarantee the outcome.

His wife Anna was beside herself when confronted with this incredible choice. We were all stunned at the horrendous turn of events and wondered how this could have happened! Pete was only thirty-eight years old. Babbo and Anna desperately tried to find other solutions, but the doctors insisted there were none. Finally, they all decided to take the risk. Pete was operated on and patiently endured weeks of painful recovery, assisted by his devoted wife.

However, after a couple of months of reprieve, the cancer spread rapidly through his body, and on March 29, 1969, on Palm Sunday, Pete was gone. I am sure after all his suffering Pete made a glorious entrance in heaven, like Jesus was making His entrance in Jerusalem. When the end came, Anna and Toni were at his bedside in the hospital. In a way, Anna never really recovered from that loss. They were so much in love with each other.

Losing Pete at such an early age made me question why death was allowed to take a loving husband from such a devoted wife and a loving father from two adoring little girls. It was not fair! But then, no one has the answer to this ageless enigma. Only a strong belief in a God that has all under control gave me that inner assurance that everything happens for a reason.

Again, time moved on, and in the summer of 1970, I traveled to Hollywood, Florida to spend a month of vacation and relaxation with the children. Perhaps because it reminded me so much of the African climate, I fell immediately in love with Florida. Most of all, I liked that there was no winter there! No shoveling snow, no icicles dangling from bare branches. No need for boots, heavy winter coats, gloves, and scarves! No soot from steaming radiators!

I wanted to pack and move immediately. The doctors agreed it would be a good move for Richie, as sunshine was considered a healing factor for his psoriasis and the bronchitis that gave him a lot of trouble and caused him to have bouts of heavy coughing.

Richie resisted the idea at first. He did not want to move far from his brothers or New York, where he had lived for so many years, even though some of his friends had already moved to Hollywood. As his cough became more acute, he finally consented and allowed me to go to Hollywood and buy a temporary home. A foothold would give us more time to look for a permanent residence in a neighborhood convenient to our needs.

I sharpened my business skills, and in the summer of 1971, I returned to Hollywood with Linda and Vinny and bought an almost new duplex with lots of space for our family and a front apartment suitable for Babbo and Toni, who wanted to move with us to Florida. I was happy that everything had gone smoothly.

I was in the process of moving into the duplex when a frantic phone call from Babbo reached me as I was unpacking.

"Emilia?" Babbo's voice was shaky and hesitant. "You have to come immediately. Richie has been admitted to the hospital with a severe cough and high fever. He needs you here."

I told him I was catching the first plane for La Guardia the next morning with Linda and told him to have someone pick us up at the airport. Vinny had applied for classes at Broward Community College, and he was to begin school in a few days. Ricky had transferred from Adelphi University on Long Island to the University of Florida in Gainesville. We had no idea then that life for us was going to change. A new tempest took aim and barreled toward our lives without warning and without mercy.

 **CHAPTER 22**

A NEW BEGINNING IN FLORIDA

I arrived with Linda at La Guardia Airport late the next morning. My brother Andy was there with Babbo, ready to drop Linda at home and drive me directly to the hospital. We arrived just in time to meet Dr. Balducci as he was leaving Richie's room, so we followed him to a waiting room down the hall.

He looked serious and was cautious in choosing his words to describe the results of the X-rays of Richie's lungs taken the previous day.

"I am sorry, Emilia, but your husband—" He lowered his voice and hesitated, trying to soften the blow he was preparing to inflict. "Your husband is very ill. The X-rays show a large tumor in one lung. I have consulted Dr. Giordano, an excellent lung specialist affiliated with this hospital, and I would like to page him now and have him come here to talk to you. Is that okay?"

"Yes, please! I would like to know his opinion as soon as possible," I answered as I my knees buckled under the weight of his words.

Dr. Giordano was still in the hospital making his morning rounds, and he joined us in the waiting room a few minutes after his page.

"Mrs. Zecchino, your husband has to be operated on immediately. His left lung is covered by a large tumor. He may have a chance of survival if we remove the lung completely. We will know further what to do after we analyze the tissues. Do you agree?"

I was shocked at the gravity of Richie's condition. He had complained for months about his shortness of breath, hacking cough, and night sweats, but he always resisted my advice and kept postponing his visit to the doctor, with the excuse that sometimes he felt so much better. Stubbornly, he had neglected himself, and for a long time, I found it hard to forgive his irresponsible behavior.

It was late August, and the operation was scheduled for the last Monday of that month. When it was over, Dr. Giordano gave us the grim news. The lung he had removed was full of cancer, and he hoped he had taken all of it away. To inject in us some hope for a recovery, he suggested radiation treatments to eradicate any remaining cancerous cells.

"I cannot guarantee the outcome of the radiation, but this is the only remedy we have available at this time," Dr. Giordano said. He did not avoid the truth. He just stated the raw facts, and I was grateful that he did not make any sugarcoated statements. When Richie recovered sufficiently, twice weekly, we made the five-mile trip to the clinic where the radiation treatments were given. In the beginning, the powerful radiation left him nauseated and weak for hours. Gradually, he began to tolerate the treatments, and for a short time, he seemed to rebound and regain a small amount of strength.

Babbo had made plans to visit his home town in Italy months before our lives took such a frantic turn, and I convinced him it was all right to leave, even though it was just after Richie's operation. In mid-September, Babbo left Kennedy airport in great health, looking forward to a few months with his relatives in Bari, Naples, and Trieste.

At the beginning of December, without warning, another development took place on the other side of the ocean. A telegram from Babbo read in part, "I am coming back on flight so-and-so from Rome to Kennedy. Have Andy pick me up."

Why was Babbo coming back so soon? I had a feeling that something ominous was in the air.

When Babbo arrived at the airport, he asked to be taken to the hospital immediately. He was having terrible chest pains and back pains, and he wanted to see a doctor as soon as possible. I had never seen Babbo so pale and emaciated. What was going on all of a sudden? We rushed him to the emergency room, and Dr. Balducci admitted him immediately to the hospital and ordered X-rays.

The next day, the results were in, and the only thing I remember said by Dr. Balducci in the waiting room was, "There is nothing we can do. We cannot operate. The cancer in both his lungs is one of the most progressive. It has advanced and spread all over. At the most, he has three months to live."

His voice trailed on as he explained other details to Andy. I heard nothing of what was said. Only the words, "He has three months to live" kept ringing and ringing in my ears, and I couldn't stop their awful sound.

No operation? Nothing could be done? Impossible! Babbo was such a part of our lives. Losing him at this time was too hard to accept. I could not understand how one calamity could follow another without mercy or compassion. I felt almost crushed and beaten by the heaviness of so much sorrow.

Then I did what usually was my custom: I turned to fervent prayer, and as usual, it was there that I found the strength I needed each day to overcome the stress, the grace to endure the conflicts, and the comfort and love of a God that in my sorrow and pain was tenderly drawing me with His silent presence much closer to Himself.

During the next few months, it seemed everyone needed me more than at any other time before, and looking back, with God's grace, I managed to hold on and be the pillar everyone needed. Babbo came to stay in my home where I could tend to his needs, and the whole family spent the Christmas holidays enjoying every hour in Richie and Babbo's company, just making the best of the brief time we had left together.

At the beginning of February, both were readmitted to the hospital as their conditions deteriorated. Finally, on the eleventh day of the month, in Flushing hospital, Toni and I attended Babbo's transition into the other world.

Richie was bedridden and could not attend the funeral. His illness dragged on as new tumors appeared on the other lung, and the decision was made to halt the radiation and test a new form of treatment called "chemotherapy," just coming into the market. The side effects of this new therapy kept sending him home and back into the hospital several more times, until he just refused to go back. His wish was to stay home until the end. On the afternoon of March 30, a couple of hours after I gave him an injection of morphine, he stretched his trembling hand towards mine, gave me a faint smile, and was gone.

A widow! At first, I found it strange to carry that label. I was single again, and lonely, unable to share my life with someone else. Except . . . oh, yes! I had three children to tend to, the youngest only ten. We had been married for more than twenty years, and Richie had been the sole provider for our family most of those years. I had helped him when we had our own business, but now, at forty-four years old, I had no degrees, no skills, and no talents. I was looking at a future that had all the semblance of a dark, scary, and bottomless pit.

Should I give in to self-pity, or was there a way out of this stinking way of thinking? I woke up one morning, and there the answer was in black and white: "Black, I lose, and white, I win." That small voice within began nudging me: "Go on, go on! I am with you!"

I bowed my head and thanked God for His presence. All the trials I had been through had taught me perseverance, determination, and the perception to see a rainbow wrapping itself below the clouds as the sun chased them from above. This time again, "hope" spread its wings, picked me up, and set me confidently again on my rainbow.

Time moved relentlessly on, and it cast a soothing balm and acceptance on what I could not change. Summer was approaching, and I was faced with many projects that had to be accomplished in a very short time. The most important was to have my son Ricky's spine operated on. Several months before, while at the University of Florida in Gainesville, playing football with his friends, he had slipped and injured his back. A neurologist diagnosed him with a herniated disk, and when several procedures, including traction, failed to bring him relief, the surgeon recommended an operation.

Ricky recovered well from his ordeal and was ready to return to Florida with us, while Vinny decided to stay in New York and enroll at Bernard Baruch College in Manhattan. My other big project, selling the house in Flushing, was taking wings. Mr. Pagano, the owner of the liquor store, was willing to buy the house and paid the whole amount in cash, making the deal complete and sealed in a couple of weeks.

The last project on my list was packing our belongings and having them shipped to Florida. As the moving van pulled out of the driveway, Mr. Pagano was there to receive the keys of the house and Linda, Ricky, and I were on our way to Grand Central Station and the southbound train to Florida.

A new beginning was opening on my path and another leaf turning in my life. Little did I suspect that the future would take such incredible twists and turns. It was the beginning of July 1972, and after registering Linda in the fifth grade at Nativity School, my life became quite interesting, at least from my point of view. I liked my new surroundings, especially the sandy beaches that stretched from Ft. Lauderdale all the way down to North Miami Beach. I loved to take friends and relatives that came to visit us on the Jungle Queen and other sightseeing boats that navigated the intracoastal waterways, from which we admired the mansions and fabulous cars parked in front of their garages and impressive white yachts moored in their own berths in the deep-water canals. We circled Ft. Lauderdale for hours, and those rides reminded me of a modern version of the fabulous Venice I had seen years before.

"Someday," I used to tell myself. "I will buy a house on the intracoastal and perhaps even a motor boat!" I was dreaming big—and why not? I had signed up for a real estate course that was to start in January. There was tremendous growth and expansion planned for this part of Florida, and a career in real estate would be a profitable occupation that

I could attempt on my own. Meanwhile, a brand new shopping center, the Fashion Mall, had just opened on the corner of Hollywood Boulevard and 441, very close to my home. I applied for a job as a sales clerk at J.C. Penney's and was hired and assigned to the home goods department, where I felt very much at home.

It seemed I had my life happily under control until another unexpected event changed my plans. Andy came from New York to spend the Christmas holidays with us and he fell in love with Florida's lifestyle. He was working in a pizza restaurant in the city and his dream was to someday own a pizzeria of his own.

After searching the area well, he convinced me that Hollywood would be an excellent place to open a pizzeria. We could be partners in the venture. I had the money to go into business, and he would borrow from me his share and pay me back monthly as the business progressed.

The idea seemed appealing, especially because I had a flare for cooking. I could trust my brother, couldn't I? I decided to put my real estate plans on the back burner and venture into the business world. We were very lucky to pick up the newspaper one day, and in the "Business for Sale" section, an ad for a pizzeria caught our attention. We lost no time in asking the owner for an appointment and soon were negotiating with Louis Donar for the acquisition of Pop's Pizza. In less than a month, Andy and I were operating the pizzeria with the help of two wonderful employees, Ann and Irene.

The ladies flipped pizzas at a speed that would have made any pizza man green with envy. They were fabulous! At that time, Pop's Pizza was a simple take-out business, selling *only* pizza in different sizes and with a variety of toppings. The entrance of the establishment looked more like an office then a pizzeria, but in the back room, two large mixers churned pizza dough with great efficiency, and four sturdy Blodgett ovens baked dozens of flawless, fragrant, golden-crusted pizzas.

Business hours were between 4:00 P.M. and 11:00 P.M., and during those hours, the phone rang almost continuously, especially on weekends. Business bloomed, and so did my hands. I learned to flip pizzas almost as fast as Irene and how to mix pizza dough and pizza sauce from Andy's recipes. Everything was going as planned, and Andy seemed happy in his new position. For the first time, he was an entrepreneur instead of a worker. He learned to give orders well, instead of taking them.

He began to enjoy his freedom a little too much, letting the lust of his eye chase the pretty women buzzing around him. I began having serious apprehensions regarding his behavior. His wife and only daughter were still in New York, preparing to join him soon in Florida. What if his wife found out?

To make things worse, we had different opinions on how to run the business. As the population in Hollywood increased, more Italian restaurants and pizzerias were opening in various parts of the city. Competition was creeping up, and we had to do something about it. Andy was happy to keep the business as it was, even though our most steady customers and friends kept pressuring us to add more items to the menu, or to change the take-out pizzeria into an Italian restaurant, as one was much needed in that neighborhood.

I loved my brother dearly, but I knew how stubborn he could be. Nothing would convince Andy that the change was necessary, until one day, out of the blue, the opportunity to make the change fell into our laps. The owner of the Roasted Chicken Restaurant a few doors away from us declared bankruptcy and closed its doors. I wanted to seize the opportunity, but Andy resisted the move. Finally, the landlord called to tell us that two individuals wanted to open an Italian restaurant and sign a lease on that location. Were we interested in making the move? He was giving us first right to a new lease. Andy was left with only one choice, and he agreed to make the move.

After a few months of renovations and numerous aggravations with the contractors, the city's inspectors approved all the plans and licenses and we finally opened Pop's Pizza and Italian Restaurant with the capacity to seat as many as eighty guests. The menu had all the popular Italian specialty dinners, from the favorite eggplant *parmigiana* to the zesty veal *saltimbocca*, from the delectable minestrone soup to the mouth-watering cream-filled *cannolis* and *tiramisu*. Espresso and cappuccino were a must-have, together with Chianti, Bardolino, Verdicchio, and Valpolicella wines, just to name a few.

We hired two waitresses and two waiters to tend the tables, two dishwashers, and to help in the kitchen, two cooks—a middle-aged married couple, Irma and Johnny—who had reputations of being masters of Italian southern cuisine. They had a special talent for making everything taste delicious, and I was in heaven, having found the rebirth of my passion for cooking and substituting when Irma or Johnny needed a day off.

During this time, Andy's wife Lucy and daughter Andrea finally moved to Florida. Lucy's help in the business brought much-welcomed relief as we took turns working the night shift. The restaurant became very popular, and lines continually formed in front as well as in the back for pizza pickup. Business was great, and we even had several players of the Miami Dolphins as regular customers. Things were looking up, and I was enjoying some calm, but peace began eluding me again.

Andy and Lucy's relationship became strained when Lucy learned about Andy's escapades. They tried to work it out, but their efforts were in vain, and they ended finally in separation. While I loved my brother, he had a lot to learn as a businessman and a family man. A few months after, I learned he had consented, without my knowledge, to hosting the Hollywood Hills High School football team after their games on weekends. I thought that decision was wrong, and it put our business at risk because we could not seat other paying customers when the entire team took up all the tables in the restaurant. Business began to decline, and in a few months, we came very close to closing the restaurant altogether. I was frustrated at the prospect of seeing my work and money going down the drain.

The only way to survive was to close Pop's Pizza, modernize the interior again, and reopen as a white tablecloth restaurant under another name with a more sophisticated menu. Andy was reticent at first, but then agreed to try it. For the money needed to make the changes, I had to apply for a second mortgage on my home and give Andy an extension on his note, while also increasing the amount he owed to me. This time, I was assuming a tremendous risk. Was I overextending myself, or was I on the right path to recovery, hoping that Andy had learned his lesson? We went on with the plans and reopened a few months later as Trevi's Italian Restaurant.

Gone was the pizza production, but following my suggestions, a large mural depicting Rome's world-famous Trevi Fountain welcomed cheerfully hungry guests, while tucked away in one corner of a make-believe garden, a real fountain bubbled pleasantly as happy diners dropped coins as if in the real fountain. We sent the money collected to our favorite charity. My prayers every morning and night were, "God, please let Andy see the light and learn from his mistakes." I know that God was listening, even though other crises were brewing in my private life and would hit me like a bolt of lightning.

After his graduation from college, my older son Ricky decided to go his own way and severed all affiliation with us. For seven years, I had no idea where he was. My other son Vinny fell under the blow of a terrible sickness. In the middle of his third year of college, severe mental depression put a halt to his promising future forever. He kept having bouts that sent him back and forth to the hospital, while doctors experimented on his condition with new drugs.

221

From the point of view of a mother who had to bear the stigma attached to mental illness, I can only implore: Please have compassion for the mentally ill. Like the sadness I felt when Mamma, Richie, my brother Pete, and Babbo moaned in pain as cancer invaded their bodies, it was even more heartbreaking to see my son's intelligent, kind, and lovable personality fade away like a light flickering out. He became a stranger with a distorted view of life. Because the chemicals in his brain were not making the right connections he fell into an abyss, floating aimlessly within a deceptive perception of a world he had no control over.

I learned a lot about this horrible disease. Lightly called crazy and most of the time ridiculed, people with this illness are misunderstood and pathetic to watch as they try to cope with life. Deprived of cognizance, they are helpless and at the mercy of other human beings.

To mothers and fathers facing the same crisis, I say, "Have courage, and don't let the stigma attached to this disease defeat you and lead you to abandon your child." Just as the liver, heart, or lung may become diseased and lose their function, so does the brain, the most complicated organ of them all. Why be ashamed to admit or acknowledge a mental patient in the family?

Thanks to the enormous advances made in this field, Vinny today is taking new medications that restore, at least in part, his ability to cope and see the world as it really is. This is both a blessing and a curse. Able to discern the life of "normal people" and knowing he's seen as mentally ill strikes at the core of his ego, making him fully aware of the stigma attached to his condition. Even more painful is the awareness that fate has stripped him of the ability to work and be productive, keeping him dependent on others. That tortures him like an open wound that never heals!

During those challenging times with my family and the restaurant, something was brewing in the Catholic Church. Through a friend of mine, I was introduced to the charismatic movement that was spreading like wildfire in churches around the United States. I joined the prayer group meetings that were held every Tuesday night in the school auditorium behind Nativity Church.

Shortly after my baptism in the spirit, my faith was put to the test in a peculiar and humorous way. New people were joining our prayer group from parishes near and far after hearing all the wonderful testimonies of those receiving the baptism. The memory of those early days is forever chiseled on my heart. One Tuesday night as I made my entrance in the crowded hall, I was approached by Tony Tucci, the leader of our prayer group, and introduced to three ladies who spoke only Italian. Tony was aware that I spoke Italian and suggested I be their guide for the night. I was very happy to be of help, especially when the ladies told me they were coming from Rome and knew no one in Hollywood.

They told me they had rented an apartment in a motel at the beach, and before leaving Rome, had prayed with their charismatic congregation about finding an Italian family in America who would assist them in their plight. They felt I was the one God had chosen and praised him for answering their prayers. The prayer meeting over, we assembled outdoors, waiting for the cab to take them to the motel. While waiting, they gave me their names—Wilma the older sister, Laura, and Edelweiss, the mother, and then they went on to tell me the reason for their visit to the States.

Edelweiss needed a rare eye operation recommended by a specialist in Rome. Only one doctor could perform the operation, and that doctor was affiliated with the renowned Bascom Palmer Eye Institute in Miami. They had no choice but to come to the States and risk the operation before Edelweiss became completely blind. They said they would be very grateful if I could help translate the doctor's instructions, and to that, I quickly agreed.

We exchanged telephone numbers, hugged, and said, *"Buona notte!"* My new friend was to be admitted to the hospital the next morning and operated on the following day. Wilma and Laura would keep me informed of the outcome by phone.

The afternoon of the operation, Laura called me from the hospital and joyfully told me that the operation was a success. Her mother was doing fine, she said, and could she ask me for a big favor? Of course, I said yes. Laura asked if I would let her stay in my house for the night. Wilma was allowed to stay in the hospital and even sleep in her mother's room. It was understandable that Laura was afraid to spend the night alone at the beach. It was the month of January, and to complicate the situation, the temperature in Miami and Hollywood began to drop drastically. I told Laura to have the cab driver call me so I could give him directions to my home.

Laura spent that night in my house, and late the next afternoon, I received another call from her, this time with one more request: could Wilma stay at my house, too? Of course, I said yes again. After all, I had plenty of room in my home in Emerald Hills. I had three large bedrooms, two bathrooms, a spacious living and dining room, and an enormous family room that ran the length of the house. My teenage daughter Linda was the only one living with me, as Vinny was staying at the Retreat for a few weeks to stabilize his medications. Laura and Wilma were welcome to share his bedroom for a few days.

In the evening, Laura and Wilma came for dinner at the restaurant and to my home for the night. They were very happy that everything was going well with their mother, and thanked God for finding in me such a generous friend.

Wilma's husband was due to arrive in Miami the following week. A few days later, around 10:00 A.M., I received a frantic call from Wilma. The hospital was ready to discharge her mother. Could she please bring her to my house? I said yes again, and now I had three guests to accommodate. I was glad I had enough room for all of them.

It was around noon the same day when again the phone rang. Wilma's frantic voice was barely audible. "Please help me!" She was in tears and sounded desperate. My heart beat fast as I expected tragic news. "Please, Emilia, the hospital handed me a bill for four thousand dollars and want to be paid immediately. If not, they will not release my mother until some other arrangement can be made, and that may take a few days and cost so much more money!" Between her sobs, I heard her implore, "Can you please loan me the money?"

I was stunned, confused, and bewildered. Four thousand dollars was all I had in the bank, as business had been slow at the restaurant for several weeks. I needed that money to pay the mortgage and other bills. Could I risk giving all I had to strangers? After all, what did I know about them? They had dropped into my lap, and I had no clue of their background.

Even though Wilma assured me that her husband was bringing the money in four or five days, I struggled with the choice I had to make. As a Christian, I had to be faithful to Jesus' teachings that "you are your brother's keeper," but could I risk all my savings? I spent a lot of money remodeling the restaurant and was behind in several payments. My lifestyle was being threatened, and I had to make a fast decision.

Finally I realized that everything I had belonged to God, anyway, and if He wanted me to give it to someone, so be it. I heard myself say to Wilma, "Okay, Wilma, come and get it!"

Five days later, Wilma's husband arrived carrying a couple of large suitcases. Once inside the house, after the usual formalities, he opened a suitcase and removed one of the well-packaged *panettones* he had brought from Italy. He set the package on the dining room table and asked us to watch closely. Gently he removed the paper, then the heavy carton, and finally, he opened the *panettone* with his bare hands.

To this day, I remember the astonished expression on all our faces at the sight of the bundle of hundred-dollar bills that rolled out of the *panettone*. I was stunned when Wilma counted *eight* thousand dollars and handed it over to me with a thousand "Grazies!" She insisted I take it as God's reward. After so many years, I am still in touch with Laura, as she is the only survivor of the three, and we often laugh, remembering that day.

Trevi's Restaurant was doing very well, but Andy all of a sudden wanted to get out of our partnership and return to New York. That turn of events I had not anticipated, and needing help to run the business, I consented to Andy's plan to sell his share to a cousin of his ex-wife Lucy, who was willing to give him cash.

I knew Fred and Trudy only slightly, and now I was going to share my life with people who were almost strangers to me. Was I making the right choice? Only God knows how many prayers for help I sent up on the day I signed those new contracts and opened a new door to my future.

CHAPTER 23

THE BIRTH OF HOLIDAY FOODS

That door opened and shut almost as fast as I blinked! Evidently, Fred and Trudy thought running a restaurant would be a piece of cake. Well, they had it all wrong. Operating a restaurant is one of the most demanding and labor intensive occupations on earth. Doing it right requires long hours of work and giving up weekends and holidays. It became evident to them pretty quickly that they had made a great mistake. They told me they could have made a lot more money by investing in something else. Unfortunately, many harbor the notion that going into business makes you an instant millionaire. What folly!

Six months later, around June 1979, Fred and Trudy were fed up with the restaurant and spread the news of the intended sale of their shares in the corporation. Luckily for them, at that same time, Irma and Johnny, who wanted to go back to New Jersey, knew an Italian chef working downtown in another well-known Italian restaurant. The man was interested in buying Fred and Trudy's shares if I agreed to an equal partnership. Irma and Johnny assured me that Joe, the chef, was a very reliable person, married with two children and had a great reputation for an excellent knowledge of Italian cuisine.

I was not prepared for this new development. I felt alone and deserted by every one of my family. I spent sleepless nights trying to figure out what to do. No matter how many good reasons I had to carry on, I had not enough courage to manage the restaurant alone. I could have hired other chefs to help in the kitchen, but I had not enough confidence in myself. I had to make up my mind fast as Irma and Johnny had to leave to join their families in New Jersey. I had to agree to a partnership with this stranger named Joe.

Hardly a week had passed before Joe showed himself to be a twentieth-century version of Dr. Jekyll and Mr. Hyde. His personality transformed as soon as the papers were signed. His attitude was hard to comprehend, and I was exposed more and more to his violent personality.

The first few days he used mild tactics and smiles to nudge me out of the kitchen. Then he told me in no uncertain terms that he was going to run the kitchen without any assistance from me. I was to be the hostess in the dining room when his wife was not around. His wife was very kind to me, but I could sense she was afraid of him. He ordered her around like a sergeant at boot camp, and I could not understand how she could shrug her shoulders sheepishly and obey every order he flung at her.

To my consternation, I found myself falling from the frying pan into the fire. I discovered that under a phony veneer of platitudes, Joe maliciously concealed his abhorrence for the loyal customers crowding our restaurant, boasting how clever he was to make them feel special while making fun of them behind their backs. I also discovered his addiction to alcohol. At the end of each day, he had consumed a gallon of white wine, and he usually took home bags of meat, fish, and vegetables for his family, reducing the business profits. He also assumed ownership of the daily revenues, giving me no nightly account of the amounts received from our sales.

His constant complaints about the business being slow, when it really was the opposite, gave him the excuse to hand me only a couple of hundred dollars at the end of the week. I felt trapped. I had no one to defend me or stand up to this man's verbal abuses and robbery of my property and livelihood. I had no money to engage a lawyer. Andy was in New York, Vinny was sick, Ricky was nowhere in sight, and Linda was commuting daily to Davie to attend her first year of studies at Broward Community College.

I felt my prayers were not reaching God, and my heart cried out in desperation. An unexpected phone call one night brought a spark of hope.

"Hello, Emilia! This is Roy, your meat supplier. Do you have a few minutes to give me?"

"Yes, Roy, I have lots of time now that I am almost out of the restaurant. You know what I mean."

"I have an idea of what is going on, and that is why I would like to buy you out."

I was startled at first but then added quickly, "Do you want to go into business with Joe?"

"Emilia, I know him well, and he will not get away with things with me as he does with you. I know how to handle his kind. Do you want to sell?"

"Do I!" I said. "I can't wait to get out of this bondage. Are you willing to give me this price?" After blurting out my price, I heard a deep sigh on the other end, followed by a long silence. Was I asking too much? I knew we filled the restaurant almost every night and were doing a profitable business. My price was not out of the ballpark.

Finally, Roy came back with an offer. He slashed a couple thousand dollars from my original price, but he was still in an excellent range. I heard myself say yes and make plans to meet with our attorneys as soon as possible. Roy would inform Joe in the morning.

I hardly had any sleep that night. What a break and what a miracle! I felt God bathing me in a beam of radiant light, as though reaching through the eye of the hurricane that was spinning furiously around me.

A few weeks later, I was free. What a relief, and what an experience. I decided to rest for a couple of months while making up my mind about what direction to take. I thought again about getting a real estate license, but at that time, the market was not performing to par. Empty condominium buildings along the seashore from Miami all the way to Palm Beach and from the beaches way out West stood like silent ghosts waiting for the economy to come out of the recession that was choking the housing market. It was not a good time to go into the real estate business. Toward the middle of 1980, my brother Andy reappeared on the scene, begging for help. What was I to do? I had no courage to turn him down, especially when he said tearfully he had learned his lesson.

Before I gave it a lot of thought I said yes to his proposal to be partners again and to try a venture in the restaurant business. A few weeks later, we bought a quaint Italian restaurant in Ft. Lauderdale that was for sale at a reasonable price. We had to travel forty-five minutes from my home to reach the new location, but it was not such a big deal. We renamed the restaurant "Amalfi's Italian Restaurant" because the interior was decorated as a real outdoor eatery reminiscent of the Amalfi coast in Italy.

We were finally on the right track. Andy was cooperating, and our personal lives returned to the harmonious stage they had once enjoyed years before. Business kept growing, and we were looking forward at last to many years of modest prosperity.

We didn't expect the approach of a silent enemy to raise its ugly head again and slash all our dreams away. The recession that seemed to fade for a while returned with merciless vengeance to change lives and conditions around Ft. Lauderdale. The unemployment rate in Florida went sky high and businesses began feeling the pinch. One by one, they fell like dominos.

Our income was not enough to cover the expenses, and we lingered until we could bleed no more. Early in 1982, Andy returned to New York. I paid all our suppliers, leaving practically nothing in my bank account, and returned the keys to our landlord. I chose not to declare bankruptcy, as I knew that would leave a bad mark on my credit and paralyze me for years. I could not afford that risk. I hoped for times to get better someday; I just didn't know when.

Before looking again for a job, I needed more time to reflect, and I rejoined the prayer meetings at church and my old friends. I had kept in touch with them whenever I could find time to host a party and show off my entertainment skills. One evening, my friend Regina Shearn, a professor at Florida International University who was attending one of my get-togethers, gently put a bug in my ear.

"You should go into business with Lena," she said casually. "She likes to give parties, too, and together you could open a catering business!"

"Open a catering business?" I stared at her, concentrating on the meaning of the word *catering.*

"Yes, catering! The food provided at weddings, cocktail parties, graduations, and so on."

She went on to explain how her own mother had done that for years up north, and she thought Lena and I would be wonderful partners in a venture where we both could find pleasure in cooking and setting up ornate buffet tables with lovely presentations.

I sure liked that idea. I felt something dormant in my soul wake and soar to the surface of my brain. I liked the word *catering*, and I made up my mind immediately to learn everything about it. I thanked Regina for the wonderful suggestion, and I still thank her now, as we have remained very good friends.

Lena and her husband Johnny were part of my circle of friends, and when we met at our regular prayer meeting a few days later, I mentioned Regina's remarkable suggestion. Lena, too, felt it was a terrific idea, but she and her husband wanted to think about it and call me in a few days with the answer.

Meanwhile, I wasted no time going to the library and looking up as many books as I could find on the operation of a catering business. I was familiar with the production of large quantities of food from my days in the restaurant business, and I was familiar with setting prices that could bring a profit after covering the expenses. I felt I could handle the operation with or without Lena. I liked the concept of catering, and even more importantly, I heard that little voice in my soul inspiring me to go ahead.

I began looking for a suitable location. All I needed was a small commercial kitchen with low overhead and parking space for three or four cars. It could have even been hidden away in a back street, as all the food would be transported, anyway. I searched the "business for sale and rent" ads of the local newspapers every weekend until an ad appeared that contained everything I was looking for. The ad read, "For Sale, because of illness: 'The Wedding Cake Shoppe, specializing in wedding, anniversary, and shower cakes, and also buffet catering and party platters."

I called the owner, and he said I could go right over to see the premises. I jumped into my station wagon and reached the location in record time. It was located in downtown Hollywood on 21st Avenue. This is a one-way, south to north, three-lane highway flanked on one side by a railroad operating freight trains and by another three-lane, north to south highway called Dixie Highway on the other side of the tracks.

The shop occupied one of several medium-sized warehouses in a building along 21st Avenue, a very commercial neighborhood. Parking in front of the shop was possible only by sliding the car over the sidewalk and obstructing one of the lanes of the highway. Additional parking was way in the back, around the building. I managed to park in front and knocked at the door with the "Wedding Cake Shoppe" sign on top.

Mr. Denis, the owner, let me in the front room that doubled as an office and waiting room. Pictures of fancy cakes, large and small, and buffet arrangements hung on the walls. Mr. Denis explained proudly that his wife was the creator of such beautiful pieces. Unfortunately, she was confined to a wheelchair following a stroke that had incapacitated her a few months before; hence, the sale of their shop.

He took me then through a door that opened into a room where they kept the supplies and then through another that opened into a large commercial kitchen. My eyes fell on the two Blodgett ovens stacked on top of one another under a hood against the back wall. These ovens were perfect for cooking food in large quantities. On the opposite wall a three-compartment, stainless steel sink with floor drains also seemed in very good condition. The stove was similar to those used at home and so were the two large refrigerators. Two working benches, an assortment of pots and pans, and a few chafing dishes made up the rest of the fixtures for sale. This is perfect for me, I thought.

It wasn't much, but it was just enough to start a small business, with all the necessities already in place to operate a commercial kitchen. Mr. Denis hoped to get fifteen hundred dollars, he said, for the contents. I replied with an offer of one thousand if I could come to terms with the landlord. Mr. Denis put me in touch with Vince, the carpenter next door, who was in charge of collecting the rents from all the units of the building. I was able to persuade Vince not to raise the three hundred-dollar rent Mr. Denis paid monthly and to agree to let me stay for a year without a lease. The deal was sealed with Vince, and Mr. Denis accepted a check for one thousand dollars, dated November 23, 1982. I still have that check framed and hanging on my office wall as a witness to the humble beginnings of a business that, *only in America,* through sheer hard work and common sense, grew into the millions.

Lena and John joined me in the new venture. We formed a corporation, and we named the business "Catering by Lena." I wanted her to feel comfortable, as this was the very first time she was part of a real business. Johnny was a mailman, and he helped us on weekends. We worked very well together, but in our first year without a Yellow Pages advertisement, we booked only a few parties. During the first Christmas holidays, we catered a few social affairs our friends from church held in their home or office. Regina recommended us at the university where she was teaching, and we began to get orders to cater several parties that kept us busy for the summer months.

Our first year in business was very slow. We grossed only $25,000, and by the time we paid expenses, we had no profit. I ran out of money completely. In July, I had no way to make a mortgage payment and was forced to ask the St. Vincent de Paul Organization for help. They paid the mortgage that month, and I thank them to this day.

Slowly, by word of mouth and advertising in the Yellow Pages, business began to pick up. We learned to dodge the many unexpected incidents that popped up out of nowhere, quickly transforming small disasters into fits of dry laughter. No matter how careful we were, we always left something behind, which forced us to become creative in very strange ways.

One incident that still brings me lots of laughter happened the Saturday after Thanksgiving 1983. Our friend Mary asked us to cater a holiday dinner with all the trimmings for fifty guests. It was going to be held at the motel she owned on Hollywood Beach. The guests were mostly priests, nuns, and teachers from Chaminade High School, and we knew many of them. We definitely wanted to impress this crowd. For three days, we shopped, cooked, decorated, assembled, and made every effort to show off our talents. In other words, we worked our butts off.

Finally, it was time Saturday afternoon to load the station wagon and head for the beach. We parked the wagon in front of the shop with the motor running to keep the air conditioning on. We took turns with the help of Helen and her sister Sally, our part-time waitresses, loading the wagon with the chafing dishes and table supplies first, then the beautifully decorated platters and trays that would have made the buffet look absolutely stunning. We had loaded everything and decided to go back into the kitchen and make sure we had everything on our packing list. Our inspection concluded in a few minutes and we opened the door to the outside. To our horror, the station wagon was *gone*!

We screamed, yelled, cried in disbelief, and finally called the police. The hardest part was calling Mary and telling her that her guests were going to fast that evening: the station wagon with all its contents had been stolen. She had to find another way to feed them. The cops were in our shop asking tons of questions, and we could not leave until they finished their investigation. We had no idea how long that would take.

Mary was sympathetic, and although she was left in a bind, she had only words of encouragement.

"Don't you worry, Emilia. I will notify the priests, and we will come up with some other solution for the dinner." Soon after, Father Dan was on the phone.

"Everything will turn out all right, Emilia. We are all praying for you and Lena. Trust God to bring this episode to a quick ending." Father Dan's voice was calm, and it fell like soothing balm on my frightened heart. About fifteen minutes later, a call came from the police station to the cops that were with us. The conversation went something like this:

"Really! Wow! Do you mean it is there? No accidents involved? That's great! We'll pass on the good news!" The cop hung up the phone and turned to us with a smile. "They have found your station wagon!" he said.

"Do you really mean that? Where is it? Can we go and get it?" I was so excited I wanted to fly to where it was located. Then I stopped, thinking that most likely, everything in the van had been damaged, especially the food, and that thought pushed me to another level of anxiety. The cops kindly suggested locking the shop and following them. When we arrived in Pembroke Park, approximately five miles from our shop, the cops turned on a side street, and there against the curb was parked my station wagon.

I jumped out of our friend's car followed by a trembling Lena. We walked towards the station wagon and peeked through the back windows. Then we turned to each other in disbelief, amazed. Everything was intact, even the fancy trays. What a miracle! Now if the cops would only let us go, maybe…maybe we could still be in time to cater the party for Mary, but there was no way to budge the cops. They had to do their work and tow the wagon to the police station to search for fingerprints. They wanted to find the culprit.

The cops called a tow truck to the scene. A chain was attached to the front of the wagon and it was dragged to the police station a short distance away. Almost three hours later, we were free to leave the police station and return to our shop with all the contents in perfect form. The weather miraculously cooperated that night and the temperature stayed very cool, which kept the food safe enough to put it back into our refrigerators and reschedule the dinner, with Mary's approval, for the next day.

It all turned out well. The police told us a few days later that two teenagers had seen us load the wagon from across the street and decided to pull a prank. I still wonder—how did all that food come out of the ordeal without being jostled around and ruined after being subjected to a bumpy ride at great speed? Thinking back, I believe Father Dan's prayers surely prevailed.

The Christmas holiday season normally is the busiest season for caterers. Our second year in business approached with greater expectations on our part. We were already booking several Christmas parties, ranging from large cocktail affairs to sit-down dinners. We had to hire several waitresses, waiters, and bartenders.

Meanwhile, to our surprise, phone calls arrived with strange requests. Customers we had catered various parties for were interested in buying the homemade, frozen hors d'oeuvres we served at our parties. Requests were coming in anywhere from five dozen to as many as ten dozen.

What terrific opportunities! We began packing and selling in plastic containers dozens of crabmeat wontons, spanakopitas, empanadas, almond dates wrapped in bacon, and cheddar cheese puffs, just to name a few.

Word of mouth spread fast, and I recognized that this side business could be developed to increase our income. Lena did not see it the same way. She could not see the point of selling tiny morsels for a few cents per piece. To make a decent profit, we would have to sell thousands of them, she reasoned. In a way, she was right—enough orders to allow us to produce large quantities were necessary to make selling hors d'oeuvres worthwhile. Lena was also having second thoughts about staying in business, since the landlord now insisted we sign a five-year lease. Sometime during the spring, Lena and John decided to call it quits and sell me their shares of the corporation for the five hundred dollars they had paid for them only two years before.

I was now alone and free to make any decision on my own. During previous years, I had had to share my life and views with other people, thinking I needed help. Well, I had been wrong! The first thing I promised myself was to never, never, never go into business with anyone again, not even my brother. I swore that from then on I was going to make it only with the help of God. No more partnerships!

First on my list was a name change. I called my lawyer and the name of the company became Holiday Caterers. I thought it had a happy, festive ring to it and was easy to remember. I kept Vince at bay for a couple of months, then signed a lease for five years, as he requested. For some reason I expected the business to grow—but I never imagined my little company in a few years would be known as one of the best food companies in the United States.

I bought an answering machine for my office, and that summer I went to work at the Seafare Restaurant in Dania Beach. I got a job assembling the salads on the menu. That little extra money kept me going until the beginning of the season. At the Seafare, my coworkers called me Emily, and that name has stayed with me ever since. I also met Steve, the expediter, and when he told me he was also a bartender, I hired him to tend bar at the weddings and cocktail parties I was booking for the Christmas season.

After work, I always stopped by my shop to check the answering machine for messages. I was surprised at how many people called, leaving their phone numbers and sometimes even orders for hors d'oeuvres. That machine had just been introduced, and for me, it was the greatest invention on the market. Before I went to work, I filled and delivered every order, saving every dollar I could earn, aware that I had to roll all my profits into the business to keep it growing.

I was now the master of my fate. I worked hard and hired good help, and it seemed like everything fell into place. So much so that one day, after quitting the Seafare, around November, I received a phone call that jolted me like a lightning bolt.

"Hello, Emily! This is Steve Bruno. How are you?"

"What a pleasant surprise, Steve! I am doing well. How is Evelyn?"

I was happy to hear Steve's voice. We had been friends for many years, all the way back when we lived in New York. Steve had moved with his family to Fort Lauderdale around the same time I moved to Hollywood. I was closer to his mother Evelyn, but because of our demanding jobs, we had not seen each other for a while.

"What are you doing now?" I asked.

"I am one of the catering managers at the Diplomat Hotel, and I called because I heard you are making and selling hors d'oeuvres. Is that right?"

"Yes, it is," I said, a touch of pride in my voice.

"Do you think you can sell some of them to the Diplomat? They can't get this week's delivery in time from their supplier. They need crabmeat wontons. Do you think you can make them?"

I was silent for a few seconds, and then I thought what the heck; I can make anything for anybody, even the Diplomat Hotel. I heard myself say, "Yes, I sure can. When do you need them for?"

"I will need them for Friday morning, not later than twelve noon."

"Okay, Steve, no problem," I answered nonchalantly. "How many dozens of crabmeat wontons does the Diplomat need?"

Loud laughter made me pull the phone away from my ear. Then Steve said, "I need three thousand crabmeat wontons. Can you handle that?"

I almost fell to the floor. "Did you say three thousand pieces? Let me see—" My heart raced as I grabbed the calculator and divided twelve into three thousand and came up with two hundred and fifty dozen. No way could I make that amount of wontons in such a short time!

Sadly, I started to say, "Steve, I don't think—" I suddenly stopped and heard myself say in a calm, businesslike voice, "Okay, Steve, I will make them. Three thousand crabmeat wontons for the Diplomat Hotel delivered on Friday morning. But what should I charge per piece?"

I began writing the order on a pad.

Steve was nice enough to give me some tips on how to pack them— use shrimp boxes and pack about twenty-five wontons in each—and on how much to charge per piece. The other company's wholesale price was nineteen cents each for wontons, and he suggested I stay competitive and charge the same price. He also gave me the impression that if the chefs liked my wontons, they might keep me as their supplier and buy other hors d'oeuvres if they met their quality standards.

When I hung up the phone, I was shaking. Wow! Me sell hors d'oeuvres to one of the most prestigious hotels in South Florida? Was I dreaming? Reality set in as I began to ponder how to keep my commitment.

After a few deep prayers for help to the Almighty, I calmed down and assessed my predicament. I needed a plan that was feasible. First on the list was hired help. Who could I call to help me roll the wontons? I thought of my good friend Rose. She was out of a job and needed to work. She could come to the shop early in the morning and help me prep the filling. In the evening, my sister Toni, my daughter Linda, and another friend, Helen, could come in after work, and I would teach them how to fill and fold the wontons so that we'd hopefully have the order complete in a few hours. That night we were folding and frying wontons till midnight.

I had to figure out how many pounds of each ingredient I needed to make three thousand wontons. After some quick arithmetic, I had a shopping list for the food and the packing supplies. On my way to the market, my heart sank when I realized I had only a couple of skillets to fry these wontons. I needed a deep fryer, at least a commercial, top-of-the-counter fryer that would speed up the frying process. I stopped by Lee's Equipment and bought one on the spot. When I had everything in the house and figured out all the expenses, I knew I was losing money on this deal. I was risking the little capital I had saved in the bank, but I also knew that this first order gave me a chance to stick my foot in the door of the Diplomat, and I felt compelled to seize the opportunity at any cost.

By Friday morning, the wontons were taken out of the , freezer, packed in shrimp boxes, and I was on my way to the Diplomat. Dozens of trucks were also delivering merchandise to the hotel, and I still can't figure out how was I able to navigate through that maze. At the loading dock, I paged Steve, and he unloaded the wontons and took them to the kitchen with my invoice attached to one of the boxes. He then told me to wait. A few minutes later, he came back with an envelope containing the check. As he rushed inside again, he said, "Thanks, Emily, for not letting us down. The chef will be very grateful."

When I got back to the shop, I took the check out of the envelope and stared at it, fascinated, for a long time, reading over and over: Diplomat Hotel and Resort to Holiday Caterers, five hundred seventy dollars. It seemed impossible!. And yet…bells began ringing in my ears. This is only one of the hotels! What if I sell wontons to the Marrriotts? And the Sheridans? And the Hiltons? What if they also like my franks in the blanket and spanakopitas and…

Could I dare entertain such grandiose dreams? The answer was short and to the point: "Yes, I can." Those ambitious thoughts set me on a path I had never expected to take, not even in my wildest dreams.

CHAPTER 24

THE S.B.A. TO THE RESCUE!

By 1985, Holiday Caterers began to be known as one of the most reliable in the Hollywood community and one that provided some of the best food. Lacking money for advertisements, I had to rely on word of mouth for increased sales, and the word spread in every direction, like feathers in the wind. When you think about it, the food is the only item you remember long after a party is over. I made sure the food I prepared was always delightful to the eye and delicious to the palate.

For ideas, I searched many cookbooks and bought every issue of *Bon Appétit, Gourmet,* and *La Cucina Italiana* magazines. I became the greatest fan of Martha Stewart. I read her two very colorful and informative books, one published in 1982: *Entertaining,* and the other just off the press in 1984, *Hors d'oeuvres, the Creation and Presentation of Fabulous Finger Foods.* I also read cover to cover a book left to me by Mr. Denis entitled *Catering Handbook.* It helped me understand the do's and don'ts of the catering business. I learned a lot from the experts, but always added extra touches that gave each recipe or presentation I made my own individual signature, never skimping on quality, even if I sacrificed the profit. I really enjoyed my work.

By Christmas 1985, catering requests were coming in from Miami to Palm Beach and I was booking parties as small as twenty people to as large as one hundred people. I also learned how not to over extend myself when, to fill an order, I had to be up all night, and I mean twenty-four hours at one stretch, to prepare food for a party I thought I could handle.

I needed more space and more commercial refrigerators. I also needed *money.* Bob, the owner of Hollywood Equipment, a restaurant supplier near me, had one used commercial refrigerator and one freezer that would fit perfectly in my kitchen. The price: $2,000!

Where could I find that money? I was in a bind, and then I remembered Ruth Berger, my very good friend from Flushing and my ex-landlady. I mustered all my courage to pick up the phone and call her. I had never asked to borrow money from anyone. My pride getting in the way, I almost put the receiver back on the phone.

Then I remembered I had to keep the business going at any cost. The rent had to be paid, and I had to keep it going for my son Vinny, who was now well enough to spend a few hours a day giving me a hand without the pressures of a regular job, making him feel somewhat useful. I would have loved to have my daughter Linda work with me also, but she had just graduated from F.A.U. with a marketing degree, and we thought it best for her to acquire some experience with a large company. Moreover, she could make more money in a regular job and put in extra time working the parties on weekends with me.

When I heard Ruth's voice on the other end, I felt so much better to hear her sincere words of optimism and support. She was very gracious and understanding of my plight and told me she would have the check in the mail the next day. I went back to the equipment supplier to make sure he had not sold the refrigerator and freezer. To my dismay, he had, but he promised that he was getting more in and told me to come back in a couple of days.

I still get a knot in my throat when I think about the events that followed three days later. Ruth's letter arrived, and when I opened it, a check for four thousand dollars fell out of a note that simply said, "You will need the extra I'm sending you. Enjoy and God bless!" She sent me double the amount I had asked for! With tears streaming down my cheeks, I thanked God for my very, very special *one of a kind* Jewish friend. Without wasting time, I got in my beige cargo van (I had traded in the station wagon) with the Holiday Caterers' logo painted on both sides, and headed to see if Bob had received the equipment.

Another surprise was waiting for me as I entered the showroom. Bob pointed at a couple of stainless steel refrigerators and freezers that looked almost new. I opened their doors and gasped in amazement! These two fixtures, unlike the other two, had slots inside exactly the way I needed them for storing the hors d'oeuvres. Was this another of those God incidents? He always turned good out of bad circumstances. Here I had the unequivocal proof.

Just as Steve Bruno had predicted, the Diplomat Hotel began ordering more products. Needing more space, I asked Vince to let me lease the warehouse next to mine that had just become vacant. He was thrilled to rent me the empty facility, and I was able to hire more staff to make hors d'oeuvres in Warehouse #2. By this time, I knew I was into something big. If the Diplomat was using my products, why not try to sell to other hotels?

Was it possible?

The catering business was growing, and so was the wholesale part of it. I needed to hire more staff for both divisions. It was quite common then for waitresses, waiters, and bartenders to knock at a caterer's door and ask for work. One day, one of those knocks brought in Joe and his wife Grace. We liked each other immediately, and I hired them on the spot. Both were excellent at tending bar and serving guests and quickly became very skilled at making hors d'oeuvres, even supervising other workers.

Another knock at the door a month later introduced me to Licia, a very talented lady who had worked for other caterers but was now looking for a job. I hired her immediately, and she created for our buffet parties some of the most beautiful fresh fruit and vegetable displays I have ever seen. They were works of art and greatly admired by every customer. It seemed that without even looking for them, the necessary people were joining my company and I was growing and growing and growing.

Around the middle of 1986, my daughter Linda got married and moved to Marco Island, while another event fell in my lap, mitigating the void. Steve Bruno came back with another request from Gene Wigger, the catering director at the Diplomat. Could we make *canapés*? These were labor-intensive creations and usually demanded a high price. I used to call them open-faced sandwiches, and on rare occasions, I had served them on ornate trays or fancy mirrors when I was catering a more up-scale function. They made such an elegant presentation.

Of course, I said yes to Steve immediately, and the next day, David, the garde-manger chef of the Diplomat came over my kitchen to show us exactly how he wanted them to appear. From then on, to my delight, I put Licia in charge of that department, and we supplied canapés for the Diplomat for several years until it closed down, heavily damaged by a nasty fire.

Another big break came when Gene Wigger quit his position there. He was hired at the Marriott Harbor Beach Hotel in Ft. Lauderdale. Noticing the difficulties the garde-manger chef was having at the Marriott to make canapés, Gene suggested calling Holiday Caterers to supply them. I was called to visit their kitchen and look at their creations so I could figure out whether I could duplicate them. Looking at their samples, I assured them I was very able to supply them. That morning, I went back to my kitchen with a new prestigious customer on my list.

Was I excited! Now I was sure there was a future in pursuing the wholesale part of the business. With the catering division, I was limited to a small part of south Florida, but with the wholesale division, my potential was limitless. I could grow not only in South Florida, but also over the whole state. In time, even the whole United States could be within my reach!

Wow! The vision that had started as a tiny seed was becoming a giant tree. Could I dare? Could I expect God to do great things in my life? Yes, I could. Encouragement came unexpectedly from someone very well known in the food industry and with a lot of power to make things happen. I was catering a wedding that weekend, and during the function, I noticed a gentleman approaching the buffet table several times, adding food to his plate from the chafing dishes and smacking his lips every time he put some small morsel in his mouth.

Curiosity creeping up inside me, I felt compelled to introduce myself and ask how he liked the food. He was tall, on the heavy side, with bright eyes and a kind smile that complemented the soft tones of his voice.

"Excellent, Emily! Your food is simply delicious! Look how many times I have helped myself! I can't resist the flavor!"

"Thank you so much for the compliment!" I said.

"By the way," he added, "I really liked the hors d'oeuvres. Did you make them yourself?"

He put his hand in one of his pockets, pulled out a business card, and casually handed it to me. I barely glanced at the card, put it down, then quickly looked at it again and gasped when I recognized the name and logo. I was talking to the legendary Joe Sciortino, well known C.E.O. of the huge Sysco Food Service Company, the largest broad line food distributor in Florida.

Taking advantage of the moment, I asked him if, in his opinion, I had a chance of marketing the hors d'oeuvres.

"Emily," he said, putting his hand on my shoulder, "I know you are selling this product direct to some hotels in the area. You have a great line, and if you decide to put it on the wholesale market, I promise you I will make sure we pick it up."

I was ecstatic. Sysco carry my product? Every one of the fifty states has one or more Sysco houses in their territory. Gradually, I could approach other houses. The future looked extraordinarily bright. Soon, I was ordering simple, wholesale catalogs from a printer close by and mailing them to all the hotels in the area. I was becoming really ambitious! Anticipating many orders, I leased another empty warehouse (Warehouse #3) next to mine, and installed a 12' by 12' walk-in freezer to store the hors d'oeuvres and a 6' by 6' walk-in refrigerator to store the food supplies. I was growing in leaps and bounds in sales and square feet of working area, reinvesting every dollar I made right back into the company.

By 1988, I was selling my line of gourmet frozen hors d'oeuvres to several Marriott hotels, Sheratons, Hiltons, prestigious country clubs from the east to the west coast of Florida, and even a few products to Disney World's hotels. As the business increased, so did the expenses. We delivered locally with the used cargo van I had purchased about a year before, but now I had to contract with Alterman, a shipping company that transported exclusively frozen foods throughout the states. During the year I also leased Warehouse #4 (next to #1) and Warehouse #5 in the back of the building, where I had to install a large 15' by 30' foot freezer.

I was expanding fast and building a great relationship with executive and banquet chefs from many hotels around the area. I gained popularity when they realized they could depend on me and call on me with special requests. I never promised them anything I could not make or deliver on time. I understood the enormous pressure the chefs are under in the hotel's kitchens, where numerous banquets are going on at the same time, and I did my best to prepare everything to perfection and make them look good.

One time, the chef of a prominent hotel placed an order for ten thousand canapés, to be ready in two days. The hardest part for me was getting the supplies in and then organizing production and coming up with an efficient assembly line that could cut the processing time down. For one full day and way into the night, the whole plant, all thirty-five employees, scooped, sliced, cut, and piped the mousse; sliced the meats, cheeses, and olives; spread compost butter and caviar on multi-shaped mini toasts and tartlets; and then decorated them with tiny leaves of parsley, dill, and tiny florets of truffle paste. Cherry tomatoes, cucumber rondelles, Belgian endive leaves, celery sticks, artichoke bottoms, and the decorated toasts and tartlets were gracefully lined up on top of sheet pans. The order of ten thousand canapés was completed by midnight and delivered the next morning as promised.

By watching my competitors' displays at food shows I attended at the Convention Centers in Miami and Orlando, I learned to introduce, pack, and market frozen hors d'oeuvres as they did, but I always kept my eyes open for new ideas and ways of doing things. One day, I was assembling a beef wellington order for a party we were going to cater that evening, when I thought I would try to make a mini version to add to my list of hors d'oeuvres. As far as I knew, there was no mini beef wellington on the market. Sure enough, the new creation looked and tasted so delicious that it became one of our best sellers, and afterwards, it was much imitated in the industry.

Someday, I said to myself, my company will be inside one of those booths! Wishing was one thing, but how could I make such dreams come true? The more I dealt with the hotels, the more I thought about dropping the catering and retail part of the company and concentrating on the wholesale part, where sales could reach every state in the United States. I needed to move into a USDA (United States Department of Agriculture)-inspected facility, where I could have everything under one roof and not split into many rooms. I also needed to be in a USDA plant to be able to ship out of the state.

Salespeople and business friends suggested I look into finding venture capital, but the thought of having to deal again with other people that would almost become partners made me give up that idea immediately. Was there another way to get capital? I turned to the banks, but when I could not provide them with collateral, they turned me down. I thought that was the end of all my hopes. One day, a flyer arrived in the mail and caught my attention. Was this another of God's incidences?

I usually threw away all the advertisements, as I had no time to read them, but this time my eyes fell on the large black letters on the golden paper that said something to this effect: "The S.B.A. (Small Business Administration) wants to loan capital to any entrepreneur willing to start up or expand a business. This is a government program that helps small businesses expand and hire more employees." There was a phone number and a location to contact a representative for guidance and advice. Could it be possible? The government wants to give money to business people? I read the flyer repeatedly and then decided to call. What the heck? I had nothing to lose.

I made the phone call, and to my surprise, someone at the other end seemed very interested in knowing more about my type of business and my need for capital. They gave me an appointment for the next day. The address they gave me was the Florida Atlantic University branch on Commercial Boulevard in Ft. Lauderdale, and the office to go to was the Small Business Development Center (S.B.D.C.). I arrived there with my son Ricky, who had come back into the family fold with his lovely wife Gabriella and a gorgeous little girl, Daniella. They both worked with me, and so did Martha, Gabriella's sister, and Carlos, her father.

After a brief wait, we were introduced to a wonderful lady by the name of Rona Helman. I was impressed by her interest in my company and kindness toward me. She spent more than an hour explaining in detail the benefits of this program and how I could benefit from it. I had mentioned that I needed close to three hundred thousand dollars to build the plant, and she seemed to think I could qualify for it. There was only one catch. I had to be willing to put up my home as collateral. Rona gave me a bunch of papers to look up, fill out, and if I consented to the terms, bring back to continue the process.

"Go home, Emily," she said with a smile. "You have a great company! Don't be afraid to apply for this loan. It is a big decision to make, and I think you will make the right one."

It seemed she believed in me. I went out of the office with stars in my eyes. Could it be possible the American government was willing to gamble on a sixty-one-year-old woman who should be thinking about retiring instead of running a business of that caliber? Should I try it? Many of my friends discouraged me, but I knew I had to follow that small voice whispering inside. My intuition kept telling me, "Go on, Emily, go on!"

The biggest obstacle seemed to be putting up my home as collateral. What if the business failed? My home was the only security I had. At my age, I was facing being alone again. My son Ricky, not quite happy with his work, was thinking about leaving and pursuing another road, and soon after, he moved away. My son Vincent was having bouts of illness and spending less time in the plant, while Linda and her husband had moved to London. I was alone making such a crucial decision.

I attribute the courage I had to risk it all to prayers and the belief that God was with me all the time. When I thought about making that drastic leap of faith, I felt confidence in the inner part of me. I filled out all the papers and went back to the S.B.D.C. and Rona. I signed the application for the loan, and I was told to come back with a marketing plan to present to the bank. In no time at all, I was approved for a two hundred seventy-five-thousand-dollar loan to be paid back in eight years and at a very reasonable interest rate.

What a miracle! *Only in America* could this happen. My home was only worth seventy-five thousand dollars at the time, and the American government was willing to take such a risk on a little old lady from Italy. The only thing I could say was "God Bless America." What happened with that money would demonstrate exactly what the proverbial American Dream is all about.

CHAPTER 25

OUR NEW MANUFACTURING PLANT

First on the agenda was another company name change from Holiday Caterers to Holiday Foods. I was leaving the catering world behind and entering the world of food manufacturing just as I finally had some help from a family member. Although I wasn't happy to see my daughter go through the pains of a divorce, I was glad she could join my company and be a vital part of it, just as I was making such drastic changes.

I had all the documents necessary for Nations Bank, the bank that would disburse the loan, with one exception. I had to submit accurate plans for the plant before they could release any money. For days, I searched for a facility suited to my purpose. I wanted a location in Hollywood that had a possibility for growth and a large enough parking lot to accommodate all the employees I intended to hire. I surveyed many warehouse complexes in the neighborhood and nearby communities, but nothing suited my needs.

I almost gave up hope as this dream kept moving farther away, when one blessed day, as I returned home after a long, stressful, and busy day at work, something phenomenal happened. Driving north on 21st Avenue to reach Sheridan Street, about five blocks up from my the present location, a huge sign with the picture of several buildings flashed by my right side window. I made the first U-turn and went back for another look.

I stopped the car, looked at the sign, and my heart started to beat with excitement. Here at last, almost under my nose, was what I was searching for. On the lot in front of me, empty for years, a large board displayed a sketch of three buildings with several warehouse spaces that were going to be built on the site and be put up for lease. I jotted down the telephone number and went home with sugar plum dreams in my head. The design of this group of buildings on that board had everything I needed, as though they were designed just for me. What I liked most was the large number of parking spaces shown in the picture. I could have never imagined that in a few years, I would occupy most of those warehouses. Was that another of God's incidences?

Early next morning, I called the number listed on the board and arranged for an appointment with the agent in charge. He showed me the plans for the front warehouse and pointed to the very first one on the corner with six thousand, five hundred square feet of space and two thousand dollars per month rent. The figure was reasonable, and told him I would come back with the answer in a couple of days. Now that I had found the locality, I had to come up with six thousand dollars to cover the first and the last month of rent plus the security deposit.

I was faced with another great dilemma, as I had nowhere near that amount in my bank. I had more than that in assets, but it was all tied up in receivables. Again, I had to turn for help to other old friends from New York City, who had retired and were living nearby. Sam and Sally Vecchio were real business people. For many years, they operated a large Italian bakery in Manhattan, producing a delicious Italian "crusty" bread and proudly marketing it wholesale and retail. They had also a profitable Italian specialty grocery store. I had confided in them all of my business's evolution and I knew they would understand my circumstances. I hesitated at first, and then I picked up the phone and dialed Sam's number.

"Hello, Sam, this is Emily!"

"Hi, Emily. How are things getting along in the business?"

"Great, Sam, but I have to ask you a big favor. I have found the perfect location to transfer my operation, and I have to sign a ten-year lease. I need six thousand dollars, Sam. Can you loan it to me? I have nowhere else to go!" My voice began to crack, but Sam's voice came back to me, clear and reassuring.

"Of course, Emily, we have been friends a long time. I'm happy to help. I will be there tomorrow morning with the check." Thank God for good friends, and especially for Sam!

The next day, I signed a ten-year lease for that warehouse space. Now that I had the location, I wasted no time in calling the architect to draw up plans in accordance with USDA specifications. I knew what was necessary for our production to run smoothly, but I had to figure out how best to place the equipment in the kitchen, the processing and packing rooms, and the shipping platform. Somehow, I managed to convey to the architect all our needs, and when the plans were ready almost a month later, I submitted them to the inspector for approval.

"Plans approved!" I heard inspector Gene Moomaw's jubilant voice say when the phone rang a few days later.

"Thank you, Gene," I mumbled as tears streamed down my face. That was great news, indeed. Now I could get the necessary funds to go on with construction. Sometime in January 1989, work began, with the promise from the builder to have it finished by August. That was good timing for me. It would give us time to move before the busy Christmas season, when we had to fill the usual heavy demands for large orders.

Anyone who has had to deal with builders knows how frustrating it can be. Well, August arrived, and so did September and October. Still, there was no plant to move into. The builder kept giving excuses on top of excuses, but none of them were true. He had tangled himself with other projects that kept him busy somewhere else. I was in a panic. I braced myself for a difficult season and a lot of lost business. I could not supply what I could not produce, and that loss of revenue almost wiped me out completely.

In the first week of January 1990, Holiday Foods finally passed every inspection, obtained all the licenses required, including the cherished C.O. from the city of Hollywood, and with forty-five employees transferred operations from the old location to the new, state-of-the-art plant. What a triumphant day that was!

Before beginning the actual work that first day of production, I thought it proper to thank God first. I called all the employees, including Linda, into the processing room and asked them to form a circle. The temperature felt like zero degrees, although the large thermometer on the wall registered fifty-five. We all had big smiles on our cold faces, and everyone was eager to begin work; however, I needed to express my feelings before the start of this special day.

"Good morning!" I said with a big smile, as I elbowed my way to make a space among them.

They answered with a loud and resounding "Good morning!" Then a great silence fell in the room, and all eyes and ears turned toward me inquisitively.

"Isn't this a great day? We finally made it!" I said with an exuberant tone in my voice. They nodded in agreement and clapped hands for several minutes. This was time to celebrate. I motioned to Maria, my interpreter, one of the Spanish-speaking employees who spoke English very well, and asked her to translate the speech I was going to make. Most of the employees came from different parts of South America, but several came from Korea, China, and the Philippines.

Jubilant first, I then felt a lump forming in my throat. My eyes welled with tears and my voice revealed all the emotion in my heart. "I want all of you to know," I said, trying to hold back the quiver in my voice, "that here at Holiday Foods we are a 'family.' I am the head of this household, and you are working for me. As you see it, you depend on me for your jobs, but I depend on you to accomplish this job. In other words, we need each other. I want you to feel like persons on a mission, the same as I have a mission. I want you to remember that each of you is special. There is only *one* of you in the whole world, and that makes you special. We all rely on one boss—God. We are all working for Him, so He is my boss as well as yours. At the end of each day, we will ask ourselves, 'Have I done my best?' In our hearts, we will know the answer!"

I looked around the room and saw their heads nodding. I continued, "During the day, if anything bothers you or if you have a problem you need help with, please come and talk to me. My door will always be open, and I will always make time to listen to you."

As Maria translated my words, their eyes filled with tears. They understood that even though I was their boss, I was approachable, and they believed I meant what I said with all my heart. And I did mean it all—the hardships I had endured at a young age and the long years of war I had lived through had made me value people, all people, more than any material object—a value I still hold dear.

"So," I continued, "I would like from now on to begin each day with a prayer. This will be a *voluntary* action." I made sure they understood that. "It will be on my time. We will meet here at eight A.M. after the second bell. Anyone who doesn't want to participate will wait in the corridor until we end our prayer time. You will be treated just the same, and I will respect the choice you make."

I felt a wave of approval for what I said and a wave of relief. I am a firm believer that when you give respect, it always comes back to you. It is also the right thing to do. In my opinion, my manager and dishwasher were equally necessary for the operation of the company, and I made it a point to give them equal respect.

"We will meet here every morning at the sound of the second bell and pray for ten minutes. Is that okay with you?" An enthusiastic and warm yes resounded loud and clear. We joined hands and closed our eyes. My prayer started like this:

"Thank you, Father, for the privilege you are giving me to be the captain of this ship. I hope to be worthy and to reflect in my actions the qualities you have shown me by imitating your life. Help me to be a good steward. Give me the wisdom I will need to navigate this ship as it begins its journey in uncharted territory. You hold in your hands our today and all our tomorrows. Teach us wisdom, patience, respect, and most of all how to love each other. Bless the hands of all these people as they bring forth the products that will bring all of us prosperity! Bless and sustain all the needy people of this world. In Jesus's name, Amen."

Looking back to that day, I must say God really answered and blessed us abundantly. In the space of fifteen years, the plant grew to cover the front building, part of the side building, and most of the back building, employing as many as two hundred people during the high season. To achieve such a feat, I believe God was with us every moment of the journey. He was with us even when, almost six months later, it became obvious we needed more space, lots of more space.

Orders came so fast I had to hire my friend, Steve Bruno, to supervise a second shift from five to ten nightly. I urgently needed larger freezers to store products. Luckily, a warehouse almost double the size of mine was still empty in the same building. I decided to lease it and leaving the large freezer behind in the old location, moved into this warehouse. Business was terrific, but another obstacle made inroads in the course "of doing business." It had a curious name attached to its back: "cash flow." That is the money needed to pay bills, and it has to come out of your income.

I learned the hard way that without cash flow you could be easily wiped out. Here I was selling to all these big names: Marriotts, Hiltons, Sheratons, the Boca West and Doral Country Clubs, and I was running out of money to pay my suppliers. What was wrong with this picture? Simple! These big name accounts paid their suppliers, me included, in thirty, forty, and sometimes fifty days. My own suppliers had to be paid in seven days—at the most fifteen.

That long wait between payments made a deep dent in my check-book and kept me in a constant state of anxiety. Every week, I had to meet the payroll that was steadily increasing and pay my suppliers to get the products I needed to make *my* products. I desperately hoped for food distributors in our area to pick up my line. I was waiting especially for Joe Sciortino with Sysco Food Service to come through with his promise and begin to carry my brand. Distributors usually paid manufacturers in fifteen to twenty days, and that would give me room to operate. I could not even get a line of credit from Nations Bank, one of many that failed and closed doors during that period. Was there a way out?

Much to my surprise, going home after work one evening, an adver-tisement on the radio captured my attention. For the first time I heard the name "Factor," and my ears stood up as they explained how they were in the business of buying receivables for a fee. Could the solution be found using their services? I made a few calls the next morning and asked for advice from several friends. All of them were skeptical, and one of them even went so far as to tell me to stay out of their dealings: "Stay away from them! They are out to get any business that is in trouble like yours," someone admonished me sternly.

As usual, I paid attention to my inner voice. I called the Factor's office, and in a few hours, the principals of that company were in my office explaining in minute detail how their services could help me. They explained that they would buy the receivables every two weeks, keeping a percentage of the total as their fee. I listened well, and when our meeting was over, I had engaged them for one year.

Thanks to that decision, my company was saved. I only had to sacrifice a portion of my profits, but that was a small price to pay. From then on, I never asked anyone else for advice, and if anyone wants mine, I have only one answer: "Follow your heart and that small voice within you!"

A few months later, another of God's miraculous incidents happened when Eugene Grey another dear friend of mine working for Union Bank, made an appointment with me, bringing the Union Bank president with him to see if my account with the failed Nations Bank was safe enough to be transferred to their bank. I had a clear view of the parking lot, and as I saw them getting out of the car, the telephone rang. I turned and saw Linda with the biggest smile on her face, telling me that the purchasing agent of Sysco Food Service had placed the first order of three hundred cases. What perfect timing! Now I could tell the bank's president that Sysco was carrying our product line, and that was a big winner for Holiday Foods. That morning, Union Bank picked up the account, and I was able to use a line of credit whenever I needed to expand.

Expand we did. Very quickly! Linda became director of marketing and sales, and she took control of strategies necessary for growth. She relied on the most prominent food shows around the country to introduce our line into new territories. Focusing first on the Florida Restaurant Show in Orlando held yearly at the Convention Center, I came home with a big feather in my hat. The first time we set up our booth in that huge facility, a large crowd gathered around to taste the scrumptious hors d'oeuvres that were sending out such wonderful aromas all around our section.

For three days, we cranked out tray after tray of our best items from our portable ovens, and for three days, the crowds kept growing around our booth. It was amazing to see the salesmen from Royalty Foods, the distributor that had several large booths across our aisle, keep coming by to comment, "What a terrific line! Holiday Foods!" They kept eating and eating, smacking their lips. "We have to tell our boss Bobby Meeks to pick this up. We could sell tons of this stuff!"

"Yes, please do!" I would say with enthusiasm. I had tried selling Mr. Meeks the line for several months, but he had always turned me down. This time, on the last day of the show, when we were almost ready to break down the booth, Bobby Meeks came by and introduced himself. Then he gave me the good news—he was picking up my line. That was a perfect fit. In the vast Orlando area, Royalty Foods had a reputation as a very upscale distributor.

Every year, Holiday Foods was getting more recognition, and our creations were very much in demand. Executive chefs were our best salespeople, and oftentimes when they were transferred to other hotels in other states, they requested my line be brought in. Food brokers were knocking at my door, as they wanted to be our representatives. It was very satisfying to know my creations were being served at the banquets of prestigious hotels like the Breakers, the Ritz Carlton, the Boca Resort, and the Peabody. They were even served on Air Force One!

Linda traveled with our executive chef to set up our popular booth in many food shows around the country from Las Vegas to New York, from Alabama to Chicago, California, Wisconsin, Tennessee, from Washington, D.C. to New Orleans. Her grueling schedule kept her on the go for several hours a day interacting with potential buyers wanting to know how to receive a shipment. Business was increasing at a fast pace, and so was our work space and the number of employees. Almost every year, we had to add another warehouse, in which we built yet another processing room or freezer storage.

In 1995, Linda and I decided to venture into cyberspace and add a catalog division to our line and post it on the internet. We set aside one of the warehouses, and arranged it with a separate packing room and large freezer to hold the products and the shipping boxes. The front office was enlarged, and several desks with their own phone extensions were placed in cubicles. We had catalogs printed and mailed out in many directions, and we taped a thirty-second commercial to air locally for the holidays.

Meanwhile, much to my surprise, I received a request from the chef of a large Southeast supermarket chain to supply them with a retail box of our hors d'oeuvres. He preferred a black background with colorful pictures on the box. They were each to contain three kinds, twelve pieces per box, and we would have four different pre-packaged varieties to choose from. That put a lot of pressure on me, but it seemed a great idea to expand in supermarkets. That venue fizzled out when the chef that made the request fell from a ladder and was so badly injured he had to quit his job, causing my project to come to a squeaking halt.

In the middle of all those preparations, a phone call from Gene Wigger brought with it a very special offer. Was I interested in a brief television infomercial on the Food Network as part of a segment in the "Best of Modern Cuisine with Robin Leach"?

Gene was working for WTDT (Worldwide Target Demographic Television), a Deerfield Beach television production company. He explained that the company was taping segments featuring a variety of food and drink products geared for the Christmas holidays, and he thought my hors d'oeuvres were a perfect fit for that show. The price attached to this three minutes' exposure? Just $32,000 thousand dollars.

Who would have refused the opportunity to be associated with the fabulous Robin Leach on national TV, the celebrity who used to sign off with his famous catch phrase, "Caviar dreams and champagne wishes"? Not me! I told Gene I wanted that slot.

A few days later, we arranged to tape part of the segment in my plant and part at the Boca Resort Hotel. Executive Chef Bryan O'Neal consented to let WTDT tape the segment in one of their most sumptuous banquet rooms. The hors d'oeuvres were to be sent to the hotel, and Chef Bryan would display them on his gorgeous buffet tables. I knew Bryan well, as he often called in to have us make special items that used his own recipes. He was one of our nicest customers.

The production company promised to air the infomercial the first week of the month of November and run it for one week. It would be perfect timing. At the completion of all the taping, the producers brought me the proofs of the tape that would be aired for my approval. It looked terrific—all of it, including interviews with Linda and me. I prepared the offices in the catalog division bay with five desks and five telephones, hired and trained five extra ladies on how to take the orders, and trained others on how to pack with dry ice and ship Federal Express.

Everything and everyone was ready to take the hundreds of orders we expected for the first week in November; however, at the last minute, WTDT called with a change in the proposed airing. They could not tell me why, but they kept pushing it back first one week, then another week, and then another week after that. The month of December arrived with no infomercial in sight.

I was furious! I had met all the terms of the contract and WTDT kept giving me the run around. Finally, they notified me that it would be aired from the 17th to the 21st day of December, just before Christmas week. In my opinion, it was too late to generate any sales for the holidays. Still, getting national exposure on a show with Robin Leach had to produce some results.

I huddled with the girls in the office and we waited every day for the telephones to ring, but no calls came through the first day or any other day of that week. Was that possible? The infomercial was being aired, and I saw it every day at home. It was a beautiful infomercial with Robin Leach's voice enthusiastically proclaiming the great qualities of Holiday Foods and showing off the mouth-watering hors d'oeuvres on the exquisite tray arrangements set out on the buffet tables.

Was it possible that no one was interested in those items? Not even one phone call from a commercial that was aired nationally? How could that be? I closed down the offices in the warehouse and had to lay off the nice ladies I had trained for that job. I wondered why it had been such a failure. Well, I said to myself, I guess I was hoping too much. I win some and lose some, including $32,000 for a commercial no one was interested in. That was a bitter pill to swallow!

I didn't know that something very unusual had happened. Around the end of January 1996, I was summoned to the phone to speak to a person who wanted to explain something very important. I picked up the receiver, and a man, I don't recall his name, asked, "Did your company place a commercial on the Robin Leach show in December?"

"Yes," I answered, perplexed. "And why do you ask?"

"I don't know whether you are aware of it, but the telephone number at the end of the commercial was a wrong number!"

I gasped and grabbed a chair to sit down as a burst of anger and disbelief made my legs tremble. I could hardly say a word. The voice continued, "I wanted to place a large order for the holidays, and your products looked so appetizing, but when I called the number on the screen, an oil company in Pennsylvania answered the phone. They were very upset and irate because their telephone had been ringing constantly, asking for Holiday Foods, interfering with their business."

What a shock that was! I thanked the gentleman for his information and the oil company's phone number and said good-bye.

The infomercial had worked after all, but how could WTDT have made such an error? That wasn't right. My head was spinning, and I could not change what had happened, but maybe I should engage a lawyer and begin a lawsuit. Meanwhile, I called Aero Oil Company in New Oxford, Pennsylvania, and apologized for the inconvenience.

A week later, I received a letter from the company's controller that said in part:

"I have reviewed the events of December 17 through December 21 1995. During this period, an advertisement was broadcast using an incorrect 800-telephone number, which resulted in many phone calls that were meant for your company. These calls disrupted work in our delivery operations center, causing lost time, customer complaints, and delays in scheduling deliveries to our customers. The problem was finally reduced by Aero placing a block on calls outside of Pennsylvania." Then he went on to demand compensation for Aero's additional phone expense, lost work time, and repair of business relations with their customers.

I understood Aero's predicament and their right to demand compensation. We did get together eventually and put the matter to rest. As for WTDT, they had several outraged customers that one way or another had been swindled. A few months later, the company declared bankruptcy and vanished like smoke. I thank God I was able to escape without a scar from the devastation that Hurricane Andrew inflicted around us, but the scars left from the wounds inflicted by an unscrupulous businessman were painful for long while.

CHAPTER 26

"SPECIAL ORDERS" AND HOW WE FILLED THEM

Holiday Foods' name spread around South Florida at a pace I had never imagined. The popularity of the brand was much aided by the many news articles and awards that appeared in the *Miami Herald*, *Sun Sentinel*, *Money Guide, Inc., Boca Raton Magazine* and several S.B.A. publications. In many ways, in fact, I became a poster child for the S.B.A. I received the "Pace Setters" award from the *Miami Herald* on November 16, 1992, the "Small Business Person of the Year—South Florida District" from the S.B.A. in 1999, and the "Breaking the Glass Ceiling Award" from the Greater Hollywood Chamber of Commerce in 2002.

One very special honor the S.B.A. gave me was on November 16, 1995, when they brought a Russian delegation of about ten people, both men and women, to tour my plant. These Russian business people were brought to see how here in America, a woman like me, with no business education, but with determination, hard work, and most importantly, assistance from the government, was able to make it as big as I had. The Russians were impressed, indeed, also kind, and inquisitive. I kept in touch with some of those ladies for a few years, though as usually happens, our busy lives took other directions, and our contact with each other faded away.

If the Russians were impressed, I was even more so when the S.B.A. official escorting the group told me he had chosen three companies in South Florida to demonstrate how we do business in America: the Motorola Company, the Publix Supermarket Depot, and Holiday Foods. Can you imagine? Me in the company of such giants! *Only in America!*

I was also honored when on May 7, 2001 the S.B.A. called upon me to be a guest speaker at that year's Small Business Person of the Year Award presentation at the Diplomat Country Club. I was delighted to share the podium that day with John Offerdahl of the Miami Dolphins fame.

It is said that advertisement is the soul of a business. I was finding out just how much that is true—and much of the advertising for Holiday Foods cost us nothing, because articles about the company and me appeared in local newspapers, contributing to both my notoriety and success.

I think a friendly, honest relationship with chefs played a great part in the high reputation I had gained among them. I cultivated a great rapport with the chef's teaching staff at the Broward Culinary Art Institute in Ft. Lauderdale, at the Cordon Blue Culinary Institute in Miramar, and the Johnsons and Wales University in Miami. When the teachers gave lessons on the making and formulation of hors d'oeuvres and canapés during their curriculum, they would call me and ask if they could bring their class over to see firsthand how they were manufactured in a plant that specialized in those items.

I was always pleased to walk aspiring chefs through the processing rooms. I thought that in the future, some of them would become great chefs and they would remember to use our products. Wanting to increase their understanding of how a plant like ours operated and grew, at the end of the tour, I would have them go into the lunchroom and my chef would have ready a variety of baked mini-bites and offer the students the opportunity to taste the delicious creations. As they munched, I recounted the story of Holiday Foods and described how an investment of $1,000 had grown to these proportions. My speeches always motivated them to work with passion, to give the best of what they had to follow their vision, to hope without fear, to dream the impossible, and always, always, begin the day with a prayer.

"*If I can do it, you can do it! And this can happen* "only in America!" I would tell them.

They would leave shaking my hand, thanking me for the encouragement and the advice. It was gratifying to receive appreciative thank-you notes a few days later.

As I look back at the time I spent in that plant, I wonder how I made it through the many years of dedication and hard work. Thank God for good help and special friends like Steve Bruno, who assumed the role of general manager when the Diplomat burned down. Thank God for Linda, who took over the operations when in February 1999, I had a heart valve repaired and had to be absent from the business for more than a month.

I think of the times we had to jump through hoops to get the orders out, and some of those episodes will live in my mind forever. One morning, I entered my office and began reading through the messages neatly laid on my desk of those early morning calls that I had to answer. On top were the ones I had to answer immediately, followed by the ones not so important. On one side, I noticed a yellow pad with the handwritten note: "Urgent—call Jeff at Disney immediately."

Without hesitation, I dialed his office. We had being doing business with Disney World in Orlando for several years. They were one of our best customers, and Jeff was their food procurement agent.

"This is Jeff."

"And this is Emily. How can I help you, Jeff?"

"Hi, Emily, how are you? Thanks for calling back so quickly. I have a very special request for one of the hotels, and I am counting on you." Jeff was always to the point.

"Okay," I answered with a little apprehension in my voice. "Let's hear it."

"There is a special function booked for Saturday at one of the properties, and the chef needs one thousand chicken breasts filled with special ingredients. I know this is a short notice, but you have to do it; it's very important!" With that introduction he listed the ingredients that would be part of this special recipe—and yes, "special" is a good word to describe the rare and hard-to-find ingredients. I scribbled as fast as I could on the pad I had in front of me.

"Jeff, how can we possibly find these items in such a short notice?"

"Don't worry, Emily," Jeff assured me. "They are being delivered to you in the next hour or so. I called the suppliers myself, because I know they always oblige me."

That was so true. Every manufacturer and supplier in the nation wants to do business with Disney, and the lucky ones like me who got orders from the "Happiest Place on Earth" made haste to fill their demands, no matter what. Disney business was not only good, steady business—Disney always paid on time.

"Call me back with the price, and try to keep it low, okay? We will have our truck pick up this order on Friday morning, and probably I will add other items to it. Thanks, Emily."

His phone clicked, and I stood there quietly for a minute, thinking about the next steps. This was short notice, even for Disney. It meant that in two days, we were going to squeeze production of one thousand chicken breasts, prepared according to a special recipe, between all the other orders coming in, but I knew Holiday Foods was up to the job. We had to add a double shift, and with all of the employees of the meat room, the order was done and ready to go on that famous Thursday.

Another order that stands out in my mind is the one we received from a Texas Convention Center, this time for a special request of thirty thousand canapés. Yes, you read that right! *Thirty thousand!* For two days, the whole plant worked on that order and had it ready when the truck arrived from Texas to pick up the canapés.

And how can I forget that memorable Friday when Al, a loyal distributor in our area, called us with his special request? Being Friday, the phones were ringing constantly that morning in the customer service area. Liz, one of the girls in that department, buzzed me.

"Emily, Al is on the line and wants to talk to you. He said he needs something very special for Boca West Country Club." Al was the best salesman any company could hope for. Sometimes, however, he made me nervous. He was working for North Star Seafood Company, and his company's sales covered most of the southern and middle part of Florida. Al sold our products to some of the top hotels and country clubs in our area, and if he had a request for something special, I was more than happy to make just about anything.

That is how Holiday Foods became indispensable to the chefs of some of the most prestigious hotels and country clubs in Florida. I knew the pressure they were under. I had then and still have a lot of empathy for these great chefs, because I had walked in their shoes. Having been the owner of two restaurants and having been in the kitchens for many hours, I know chefs are under great pressure and deserve mountains of respect. They also deserve reliable service. I always filled their orders on time and never made promises I could not keep, and thus deserved the best name on the street.

"Okay," I said. "Pass him on to me."

"Hello, Emily. How are you?"

"Fine! Fine! Al, what is it this time?"

"Well, I have a special request from Chef Garry at the Club. He wants you to make him 2000 franks-in-a-blanket, and no, he does not want the regular ones. This is what he wants: take a regular frank, cut it in three parts, and roll each part in puff pastry. Can you do that? He said he will put them on his menu and order them all the time!"

"Okay, Al, that is easy to do. They will be ready in a few days."

"Oh, no Emily! He needs them tomorrow!"

"Tomorrow? How in the world… Let me call you back." I began to panic. I paged Danny, our executive chef, asking him to come to my office. Two minutes later, he appeared with a puzzled expression on his face.

"What is going on?" he asked. "Another immediate request?"

"Yes, Danny, we are going to make…let me see…2000 franks… Let me see, what name shall we give them? I know: 2000 Franks *a la* Garry!"

"Franks *a la who*?" inquired Danny, sounding a little annoyed. Slowly, I explained the order that had come through and asked him to take care of it. He knew that when I committed to fill an order, there was no room for hesitation. Grumbling, he turned on his heels and proceeded towards the processing rooms in the back.

Suddenly, he stopped and turned again toward me. "Sure!" he mumbled sarcastically under his strained lips. "I bet Garry said this was a pop-up, right? I am sure he had this order on his desk for a few days! He thinks he can snap his fingers and—" Danny was sounding very frustrated.

At that moment, I found it necessary to refresh his memory and bring him back to reality. "Danny," I retorted in disbelief, "have you forgotten how many times you called me with these same kinds of requests that used to drive me insane? You were working at the Marriott Harbor Beach then, and when you were promoted to executive chef at the Marriott Biscayne, do you remember, Danny, how many times you made me jump through hoops to fill your special orders?" I fumed as I remembered those days. "Were those always 'pop-ups,' as you used to call them? Maybe you waited for the last minute to call them in. Now I know the truth. " I continued with mockery in my tone. "It is different now that you are on the other side of the fence and sitting in the hot seat. You have been working here several years now and are still surprised at what happens in this plant?"

I just shook my head, puzzled at his attitude. "Come on, Danny, don't complain. We have a large staff here and you can coordinate production in no time. Just move some of the people from #1, some from #4, and add them to #3. Let them all work together, and you'll have the order ready for Al as we promised. Think about the benefits you have by working here. No night shifts into the wee hours of the morning, no work on holidays or Sundays!" I tried to bring some humor to the situation.

"Okay, okay!" I heard Danny laugh as he made his way out of the office. That was Danny!

CHAPTER 27

THE END OF THE LINE

I could spend hours and hours reminiscing on the past, but today, my album of memories is posting the last pictures of this extraordinary adventure.

I see myself on the morning of January 20, 2006. I have a very important appointment to keep. Today, this ship called "Holiday Foods" will change skipper. My journey is coming to an end. I have reached my destination and anchored in a quiet lagoon. My future is about to become a life of pleasure and long-needed relaxation. I have to be at the lawyer's office by ten with Linda, where we will sign a contract with the Schwan Food Company, transferring ownership of Holiday Foods to them. I step out of my office and into the cluster of offices that made up the brain of Holiday Foods. From here, business has been conducted with great care and precision. Here orders for our products are received and scrupulously filled.

Being the top of the season, orders have been coming through very fast, and even the fax machine has been busy spitting out the orders on neat long sheets of paper. All the noise generated has been music to my ears, but now it is time to go.

"Mom, we better leave if we are going to get there to sign the paperwork on time," says Linda, tapping me on my shoulder. I reach for my bag and start toward the exit door, assuring everyone that we would be back in a couple of hours. We climb again in the SUV and head for the attorney's office. Hardly exchanging a word to each other along the way, we arrive about ten minutes earlier than we had expected. I look at her beautiful face and can see the emotional and physical exhaustion that I feel. I again ask myself if we are doing the right thing. We have a very successful business that took years to build, and we are going to place it in someone else's hands.

Well, that's that, I say to myself as Linda helps me out of the SUV.

"Cheer up, Linda, let's look forward. Anything you want to say?" I ask to see if she has any last-minute regrets.

"No, Mom," she says quickly. "I just want it to be over soon, so we will be free. It is time that you think of yourself and make a life—a real life with no more worries." I agree with her and we walk towards our attorney Charlie Morgan's office. Linda opens the door, and we look at each other as we make our way through. I know she is trembling on the inside, just as I am. We turn the corner, and there is Charlie's office.

Again, Linda opens the door and makes me go in first, and there we are on the cool, shiny tile floors facing a cutout image of Don Shula that is so lifelike I almost say hello to him. Charlie is a great Dolphins' fan and very good friend of Coach Shula and many of its players. It was no surprise that the walls of his office and the shelves of his bookcases are gracefully decorated with precious Dolphin memorabilia.

As we are escorted into Charlie's office, my attention falls on the stunning portraits of Marabel Morgan, Charlie's wife, adorning the walls of the corridor. I met Marabel briefly, and I greatly admire her accomplishments as a writer. She is a sought-after motivational speaker who has a soft-spoken natural beauty and a very talented artist.

Behind his large desk, Charlie is busy organizing the many bundles of paper in front of him. He quickly rises, walks briskly around, and we shake hands and exchange cordial greetings. Charlie steps back and returns behind his desk, motioning us to take our seats. Of medium stature, mature in years, with a soft voice and bearing, he makes us feel very comfortable. No one else has arrived yet.

Charlie smiles and asks, "Are you ready?"

Linda and I try to look normal, calm, and collected as we settle into the comfortable chairs. I manage to smile and utter a feeble, "Yes, we are ready."

Finally, it is here. The moment that is going to change our lives has arrived. Is it possible? Please, somebody pinch me! I glance at the tall packs of typed paper neatly arranged on the desk, and I know that their pages contain my destiny. One pack for me, one for Linda, one for Tony Jacaruso, our accountant, and one for Don Franza, our CFO. Others are for the Schwan people.

These are the contracts meticulously agreed upon after hours and hours of revisions. I have spent days going over them with my legal team and they are the results of heartrending negotiations that have taken endless months to complete. Now, in a few minutes, and with a stroke of a pen, we are finally coming to an end.

It takes a few minutes for all the parties involved to arrive. Schwan's representatives Kristy Griffin, and Kurt Battles and Brian Sattler, the Schwan attorneys, followed by Tony and soon after by Don. After the usual small talk, we all settle down and begin the task at hand—the sale of Holiday Foods, Inc. to Schwan Food Company. Page after page are passed around, read, and confirmed for approval. Impressive sounding words are exchanged, words unfamiliar to me, many of them terms used by attorneys in the exchange of their strange jargon.

I am not paying much attention to what is going on because I am sure my fate is in good hands. Charlie has gone over the whole thing with Linda and me and we know he has our best interests in his heart. My eyes keep roaming toward the high bookcases on the right wall of the office. The many rows of leather-bound law books stand as silent witnesses to the thousands of contracts that have been signed in that room, documents that have changed the course of many lives.

The moment has arrived.

"Well, Emily," Charlie says with a warm smile. "Here it is. You sign on this line."

He placed in front of me a very innocent-looking piece of paper. With the addition of my signature to it, my future will change drastically. I felt my hand tremble as I signed my name: Emilia Zecchino, President. On the other side of the page is a line for Linda Zecchino, Vice President, which she signs after me. The names of the others follow, and one by one, all sign on their lines. Our signatures are just strokes of a pen, but what weight they carry!

That little stroke has made us suddenly millionaires! Can you believe it? I know I built a great company that captured the attention of many food buyers around the country, and I received many great offers along the way, but this offer coming from such a huge company as Schwan's, has exceeded all my expectations. My main concern, of course, had been to sell it to the best company, one that would carry on the name of Holiday Foods without changing the core value of the products, and I wanted a company that would bring it to a higher level of sales.

Now, as I remember that life-changing day, the Schwan company proved to be the perfect fit. Ours was a marriage made in heaven. What makes a company great is its reputation in the marketplace, and Schwan has one of the greatest in the food industry. Holiday Foods' history in some ways reflects the history of the Schwan company. Years ago, in the small town of Marshall, Minnesota, Marvin Schwan found himself at the helm of a small dairy farm. His mother and father needed help running it, so Marvin took on the task, forfeiting his dream of becoming a pastor.

Milk became abundant, and Marvin had to think of ways to dispose of it at a profit. He thought, "Ice cream!" It was not long that the delicious ice cream he made became very much in demand in Marshall. Soon his sales and yellow gold freezer fleet of trucks expanded to sell in other towns, too. Then the trucks began to carry a bunch of other goodies all over Minnesota, and eventually to every state of the Union. What a feat!

Over the years, Schwan had ventured successfully into other specialty frozen food products that today are sold in many supermarket chains and are recognized by their popular names, such as Red Baron Pizza, Tony's Pizza, Freschetta Pizza, Mrs. Smith's Pies, and Mrs. Edwards' Pies. In Marshall, Schwan's corporate offices and manufacturing plants dominate the whole area, and almost everyone living there works for the still privately owned company, which is now a global powerhouse with more than twenty thousand employees.

Holiday Foods became part of this huge company as signatures were affixed and notarized. Finally, each of us received a copy of the contract. Vaguely, the customary congratulations and best wishes flew by my ear as we politely shook hands and said our good-byes. Bewildered, I got up from my chair, searching for words to express my feelings and could think of none. I was numb and speechless.

Suddenly, Linda's warm laughter brought me back to reality. Her arms folded around me, kissed me, and then suggested we celebrate. Charlie heard that and invited us for lunch at Shula's Steak House, joined by Kristy, the only Schawn representative who had a late flight back to Minnesota.

For the life of me, I do not remember what we ate for lunch. My mind was occupied with the next task for the day—how was I going to explain to one hundred and fifty people that Holiday Foods had changed hands and how this change would impact their lives? I knew at first that they would be shocked at this turn of events. They would be in fear of losing their jobs. It was up to me to gently break the news and convince them that, in fact, their jobs would be more secure, and that I was leaving them in very good hands. My head was throbbing. Lunch was soon over, and again we were in the car on our way back to the plant.

"We will sure remember this day, Mom!" Linda said with a smile as she maneuvered the car through the heavy midday traffic. "Now is time to be strong. I know you are not happy to have to inform all the people at the plant, but they have to know, and the sooner the better. I will be next to you as usual. Pray for courage. It will be hard, but we have to do it now. I will call Fausto, and you can explain to him first, then we will tell the rest."

Back at the plant, Linda summoned Fausto on the loudspeaker, and in a few minutes, he walked into my office. I could feel he had some vague idea that something of extreme importance was to be discussed, and as usual, he was very calm. Our dear Fausto, a bit overweight, suntanned, with a brown mustache and curly brown hair—his eyes looked deeply into mine and I knew he was searching for an explanation. I motioned him to sit in the chair in front of my desk.

A warm smile graced Fausto's round face and in reassuring tones he said, "Emily, I know there is something very important you have to say, but I want you to know that I will always support you in whatever you have to do."

That was Fausto. I knew I could depend on him for moral support and understanding. He was not so surprised when I told him that I was no longer the owner of Holiday Foods. Looking back at the happenings of the last few months, he had surmised that some changes were forthcoming, and he was delighted that a great company such as Schwan was going to be in charge of Holiday Foods.

"Fausto, you understand that I am seventy-eight years old, and it is getting very hard for me to run this company. I am so thankful that God is providing you with a great future, much greater than you could have had with me. Schwan has the resources to bring all the innovations that are needed in the next few years to make Holiday Foods a national company!"

"Yes, Emily, I understand perfectly well how hard you are working at your age, and I do appreciate the fact that you chose Schwan to be your successor, but…" His voice began to quiver as he got up and put his arms around me. "It will not be the same without you!"

"I know, Fausto. It will be difficult to adjust for me, too, but we have to be strong. Please assemble every one into the lunchroom so we can tell them the good news."

"I'll call you when everyone is there." He turned and quickly walked towards the back door into the plant.

Tears began to well in my eyes, and the sad feelings that changes usually bring on were taking over my spirit. Guilt crept into my soul. It is difficult to explain how hard it is for an owner to make decisions that will affect the lives of people that depend on you for a living. Even though I knew in my heart I was doing it for the best interests of all, I could not escape the skepticism that would be there at first. I had to find the proper words to convince them that their future was in much better hands.

Fausto was quick to assemble most of the employees in the lunchroom and called for Linda and me to address the gathering. I found myself looking at all these faces staring anxiously at me, waiting for an explanation for this unusual call. I felt the anxiety in their voices and compelling glances.

"What is going on?" "*Qué pasa?*" I heard a few asking in whispers.

Finally, Faustos's voice broke in with authority, "Please, everybody! Emily and Linda have something to tell you."

"Hi, everyone!" I said with a great smile. "There is something very special I have to tell you, and I want you to believe that it is something good."

I stopped to give Fausto time to catch up. His voice was strong as he translated every word into Spanish. "Many of you have worked here for many years," I continued. "Some as many as fifteen or more, and we are a very happy family. I always told you that although I own this company, I am not your boss. Who is your boss and mine, too?" I asked, as I often did.

They all shouted, "God."

"You are correct, and you will always work for God, no matter who owns this company. So it is with great pleasure that I tell you that as of today, the Schwan Food Company is taking over Holiday Foods."

The noise that had been muffled up to that point suddenly broke forth. "No, no, it cannot be true!" I heard them tell each other as they turned to me in shock.

"Please, please! Just listen to me," I pleaded. I wanted to soften what they thought of as a blow by reassuring them that this was the best thing to happen to Holiday Foods and its employees. "Schwan is a great company, a huge company, and all your jobs are secure with them for many years to come. Please, trust me. In a few years, Holiday Foods' products will be sold all over the United States." I tried to reassure them that the most important factor they had to consider was that under this new company, they had no fear of losing their jobs.

"I will be here for another six months, and Linda will be here for as long as she wants to be, so we are going to be around for a long time!" Yet I could see on their faces and hear in their voices that they were still unhappy and skeptical.

"I know this comes to you as a big surprise, but I want you all to give me a good look. What do you see? A very tired old lady! I am seventy-eight years old, and it is time for these aching bones to take a rest."

A rush of Ho! and Ha! hovered in the room as the ladies voiced their amazement and finally understood what I was trying to convey. I felt the unhappy atmosphere change to one of empathy. The women, all of whom were years younger than me, knew from experience how hard it was to stand on their feet all day, especially in that cold.

I reassured them that nothing would change in the company, and if it did, it would be for the better. I think I was able to reassure them. I saw smiles gradually return to their faces as they wished me good health and much happiness for my future. "You deserve it, Emily," I heard them say.

Well, it was over. My explanation was accepted, though I knew that it would take time for the idea of having a new boss to sink in. I turned to Fausto and asked him to end the meeting with a prayer, and when that was over, everyone returned to his or her stations. As they went back to their jobs, many of them said, *"Felicidades"* or *"Buena suerte*, Emily!" "Good luck!" I knew their congratulations were sincere. They had good hearts.

With a sigh of relief, I made my way toward my office, told the staff I needed some quiet time, and closed the door behind me. I slumped in the chair behind my cluttered desk, leaned backward, and closed my eyes. I was drained by all the emotions that had piled up since the morning. This was a day I would never forget, but how in the world I had made it to this point?

Surely, looking at what had just happened in a few hours, I perceived that today that elusive *American dream* had become reality. What was so special about me? There I was, almost at the end of my life, finally reaping what I had sown through years of sweat and tears. Words like "perseverance," "hard work," "sacrifice," and "passion" came to my mind. I believed in and practiced all those qualities, but there was more to my success than those character traits, important as they were and still are to my story.

What molds an individual to display such character? I asked myself. The answers were in my past. In my case, as far back as I could recall, a variety of events, circumstances, and crises had entered my life. I believe they came for one purpose only: to teach me compassion and empathy for people of every race in search of the basic needs and values universally longed for. Yes, that is true.

As I sat in that chair, my thoughts turned to the past, and pulling back the curtain of time, I remembered special people who had made a difference and touched my life, and the memories tumbled down at great speed. I felt the warmth of Mamma and Babbo's love; I sensed Richie's

269

gay laughter whispering, "Job well done!" while holding me in his arms; I felt Ruth Berger's smile as she softly whispered, "Mazeltov!" I recalled Regina Shearns's encouraging words, "You can do it!" I heard the chuckle in Steve Bruno's voice as I entered instructions for the cherished "first" order of "wontons" to be produced by our manufacturing staff for the renowned Diplomat Hotel.

To all of them, and to all others that inspired me in my journey, I will always hold a deep sense of gratitude. I will also be eternally grateful to my precious God for arranging every circumstance and placing everything in its proper order.

Reflecting on all the years gone by, I realized that it is in the process of time, through our experiences and the choices we make, whether good or bad, that we become who we are and do what we do. As God gives us the seeds, we have to be ready to water the garden, but *"only in America,"* where the fertile ground for success meets the needs of its seekers, do dreams become realities and visions take on solid form. Thank you, America! God did shed His light and grace on you. God bless America!

The Hallandale Digest

Thursday, June 17, 1993

Great beginnings!

The queen of first courses tastes success

Emily Zecchino at work in her Holiday Foods plant.

Andrew Goldstein/Digest News Photo

By Judith Stocks
Digest Food Editor

Emily Zecchino's day starts at 5 a.m.

She wakens and puts on the coffee. For the next thirty minutes she immerses herself in her bible to get grounded for the day.

By 7:30 a.m. she's at work, where she'll remain for the next thirteen to fifteen hours.

Maybe more.

And if it becomes necessary, she'll put in a night shift, too.

Unusual?

Well lots of people do it all the time. It's just that Emily Zecchino, at the age of 65, when most people are settling comfortably into retirement, is still vision-driven.

It began humbly in November of 1982, when Zecchino opened a small catering business with seed money of only $1,000. With it, she purchased as much used commercial cooking equipment as she could, and Holiday Catering was born.

From a tiny original facility just east of the railroad tracks on 21st Avenue in Holly-wood, where she did all the cooking herself, (including some back-breaking 24-hour double shifts), the business grew. And grew. And grew.

"My first year in business, sales were $25,000," says Emily. "Three years later they were $100,000."

As time went on, Holiday Catering evolved from a catering concern to Holiday Foods, a manufacturing plant specializing in wholesale hors d'oeuvres and

> *Entrepeneur Emily Zecchino came close to closing the doors of her business forever just two years ago. Sales this year are expected to hit the two million dollar mark. Changing the course of her success took more than luck.*

fancy canapes.

But, in spite of the growth, not all was rosy.

"I almost closed up 2½ years ago", says Emily. "We just had more expenses than revenue."

Zecchino, determined to try every way possible to make it work, used a factor to give her business the first turnaround it needed. (Factors are people who lend money on the security of accounts receivable.)

"I bless the factors," she adds. "even though many people advised me not to do it."

The second break came with approval to distribute her products through Sysco Food Services of Miami, the largest distributor in the nation.

Today, Zecchino is the matriarch of a $1.7 million dollar business that counts 1 chef, 2 cooks, 55 full-time and 25 part-time employees on its payroll.

Last year, she was endowed with The Miami Herald's Small Business Pace Setter Award, as one of ten small businesses honored for achievement. INC. Magazine has featured her in their pages and just last week, Money Magazine called her for an interview.

The best part of all this is that the more you learn about Zecchino, the business person and the woman, the more remarkable she becomes.

Italian born, she arrived in the United States as a war bride in 1947, unable to speak a word of English. For twenty years she and her late husband operated a grocery business in Flushing, NY and for seven additional years she withstood the grueling task of living the life of a restaurateur.

She is not at all what you would expect to find at the helm of a multi-million dollar business on the verge of yet another growth spurt that will place her in the rare category of self-made success stories. For while she is indeed driven and intensely committed, she handles herself in a subtle, dignified way that commands respect and admiration from all who come in contact with her.

Even though the business has grown beyond her wildest dreams, there is no shadowing ego to cut through . . . she is who she is. Above all else, Emily Zecchino, entrepreneur extraordinaire, is a lesson in human kindness . . . just a soft spoken women who believes with all her heart and soul in the golden rule.

Spending a day with Zecchino is like following an inquisitive, exploring toddler. Never sitting still for very long, she constantly pops up and down from her desk like a toy jack-in-the-box, tending to the endless tasks of running a food manufacturing plant with USDA approval for national distribution. The plant produces about 100 different kinds of fancy canapes and hors d'oeuvres, as well as custom-designing products, sometimes on short notice, for creative customers.

Rarely taking time out for simple pleasures, like lunch, Zecchino prefers to work right on through, and often the lunch that was heated up for her will sit for hours waiting for her to catch up with it.

She shares an office with Linda Smith, her right-hand person, who also just happens to be her daughter. Son, Vinnie, is also active on the scene, making this very much a family operation.

The portion of the small office where she sits, whenever she does, is simple . . . her brown swivel chair faces an African violet, a bottle of Maalox, assorted useage charts, equipment catalogues, reference books, cookbooks, and a few snapshots of her family.

Emily is delighted to no longer be fighting the battle of whether or not Holiday foods will make it, though she considers it a valuable lesson to recall the days when she couldn't afford to pay the booth fee for a food show to get the necessary exposure to grow the business.

"I could have moved along much faster if I would have just had a better cash flow," she adds.

Her days and nights are now spent planning for the next growth phase. Recently, two large empty bays in the complex where the business is currently located have been taken over as part of the latest expansion. Renovation of these warehouses is currently underway and plans are on the drawing board for new offices, new storage and production areas, new blast freezers, and a kosher-ing facility.

Always, Zecchino absorbs herself into the daily production activities. She is much like the mother of the plant, noticing everyone and every little thing. It is typical of her to take a few minutes out to talk to those who have dropped by seeking employment. The low-key interview is casual, friendly and caring. Much like Emily herself. She speaks kindly and with consideration to each person she encounters in a day.

Emily Zecchino is not the kind of person to be standing around and not doing something. Her constant activities are a necessary part of her constant re-creation . . . of the reach to the next level of renown. Besides, there are legions of wannabe entrepeneurs hustling and dreaming of being the next Holiday Foods. Success is like a bright light . . . and like a moth drawn to the flame, Emily Zecchino seems naturally drawn to it.

EMILY ZECCHINO'S SMOKED SALMON AND DILL STRUDELS

1 lb. finely chopped smoked salmon

1/4 lb. cream cheese, softened

1/4 lb. sauteed shallots

3 tablespoons dried dill

Phyllo dough

Melted butter

In a medium sized mixing bowl, combine salmon, cream cheese, sauteed shallots and dried dill. Mix with a spoon until well combined.

Cut phyllo dough into strips about 3 inches wide and 18 inches long. Brush strips with melted butter. Place a tablespoon of the salmon mixture at the bottom of the phyllo strip. Fold one corner over as you would to fold a flag, forming triangles. Brush top lightly with more melted butter.

Put aside until they are all completed. Place the strudels on a large ungreased baking sheet. Bake at 375-degress F. until golden brown. Approximately 5-10 minutes. Serve immediately as an appetizer.

News Prints — 920-1212

An article in *The Hallandale Digest* written by my friend Judith Stock in 1999.

Inc.

OCTOBER 1993

BANKING & CAPITAL

CREDIT

When a Single Bank Won't Do

BANKERS TALK A LOT ABOUT the importance of relationships as opposed to standalone transactions. And they

given CEO Emilia Zecchino her Small Business Administration loan failed, she tried to get a big Miami bank she

MANUFACTURERS AND DISTRIBUTORS OF
ELEGANT CANAPES AND HORS D'OEUVRES

frown on the idea of small-business customers' spreading their business among a group of banks. Yet for some business owners, using multiple banks is a matter of practicality—a way to get their credit needs met and hedge against possible bank failures. Here's what CEOs who use more than one bank have to say:

HOLIDAY FOODS
Hollywood, Fla.; $2 million in sales

When the bank that had

also did business with to take on the loan. It refused, so another small bank won her business. The large Miami bank handles payroll, so her catering employees have a nearby location where they can cash their checks.

Comment: "My old bank is after my business now, but I'm stalling. I don't want to say no, because I want to keep the door open in case I need more money in the future."

This article appeared in October 1993.

Sun-Sentinel

Tuesday, December 6, 1994

Staff photos/SEAN DOUGHERTY

Holiday Foods employee Hoa Danz makes salmon canapes as employees behind her create dishes.

HOLIDAY FANCIES

A taste of the season offered in small bites.

By JAY WEAVER
Business Writer

Inside a spotless building in Hollywood, about 900 nimble fingers are making gourmet hors d'oeuvres and canapes.

In a matter of hours, the items will be packaged, frozen and distributed to hotels, country clubs and restaurants in South Florida and other regions of the country.

It's a busy time of year for Holiday Foods Inc., but not just because of the holiday season. The wholesale specialty food manufacturer, founded with a $1,000 investment in 1982, has published a new 20-page catalog that will be mailed out this week.

The company's president, Emilia Zecchino, 67, admits being anxious about her new venture to entice affluent households with fancy frozen foods via overnight mail. "I'm scared because I've invested a lot of money in it," she said on a tour of Holiday Foods' 25,000-square-foot center.

Still, Zecchino says she likes to take well-calculated risks. So far, her hunches have paid off: Her business expects to do $5 million in sales this year.

Hotels and country clubs, such as the Omni Hotel in Miami, Marriott Harbor Beach Resort in Fort Lauderdale, the Ritz-Carlton in Manalapan and St. Andrews Country Club in Boca Raton, rely on her business as

A worker makes cheddar cheese and port wine hors d'oeuvres. Holiday Foods, with headquarters in Hollywood, has 95 employees.

if it were an extension of their own kitchens. At Thanksgiving, Holiday Foods also made 14,000 turkey dinners for hotels and restaurants at Disney World in Orlando.

Hospitality industry observers say Holiday Foods has been able to carve out a market niche by serving upscale establishments that cannot justify the cost of such labor-intensive work.

"Her business also benefits from the seasonal surge in food services down here," said Manny Mighdoll, executive vice president of the Florida Restaurant Association in Hollywood.

Holiday Foods' catalog business, which will offer frozen canapes, hors

d'oeuvres, dinner entrees and desserts to American Express cardholders, could make her company richer. "Potentially, the sky's the limit," she said.

Also, her company has been testing specialty food products for Delta Air Lines and the retail discounter, Sam's Club.

"We've had to expand because our customers constantly keep asking us to make more things," she said.

Food has always been at the center of Zecchino's life. She and her late husband, Richard, owned a grocery store in Queens, N.Y., until his death in 1972. She then moved with

Pizzeria, restaurant preceded company that cooks up food

her three children to Hollywood, starting a pizzeria and an Italian restaurant. In the early 1980s, restless to start a catering business, she began making hors d'oeuvres for special occasions in people's homes. "I like making pretty things for parties," she said.

In the mid-1980s, she met Stephen Bruno, catering director at the old Diplomat Hotel on Hollywood Beach. He gave Zecchino her biggest order at that time — 3,000 crab wonton hors d'oeuvres. She pulled it off and soon was in demand by major commercial customers. Bruno is now Holiday Foods' general manager.

Her business really grew in

HOLIDAY FOODS

■ **COMPANY NAME:** Holiday Foods Inc./Holiday Foods Catalog Division Inc.
■ **HEADQUARTERS:** Hollywood
PRESIDENT: Emilia Zecchino
■ **NUMBER OF EMPLOYEES:** 95
■ **1994 SALES:** $5 million
■ **HISTORY:** The company started in 1982 as a home catering business. With two SBA-guaranteed loans totaling $600,000, Holiday Foods expanded into a wholesale specialty food manufacturer. It just started publishing a catalog for affluent households.

1989 after she went to Florida Atlantic University's Small Business Development Center to learn how to obtain a loan. She landed two loans for $600,000, guaranteed by the Small Business Administration.

They have enabled Holiday Foods to hire 95 employees and expand its production center at 2050 McKinley St. In addition to Bruno, Zecchino is assisted by her son, Vincent, and her daughter, Linda.

Almost all of her company's employees are new immigrants from the Caribbean, South America and the Far East. Using natural ingredients, they produce by hand such hors d'oeuvres as spanakopitas, bris en croute and quiche lorraine, and such entrees as suffed chicken breast, dilled salmon and beef Wellington.

Once the items are finished, they're stored in freezers until trucking distributors transport them to different parts of the country. For its new catalog, Holiday Foods will use Federal Express.

"What I'm hoping for," she said, "is that one day some big company will buy us out."

News Prints →920-1212

This *Sun-Sentinel* Article appeared on December 6, 1994. Hoa Danz was making smoked salmon canapes'.

Money Guide

1994 Edition

$3.95

Mistakes your
Growing
___ company needs to avoid

by Mary Rowland

A healthy firm outgrows its old ways of doing business as fast as a child sheds shoes. Follow these 10 management strategies to avoid cramping your company's expansion.

MANUFACTURERS AND DISTRIBUTORS OF
ELEGANT CANAPÉS AND HORS D'OEUVRES

❶ Failing to seek new opportunities. An entrepreneur usually launches a company to fill a need that he or she perceives. To make the business grow, however, you must constantly look for new needs, either in the same market niche or in other ones. Take, for example, Emilia Zecchino, now 65. For 20 years she helped her husband run a New York City grocery store. When he died in 1972, she moved into the house the two of them had recently bought in Hollywood, Fla. and opened an Italian restaurant. By 1980 she felt her restaurant's growth had peaked. "If I reached $150,000 a year in revenues, I was lucky," she recalls. So she switched to catering, making hors d'oeuvres for private parties, and doubled her revenues by 1986. But when those revenues too stopped growing, she borrowed $275,000, using her house as collateral, and opened Holiday Foods, which makes hors d'oeuvres and canapés for restaurants and hotels nationwide. Expected gross this year: $5 million.

News Prints —920-1212

Article that appeared in *Money Guide* after an interview with a reporter in 1994.

274

One of the many articles by the *Small Business Development Center of Florida*.

Leading Small Business to Capital

■ ■ ■ ■ ■ ■

"Go and see them absolutely...before even starting a business. Lay the foundation with the SBDC," says Zecchino. "I started the business with a check for $1,000. Now I have sales over $4 million annually...It can only happen in America!"

Holiday Foods, Inc.

contributed by the Florida Atlantic University SBDC

Emilia Zecchino

In 1983, with just $1,000, Emilia Zecchino started a small catering business. There was always a big demand for the canapes and hors d'oeuvres she made. Only the freshest ingredients and no preservatives were used to make these delicious gourmet foods. After several years, Zecchino felt she could expand the business by manufacturing and distributing these products. A significant order from the Diplomat Hotel gave her the incentive to turn her expansion idea into reality. A new location was needed to manufacture and wholesale the frozen canapes and hors d'oeuvres. In April 1989, Zecchino came to the Florida Atlantic University Small Business Development Center to find out how to finance this new operation. She received advice and direction about the SBA Guaranty Loan (7A) Program and decided to apply. The loan request was funded in the amount of $275,000.

With this capital investment, Zecchino moved into a new facility, purchased kitchen equipment and supplies, and increased her product line. Her standards for the highest quality products and service were never compromised. Sales began to explode with orders from Disney World, Marriott, hotels in the local area such as the Omni in Miami, the Boca Raton Hotel and Resort, the Ritz-Carlton, and many country clubs. Again, Zecchino returned to the SBDC to discuss sales growth and management. Several options were reviewed with particular emphasis on the advantages of brokers/distributors in this industry. By deciding to use distributors, Zecchino's business increased at a rapid pace and she even had to decline many orders. She participated in many trade shows around the state of Florida and then ventured to other areas including New York, Atlanta, New Orleans, and Texas. After taking on over 10 distributors, including Sysco, she was ready for another SBA loan to purchase additional freezers and equipment to increase the inventory. The second SBA loan was funded for $300,000.

Currently, Holiday Foods is located in a 25,000 square foot facility, employs 100 people, utilizes over 20 distributors from several states, and sells products nationally and internationally. Sales revenues for 1994 were approximately $5 million. But Zecchino is not stopping yet! She is now selling to Sam's Club, and has opened a retail outlet and developed a mail order catalog. "Nothing can stop you when you believe in your product and yourself!...It can only happen in America!" says Zecchino.

Continuation of one of the many articles by the *Small Business Development Center of Florida.*

The Miami Herald

SUNDAY, SEPTEMBER 17, 1995

The War Brides

USO worker had courage to gamble –

with marriage,
new businesses

When GIs' promises were fulfilled, many women found true love and a new life in the States

By ELINOR J. BRECHER
Herald Staff Writer

In 1946, Dominick Zecchino and his brothers got a telegram in Queens from relatives in Italy. Someone should come quickly; their mother was dying.

Dominick arrived in the southern town of Conversano too late. But Zecchino, an Army veteran of the Pacific Theater who'd been discharged the previous year, decided to stay a few weeks in the land of his birth.

One day, headed for the PX at

ALAN FREUND / Herald Staff

TAKING RISKS: Left, Emilia Lorusso and Dominick Zecchino in their youth. Above, Emily at her Hollywood catering business. Six years ago, she got a $275,000 Small Business Administration loan. "I was already 60 . . . It can only happen in America."

nearby Bari, he passed a USO office and glimpsed Emilia Lorusso.

She'd been working there since the American invasion in 1944. Her father was a prisoner of war in North Africa, where the family had lived for several years.

She was 18 when they met, and "before you know, we were in love. His visa was only three months . . . but there was a law that the GIs could call for their girlfriends wherever they were, and we could come in as war brides."

Now, you wouldn't think it to look at her, but Emily Zecchino is a gambler: In September 1947, she took the gamble of her life and boarded the USS Saturn for the United States.

"I was scared," she admits. "I was in a panic, and thought I made a big mistake . . . The first day on the boat, I cried a lot. I wanted to go home."

Two weeks later, the Saturn steamed into New York Harbor. Only one sight thrilled Emilia more than the Statue of Liberty: Dominick Zecchino on the dock.

They married and opened a grocery store in Flushing, N.Y. First came two sons and then a daughter. But Dominick, plagued by wartime health problems, died in 1972, after 24 years of marriage.

"We were supposed to move

here to Florida. He never made it, but I liked it . . . So by myself, I started a restaurant in Hollywood: Trevi's. I sold that and bought one in Fort Lauderdale: Amalfi.

"In 1982, with a $1,000 investment, I rented a commercial kitchen for catering and slowly but surely the business grew."

The business is now Holiday Foods of Hollywood, employing 125.

Holiday produces canapes and hors d'oeuvres for many of South Florida's better hotels and country clubs. Zecchino, her daughter and younger son run it together. They've recently added a retail line and a catalog business.

"I got a $275,000 [Small Business Administration] loan six years ago," she explains. "I was already 60. Then I got another $300,000 loan. It can only happen in America."

Dominick could never have imagined such a thing, she's sure. "He was a lot more cautious. I take risks."

Recently, Zecchino taped a segment for a Robin Leach cable show called *The Best of Modern Cuisine.* She's also advertising on the Internet.

"This is the United States," she says. "You have these opportunities."

News Prints 920-1212

On September 17, 1995 *The Miami Herald* published several stories about the lives of WWII War Brides living in Florida. I was one of those brides!

The Miami Herald

WEDNESDAY, NOVEMBER 15, 1995

Russians tour S. Fla. businesses for strategies of success

HOW IT WORKS: Emily Zecchino, right, owner of Holiday Foods in Hollywood shows Russian business people her food storage freezer.

JEROME CONQUY / FOR THE HERALD

Russians get crash course in S. Fla.

By SHARI HENNESSY FERRER
Herald Writer

The aroma of oregano, basil and garlic drifts toward the back of the room as people crowd around stainless steel tables covered with dozens of pastry-wrapped Vienna sausages, egg rolls and finger sandwiches.

Though they've had lunch, the smell

of the mini Beef Wellington in the oven proves seductive. A few of the visitors to Holiday Foods' manufacturing plant wonder if they'll get a chance to sample owner Emily Zecchino's creations.

Assured that they will, the 13 guests begin chattering in Russian and English. Even more than Zecchino's gourmet hors d'oeuvres and canapés, however,

what these visitors crave is her success, American style.

These Russian business people are on a three-week tour of South Florida. They are part of an internship-type program funded by the U.S. Agency for International Development and coordinated by Florida Atlantic University.

They're learning about business management, marketing and finance and seeing the lessons in action through "a day in the life of a local business person," said Linda Krepel, associate director of the international trade center at FAU's Small Business Development Center.

Zecchino's Hollywood company is a great example of how to build a business, Krepel said.

Zecchino has spent 13 years nurturing Holiday Foods from a one-woman catering business to a $4-million-a-year wholesaler and retailer of frozen hors d'oeuvres and canapés.

A native of Italy who came to America in 1947, Zecchino worked in the grocery business for 20 years with her husband in Flushing, N.Y. When she moved to South Florida after her husband's death in 1972, she and her brother were partners in a Hollywood restaurant.

In 1982 she started the catering business that now has a 33,000-square-foot manufacturing plant.

With $1,000 in savings, she rented a small commercial kitchen and bought used restaurant furniture. With help from FAU's center, Zecchino developed a business plan and got two Small Business Administration loans totaling $575,000.

"It's important to know how U.S. businesses operate because many of our clients want U.S. partners," said Ellina Tretiakova, a training consultant visiting from the USAID office in Ekaterinburg, Russia.

"We got to see in practice what we learned in theory in seminars.

I think it will be of great use."

But would the same business principals that made Zecchino a success work in Russia? "Of course," said Zecchino, 67. "It works all over, in any nation."

Since arriving Oct. 28, the Russians have attended seminars and toured Motorola's manufacturing plant in Boynton Beach and Publix's distribution center in Deerfield Beach. They will visit Boca Research's manufacturing center in Boca Raton Thursday and fly home Friday.

News Prints ~920-1212

Sun-Sentinel

Wednesday, November 15, 1995

Staff photo/JOE RAEDLE

Russians study how Priscilla Gish, left, and Thelma Donaldson prepare meals at Holiday Foods.

RUSSIAN RESOLUTIONS

Group studying in S. Florida has ideas for changes back home.

By CHARLES LUNAN
Business Writer

Tatiana Belanova wants to pioneer the sale of variable life insurance in Russia. Evgueni Loretts is looking for investors to help his company market a gold mining process that eliminates the use of toxic chemicals. Viktor Boguslavski, who owns 40 percent of an instrumentation company, just wants to expand his ideas about management.

So in late October, they boarded a jet with nine other entrepreneurs from Ekaterinburg, Russia, and flew to Miami compliments of the U.S. taxpayer. They have spent much of the past two weeks sequestered in classrooms and computer labs at

Florida Atlantic University in Boca Raton, studying strategic planning, U.S. economic policy, quality management systems and learning how to navigate the Internet on personal computers.

Their visit is part of a training program the U.S. Agency for International Development established in the last few years to instill Russia's most promising entrepreneurs with American capitalist knowhow. The agency, which is an arm of the U.S. Department of Commerce, has hired the accounting firm Deloitte & Touche to run the program.

"Our goal is to support small and medium-sized businesses to start and survive in Russia," said Eillina

Tretyakova, manager of the American Entrepreneurial Center in Ekaterinburg. The center screened 100 applicants to select the 14 participants visiting South Florida, she said. Deloitte & Touche has established nine such centers in Russia, said Linda Krepel, director of the Florida International Trade Center at FAU.

Krepel recruited a half dozen South Florida lawyers, accountants and consultants as teachers.

"I introduced the concept that the customer is king," said Green. "You have to understand the environment they are in. For years if you put it on the shelf in Russia, it sold. But Russia is rapidly becoming a country

where there is competition. They have to make their businesses current enough to compete against the foreign companies coming in."

Named for the wife of Peter the Great, who founded the city in 1723, Ekaterinburg is located at the border of Europe and Asia near some of Russia's largest gold, copper and iron mines, said Tretyakova. About half Ekaterinburg's 1,200 industrial enterprises have been pri-

Group of Russians study capitalism in South Florida

vatized, said Tretyakova. Many are learning that to survive they must look beyond Russia's vast borders for partners, capital and technology.

Toward that goal, the Ekaterinburg delegation has visited Motorola's robot-filled paging plant in Boynton Beach, Publix's vast distribution center in Deerfield Beach and the *Sun-Sentinel's* neighboring printing plant. On Thursday they visit Sensormatic Electronics in Deerfield Beach and Boca Research in Boca Raton.

"Today in Russia, at plants that are not part of the military industrial complex, the level of technology is much lower," said Boguslavski.

Belanov hopes to set up an exchange program that would return her to the United States to study the life insurance industry and send an American to Russia to teach marketing and insurance techniques.

"If I study this and get a license, I can go back to Russia and become the first in the field," she said. "People in Russia have to save money from inflation, which is very great."

Such plans show how far Russia's entrepreneurs have come, said Krepel.

"Five years ago when we brought people in from Russia, it took us 45 minutes just to explain the concept of the service industry," she said. "Now they are building an insurance industry."

The Miami Herald and *The Sun Sentinel* articles covering the visit to Holiday Foods by a delegation of Russian entrepreneurs escorted by officials of the Small Business Administration on November 15, 1995.

Sun-Sentinel

Wednesday, December 11, 1996

RETAILING

Emily Zecchino, left, owner and chief cook of Hollywood-based Holiday Foods, prepares bake-and-ship goodies with Wilma Valencia, foreground, and Lisa Hen. Hors d'oeuvres, below, are among a wide array of edibles that Holiday Foods sells through mail order.

Staff photos/
LOU TOMAN

Mail-order foods offer a taste of the holidays

Selection has grown as business booms

Staff and wire reports

South Florida caterer **Holiday Foods** is among a handful of specialty foods mail-order businesses that are busy baking and packing this holiday season.

"We're working double shifts," says Emily Zecchino, owner and chief cook of Hollywood-based Holiday Foods. "We do the bulk of our work wholesale, selling to distributors who then take it on to country clubs, cruise lines and the hotels. Our only retail outlet is mail order. Business is growing every year."

One look at the mail box is all the proof you need that mail-order food is booming. There are many more choices this year than there have been in the last five, food experts say.

Unfortunately, that also means there are more substandard products, and many are outrageously priced: ordinary dried pasta for $7 a pound or a brand of coffee that can be bought for $8 a half-pound in most speciality markets, being sold for $14 plus shipping.

You expect to spend more for mail-order products because of the cost of packing and shipping. And when the food must be shipped overnight, or even second-day air because of perishability, you pay even more.

Products should be made from real ingredients and be tasty to be worthy as a special holiday gift.

Following are some popular mail-order items that you still can have sent for the holidays.

(The mail-order listings include the addresses and phone numbers of the companies. Also listed is the cutoff date for orders to be delivered by Dec. 24 and the forms of payment accepted.

The credit card abbreviations are: AE for American Express; DC, Diners Club; D, Discover; MC, Mastercard; O, Optima; V, Visa.)

Mail-order food selection grows as business booms

SAVORIES

Holiday Foods' catalog division sends mini quiche Lorraine with seafood or mushrooms at $36 for 50 pieces or $62 for 100 pieces; with salmon and onion, $40 for 50 pieces and $70 for 100 pieces. Shipping is included.

Suite No. 3, 2050 McKinley St., Hollywood, Fla. 33020; 954-921-7786, 800-877-7434. Dec. 14. AE, MC, V, D.

News Prints 929-1212

This article appeared in the *Sun-Sentinel* on December 11, 1996.

BOCA RATON

Each big step in the development of Holiday Foods has required a creative leap of faith by Emilia Zecchino.

Food also can create an emotional bond with loyal consumers, as EMILIA ZECCHINO discovered. She started a little home-based catering service that grew into a large food preparation company, Holiday Foods of Hollywood, specializing in canapés and other types of appetizers. A widowed Italian immigrant, Zecchino came to South Florida by way of New York, where she and her late husband had a small grocery store. Her first business ambition in South Florida was to try real estate. Instead, she invested heavily in a restaurant venture that went bust. "That was in 1981," she recalls. "I lost a lot of money." Undaunted, in 1982, she launched her current business, catering weddings and house parties.

After making her first big sale to a commercial customer (3,000 lobster wontons to the old Diplomat hotel in Hollywood) Zecchino began making her appetizers in bulk for hotels and country clubs around South Florida. As chefs she worked with here moved to jobs elsewhere in the United States, they kept calling her, placing orders for her appetizers. Food distributors serving cities throughout Florida and across the nation took notice and added Holiday Foods to their vendor lineups. Now, food distributors account for most of the company's sales, about $10 million a year.

Throughout her career, Zecchino has been sustained by a love of food and entertaining, and a passion for doing things her way. "Believe me, I buy every *Gourmet* magazine, every *Bon Apetit* magazine," she says. "I have a wall full of cookbooks. I love the pictures. But when I cook, I never look at any of those recipes. I make up my own."

Each big step in the development of Holiday Foods has required a creative leap of faith by Zecchino. When sales to hotels and country clubs began to soar in the early 1990s, cash flow became anemic because working with larger customers meant waiting longer to get paid. Against the advice of friends and associates she consulted, Zecchino responded to the cash crisis by going deeper into debt and ultimately pulled her company back from the brink of insolvency. "I was really bleeding," she recalls. "I almost lost the business."

Her faith in good fortune may be stronger than most because of her harrowing experiences as a girl growing up in war. During the early stage of World War II, she spent almost a year imprisoned with her family and other Italian citizens in a British-run concentration camp in Ethiopia. Her father, an Italian army officer, was sent to Ethiopia when it was controlled by Italy, before the Brits arrived, and had brought his family with him. Her father remained a prisoner of war for six years. The British sent her and the rest of her family back to Italy on a 40-day sea journey that proved more dangerous than their 10-month concentration camp stay. "We came very close to being bombed by submarines," Zecchino says. "For 40 days, we didn't know if we were going to live or die."

That kind of horror puts a business crisis into proper perspective. Indeed, facing such danger as a child may have emboldened Zecchino to face the risks of business ownership as an adult.

"Always when I thought that it was all over, something happened that made me go ahead," she says. "It's my faith. I know there is a God." ✦

This article appeared in the May/June 2004 issue of the Boca Raton Magazine

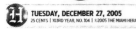

The Miami Herald

TUESDAY, DECEMBER 27, 2005
25 CENTS | 103RD YEAR, NO. 104 | ©2005 THE MIAMI HERALD

BROWARD FINAL

MiamiHerald.com

BR1

TINY BITES, BIG MONEY

CANAPES AND HORS D'OEUVRES HAVE GROWN INTO A $9 MILLION-A-YEAR HOLLYWOOD ENTERPRISE.

BY NIKKI WALLER
nwaller@MiamiHerald.com

When Emily Zecchino looks at a circle of crustless white bread, she sees infinite possibilities: curls of smoked salmon and pimentos, lobster medallions and tenderloin tips, drizzles of balsamic vinegar and daubs of Dijon.

Zecchino, 77, owns Holiday Foods, a wholesale appetizer company that occupies a 75,000-square-foot warehouse in Hollywood. Since October, she and her staff of 150 have been preparing for this time of year, the peak season for hors d'oeuvres and holiday parties.

The Italian-born Zecchino — who came to the United States as a war bride in 1947 — grew her business from scratch, turning a one-woman catering firm into a $9 million-a-year enterprise.

Her proudest creation is the mini beef Wellington, a sort of landmark achievement in the field of hors d'oeuvres and miniature foods, right up there with the mini Philly cheese steak and mini lobster rolls.

Zecchino estimates she sells more than 200,000 a year.

The mini beef Wellington also illustrates a core principle of appetizing: You can never go wrong with mini foods.

"Anything you can make big," she said "you can make small."

Another law of appetizer thermodynamics: Anything wrapped in wonton skins or bacon tastes pretty good.

When she first came to the United States, Zecchino and her husband Dominick, ran a grocery store in Queens, N.Y. He died suddenly in 1972, leaving a single mother with three children. The family moved to Hollywood, where Zecchino opened two restaurants. She sold the businesses in 1981, and on the advice of friends, opened her own catering company.

She had modest success working some weddings and graduation parties, making main dishes and desserts, but her heart was in hors d'oeuvres.

THE WONTONS

Then came the crabmeat wontons. A friend in the catering department at the Diplomat Hotel called with an urgent request. The hotel was planning an event and needed some appetizers. Could she deliver 3,000 crabmeat wontons in two days?

"When I heard 3,000, I fell on the floor," she said. Then she enlisted her sister, her daughter, all her friends and everyone she could find. The women worked for two days straight, pressing the pastries and packing the trays. She delivered on time, and a business was born.

"That opened my eyes," Zecchino said. "If this hotel can buy them, maybe there are other hotels that want to buy them."

She began to sell to area hotels and country clubs, and the business blossomed. At age 55, she obtained a Small Business Administration loan for $275,000 to relocate her business to the Dixie Highway warehouse, where she quickly outgrew her rented space and had to expand into adjacent spaces.

Today, that business is a 75,000-square-foot factory with four food-preparation rooms, five packing rooms and four kitchens.

"I keep saying, only in America these things can happen," she said.

Sales went from $35,000 in her first year of business to nearly $9 million this year.

Zecchino's daughter Linda, who was 10 when the family moved to Hollywood, is the company's vice president, in charge of marketing and sales.

"She's the front of the house, I'm the back of the house," Zecchino says, chuckling.

In the back of the house, 150 nimble-fingered employees press dough, spoon savory fillings onto squares of puff pastry and pinch them into little purses.

Zecchino works with an executive chef, Dan Kucera, to dream up new savories that can be deep-fried, skewered or wrapped in phyllo dough.

This year's new models include the beef firecracker — beef and jalapeño cheddar tucked in an egg roll wrapper and twisted at the end to look like a popper, as well as the risotto and Gorgonzola croquette, a distant cousin of Southern Italian *arancini*, deep-fried balls of rice, beef, peas and tomato sauce.

Like *arancini*, foods once associated with poverty in Italy, such as focaccia and polenta, have gone gourmet, a development that has allowed Zecchino and Kucera to explore new realms of finger foods.

Despite the success of new appetizers, the beef firecracker will probably never rival the popularity of pigs in a blanket. "We wish they would stop calling for franks in a blanket and egg rolls, but they never go out of style," said Zecchino ruefully.

THE MEATBALLS

And while she's at it: Enough with the Swedish meatballs, too. Try something different for once, a nice shrimp skewer or mini brie en croute with raspberry, or a canapé assortment.

As Zecchino walks through the factory she built, she stops to chat with employees, pointing out the many who have been with her for 10 years or more, bringing family members and friends on board along the way.

Patricia Giraldo manages the raw meat production room, where white-coated workers thread lobster medallions onto skewers and dredge shrimp through diced coconut flakes. Giraldo has worked at Holiday Foods for 14 years, and now her husband, two sisters and two brothers work there, too.

Zecchino beams as she opens the door to the canapé room, the last, best room at Holiday Foods. Trays of lobster medallions drizzled with balsamic vinegar and laid atop crostini, destined for the Eden Roc hotel in Miami Beach, fill rolling racks. White-coated workers carefully thread strips of pimento through olive rings. It's part art studio, part science lab.

Lisa Ming Chen, a former opera singer in her native China, directs the presentation.

Chefs give the recipe, and she creates the look of the canapé, balancing the color, variety, height and shape of each.

"I like beautiful things," she said. "That's my imagination."

Beautiful canapés, said Zecchino, come from the heart.

"There is no end to what you can do, you never run out of ideas," Zecchino said. "It is infinity with canapés."

CANAPES GALORE: Linda Zecchino, left, and her mother, Emily, far right, who founded Holiday Foods of Hollywood, talk with Lisa Ming-Chen, middle, who designs the look of their canapes.

CANDACE BARBOT/MIAMI HERALD STAFF

PHOTOS BY CANDACE BARBOT/MIAMI HERALD STAFF

FAMILY BUSINESS: Emily Zecchino, above left, with her daughter, Linda, run the Hollywood catering business Emily started alone after she moved from New York following her husband's death. They now reap $9 million a year in business. A worker, bottom, threads pimentos into olives on canapés in a kitchen at the 75,000-square-foot factory. Many of the employees have been with the Zecchinos for more than 10 years and brought family on board.

'There is no end to what you can do, you never run out of ideas. It is infinity with canapés.'

— EMILY ZECCHINO,
owner of Holiday Foods of Hollywood

News Prints (954) 926-1212

The Miami Herald article appeared on December 27, 2005 just one month before Holiday Foods was sold to the Schwan Company.

02 AUGUST 1994

AUG. 09 1994

Dear Linda,

IT WAS A PLEASURE MEETING YOU AT THE RECENT FOOD SHOW IN NEW ORLEANS AND SAMPLING YOUR COMPANY'S PRODUCTS. NOT ONLY WAS I IMPRESSED WITH YOUR LINE OF OUTSTANDING HORS D'OEUVRES, BUT YOUR COMPANY'S COMMITTMENT TO QUALITY.

YOUR MOTHER'S TENACITY IN MAINTAINING ELEGANCE / PREMIERE QUALITY / RESISTING SHORT CUTS ARE TRULY AN INSPIRATION TO ALL OF US JUST STARTING OUT. GOOD LUCK!

SINCERELY,

Dan Coueevan
Gourmet Express Inc.

A very special honor given to me and Holiday Foods by a visitor and probably a future competitor, at the Food Show in New Orleans where Linda and our executive chef tended our booth with a display of our products. 1994.

2/16/2005

Mrs. Emily Zecchino, Owner
Holiday Foods
2050 McKinley Street
Hollywood, FL 33020

RE: Field trip for our Class at the Le Cordon Bleu College of Culinary Arts-Miami

Dear Mrs. Zecchino:

We were genuinely impressed with your generosity in taking time from your busy schedule to share a field trip at your Hors D'Oeuvres operation. As we listened to your presentation, you brought alive the culinary history of Holiday Foods. To hear that you your sister and daughter started the business was heart warming. We were impressed with your philosophy, the standards you've developed and implemented, and your passion for food. Your joy of cooking came across in all aspects you presented.

Equally impressive is the passion we observed in the happy employees who talked with us, in the neat, clean and organized kitchens and freezers. The story you told about Holiday Foods' and it's attention to getting the job done, organization of business events, beauty of food presentation, quality of food and detail to food safety, surely exhibits a truly world class operation.

Many of us have expressed an interest in Holiday Foods product line and would like to contact you either on future tours or directly by email. Your friends at Le Cordon Bleu.

Sincerely,

The Food Science Class
Le Cordon Bleu College of Culinary Arts- Miami

A thank you letter from the Food Science Class of the Le Cordon Bleu College of Culinary Arts in Miami, a few days later of their tour of Holiday Foods' Plant.

us of your early years in Italy and your rise to head such an enterprise as Holiday Foods was appreciated.

More than that, your wonderful faith which has sustained you always is a sign that God does work in strange and mysterious ways.

May God continue to bless you, your family and your family of Holiday Foods employees.

Sincerely,
Eleanor Ebner
(over)

Jan. 9, 1998

Dear Mrs. Zecchino (Emily):

After reading a recent article in the Sun-Sentinal, my friend and I decided to visit the site of "a small miracle". We were happily surprised when you, yourself, came out into the parking lot as we were staring in wonder at the McKinley Street building.

Your patience and kindness in telling

We hope you take time to put your wonderful story on tape in your own voice and in your own words. It would be filed under "Inspirational".

Thank You

SPECIALIZING IN:
• WEDDINGS
• BIRTHDAY PARTIES
• CORPORATE FUNCTIONS
• FAMILY REUNIONS
• HOLIDAY FESTIVITES

Terreza's Party Planning

THE ULTIMATE IN EVENT PLANNING

Terrie Chin

SOCIAL DIRECTOR

TEL. (954) 964-1186

FAX (954) 964-1169

Dear Emily,

Thank you for your Prayers and your advise. I did get that Big Contract and I owe it to you for leading Me to the Lord. For he is Worthy to be praised. I give him the glory every day and I thank you every day

Terrie Chin

A thank you card from one of the many caterers in the area.

U.S. SMALL BUSINESS ADMINISTRATION
SOUTH FLORIDA DISTRICT OFFICE
100 SOUTH BISCAYNE BOULEVARD, 7TH FLOOR
MIAMI, FLORIDA 33131-2011
TELEPHONE (305) 536-5521   FAX (305) 536-5058

May 11, 2001

Mrs. Emilia Zecchino
President
Holiday Foods, Inc.
2050 McKinley Street
Hollywood, Florida 33020

Dear Mrs. Zecchino:

On behalf of South Florida's entrepreneurs and advocates, and the South Florida Chamber of Commerce, I thank you for participating as a speaker at the 2001 Small Business Week Annual Luncheon on May 7th. Your presentation was both informative and inspirational and was a highlight of the luncheon. You made our celebration of small business ownership a tremendous success.

I wish you continued success in your business ventures. Should you ever need the South Florida District Office, I hope that you will give us the opportunity to serve you. Once again, thank you.

Sincerely,

Francisco A. Marrero
District Director

FAM/aah

Federal Recycling Program   Printed on Recycled Paper

A thank you letter from the District Director of the S.B.A. after my speaking engagement at the 2001 Small Business Week Annual Luncheon held at the Diplomat Country Club on May 7.

286

AUG 10 1996

August 9, 1996

Emily Zecchino
HOLIDAY FOODS
2050 McKinley Streeet
Hollywood FL 33020

Dear Emily,

You are a delightful person and you have a wonderful story. I have met so few successful women who are as hard working, diligent, persistent and true to their own dreams as you. I feel so fortunate to have spent time with you on Wednesday. Thank you for taking the time out of your busy schedule to talk to us.

I learned alot and have renewed faith in myself. I would be most pleased if you would allow me to keep the door of communication open. Your professional opinion as a mentor would help me tremendously.

In any case, I thank you for your most valuable time.

Sincerely,

Judy Pertnoy, President

Judy's note touched my heart deeply for days on end!

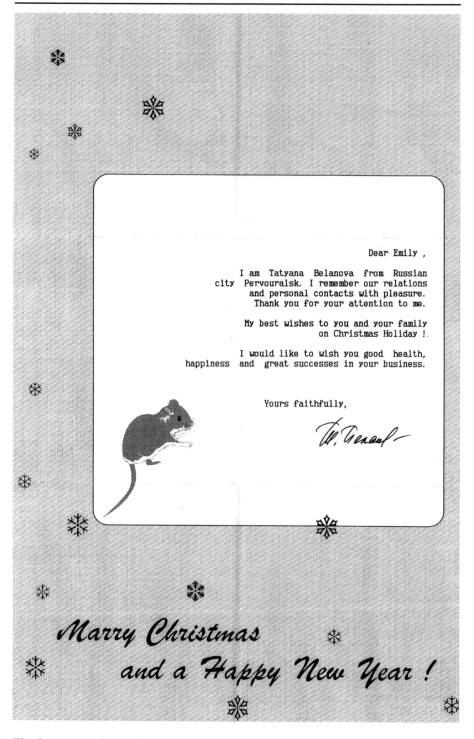

> Dear Emily ,
>
> I am Tatyana Belanova from Russian city Pervouralsk. I remember our relations and personal contacts with pleasure. Thank you for your attention to me.
>
> My best wishes to you and your family on Christmas Holiday !
>
> I would like to wish you good health, happiness and great successes in your business.
>
> Yours faithfully,

Marry Christmas and a Happy New Year !

Thank you note that arrived to me from Russia, written by one of the ladies with the Russian Delegation that toured Holiday Foods Plant with the SBCD Officers.

CITY of HOLLYWOOD, FLORIDA

GEN. JOSEPH W. WATSON CIRCLE · 2600 HOLLYWOOD BOULEVARD

ELEANOR SOBEL
Commissioner

November 5, 1997

Ms. Emily Zecchino
Holiday Foods
2050 McKinley St.
Hollywood, Fl 33020

Dear Emily,

I cannot stop talking about your hospitality and your efficient factory here in Hollywood. Thank you very much for the personal tour of your memorable facility and for the sampling of some of your delicious goodies. With a woman such as yourself as the chief executive, it becomes quite clear why your business is extremely successful. I am most impressed by the quality of your products and the immaculate condition of your plant.

I have given away the two brochures that you gave me and hope that you would be kind enough to send me more brochures for my own needs and to pass around City Hall.

I hope to hear from you after the New Year, as you expressed, about your business concerns. I also mentioned to Mayor Giulianti your invitation to her to visit Holiday Foods.

Have a happy Thanksgiving.

Fondly,

Eleanor Sobel
Commissioner

MAILING ADDRESS: P.O. Box 229045, Hollywood, FL 33022-9045 · Phone (954) 921-3321 · Fax (954) 921-3386

"An Equal Opportunity and Service Provider Agency"

A thank you note from then Commissioner Sobel, currently serving as Florida State Senator.

#HAve Nice day!

Smile God love you!

"I Love My Job!"

Hi EMELY: God bless you!
I need to explain what is make balls for me;
is health, playful, is really the job what "God"
send me to doing in your company, I feeling
so and I want to you now: when I not make

WITH GRATEFUL THANKS

balls one day make me dull, give heart-ache, etc.

I make balls from my *Lourdes Contreras*
heart, I love that and god 06/24/03
thanks I feel well. —
      Sincerilly, L.C.

thANKS to be your worker

A very heart warming note I received from Lourdes, one of my employees, telling me in her broken English how much she enjoyed scooping products into balls and how grateful she felt to be working for me!! (I simply could not hold my tears feeling her love for God and for me!)

290

1999 Small Business Awards Winners

SCORE Chapter of the Year
National
Leonard Willner, Chapter Chair
South Palm Beach SCORE

Small Business Person of the Year
South Florida District
Emilia Zecchino, President
Holiday Foods, Inc.
Hollywood

Accountant Advocate of the Year
South Florida District
State of Florida, and
Region IV
Carlos B. Pargas, CPA, Principal
Carlos B. Pargas, CPA, PA
Miami

Veteran Small Business
Advocate of the Year
South Florida District,
State of Florida, Region IV
Bernice Braden, President
Bernice Braden Realty, Inc.
Cape Coral

Small Business
Exporter of the Year
South Florida District, State of
Florida, Region IV
H. Donovan Brown, Ph.D.,
President
Donovan Brown & Associates
Lakeland

Women in Business
Advocate of the Year
South Florida District and
State of Florida
Rochelle M. Bloom, President
Crystal Collection
Boca Raton

Media Advocate of the Year
South Florida District
Michelle Vachon
Business Reporter
Naples Daily News

Financial Services
Advocate of the Year (tie)
State of Florida,
South Florida District
Frank Rodriguez
Business Development Officer
First National Bank of Naples

South Florida District
Eduardo A. Godoy, President
Business Loan Development Corp.
West Palm Beach

Minority Small Business
Advocate of the Year
South Florida District
Dania Lopez, President
Lee County Plumbing, Inc.
Cape Coral

My 1999 Award for the SMALL BUSINESS PERSON OF THE YEAR
- South Florida District, given by the S.B.A.

TO EMILY

There are two ways to live our lives:
One, as though NOTHING is a miracle.
The other is as though EVERYTHING is a miracle.
Emily made a miracle. Where everyone else saw
problems, she saw an opportunity.
We all here are part of the miracle—a part of an
American Dream come true, a part of Emily.
By her achieving the goals she set up for herself, we benefit.

I am sure we all have a story of how we relate in our lives
to Emily.
To me Emily has been a friend and a motivator of
achievement.
A friend is one who knows you as you are, understands
where you have been, accepts you as you have become, and still
invites you to grow. This is Emily to me.
Many years ago, I was impressed by the movie star Cary
Grant. One time I saw an interview of his and they told him
that every man would like to be like him. He answered, "Me,
too!"
Emily, we'd ALL like to be like you, but you are one of a
kind.
Personally, I feel fortunate to be part of your journey.
Thank you for all the help you gave me in catering
through the years and for the inspiration to achieve my goals.
My best wishes and prayers are with you forever.
Zvi (Steve) Feldman

A very special acknowledgment from my friend Steve Feldman, his words were and
still are deeply appreciated.